Case Studies in
Abnormal Psychology

Case Studies in Abnormal Psychology

Clark R. Clipson, Ph.D.
*California School of Professional Psychology,
San Diego*

Jocelyn M. Steer, Ph.D.
San Diego Family Institute

HOUGHTON MIFFLIN COMPANY   Boston   New York

Sponsoring editor: David Lee
Senior associate editor: Jane Knetzger
Senior project editor: Rosemary Winfield
Associate production/design coordinator: Deborah Frydman
Senior manufacturing coordinator: Marie Barnes
Marketing manager: Pamela Laskey

Cover designer: Harold Burch, Harold Burch Design, New York City

Printed in the U.S.A.

Library of Congress Catalog Card Number: 97-72455

ISBN: 0-395-88569-8

123456789-QF-01 00 99 98 97

CONTENTS

PREFACE

Case Studies in Abnormal Psychology presents sixteen portraits of individuals with a broad range of psychological disorders. We have tried not only to select and develop cases that best illustrate these disorders but also to tell the *stories* of these sixteen individuals, vividly conveying to the reader what it is like to live and struggle with the disorder in question. Written in language that is accessible to its undergraduate audience and with lively detail, each story brings the person to life on the page and fleshes out more static descriptions often encountered in students' textbooks and class lectures. We have based these clinical portraits on actual cases from our clinical practices, altering identifying information as necessary to protect the confidentiality of the clients.

A further goal of the casebook is to enhance students' critical thinking skills. Students are invited to be curious about the person described in each case and wonder along with the clinician about client dynamics, diagnosis, and treatment. These case explorations are designed to arouse interest and engage students in a process of discovery based on both scientific research and clinical experience. Because the book is intended primarily for undergraduate students of abnormal psychology and introductory counseling classes, it provides a clear framework for thinking about the cases with a minimum of technical jargon. The book does not conceal the fact that all clinicians do not agree on the etiology or treatment of specific disorders. Students are asked to reflect on the cases from a critical viewpoint and to raise and respond to provocative questions regarding the diagnosis, treatment, and prognosis of specific disorders.

The classification of disorders in the casebook adheres to that set out by the American Psychiatric Association's *Diagnostic and Statistical Manual of Mental Disorders (4th ed.) (DSM-IV)* and most abnormal psychology textbooks. Nonetheless, we recognize that the actual clinical manifestation of a disorder is highly complex and influenced by a variety of factors. The cases have thus been presented from a biopsychosocial perspective in order to capture this and to help students begin to appreciate the complexity of individual cases. Whenever appropriate, we examine the influences that culture, gender, sexual orientation, genetics, family systems, and so forth have on the development of a disorder. As a result, there is an emphasis on diversity in the casebook.

Organization of the Casebook

Each chapter explores a distinct psychological disorder and follows a similar format as follows:

- **The Client's Story**   The chapter opens with the individual's story. Written in an informal style, the stories describe the thoughts, feelings, relationships, family history, work patterns, and so on of the person portrayed in the case.

- **Questions to Think About**   Following each story, students are presented with a series of questions that are designed to direct their thinking about the signs and symptoms, possible causes, and contributing factors of the disorder. These questions are then addressed in subsequent sections of the chapter.

- **Assessment**   The Assessment section presents actual data collected by the treating psychologist (such as psychological tests, structured clinical interviews, mental status exams, self-report checklists, clinician observations, family interviews, and histories).

- **Case Conceptualization**   This section draws on the details of the case history and the findings from the assessment phase to understand the dynamics of the person and the disorder. Presented from a bio-psychosocial perspective, this part provides a clear framework for students to organize and understand the case. Up-to-date research supports the case conceptualization.

- **Diagnosis**   This section formalizes a diagnosis using the criteria set out in the *DSM-IV*. When appropriate, additional and competing diagnoses are given or ruled out, with a rationale for doing so.

- **Treatment and Outlook**   This portion of the chapter outlines the most common forms of treatment for the disorder. A more detailed explanation of the treatment used in the actual case is then given, along with the prognosis for the client.

- **Critical Thinking: Questions for Writing or Discussion**   Each chapter concludes with critical thinking questions that provide a springboard for further exploration.

Additional Resources

Houghton Mifflin's Psychology Website provides access to additional useful and innovative teaching and learning resources that support courses for which this book is designed. This location can be reached by pointing to the Houghton Mifflin homepage at http://www.hmco.com and going to the College Division Psychology page.

Acknowledgments

We would like to thank the following people for their help in completing this project. Jane Knetzger provided both of us with invaluable guidance throughout the process, for which we are most grateful. Her optimism kept us afloat when our own buoyancy threatened to fail us. Special thanks go to David Lee for initially proposing the casebook and for having confidence in our ability to carry it out. We would also like to thank the many reviewers, whose comments and suggestions allowed us to write a better casebook:

Cole Barton, Davidson College
Beth Benoit, University of Massachusetts—Lowell and Middlesex
    Community College
Peggy R. Brooks, North Adams State College
Joyce L. Carbonell, Florida State University
Deborah Carlin, Washington University
Craig R. Cowden, Northern Virginia Community College
Joan Doolittle, Anne Arundel Community College
Steven C. Funk, Northern Arizona University
Louis E. Gardner, Creighton University
Cheryl Golden, LeMoyne-Owen College
Robert R. Higgins, Oakland Community College
Debra Hollister, Valencia Community College
Heidi M. Inderbitzen, University of Nebraska—Lincoln
Ronald W. Jacques, Ricks College
V. K. Kumar, West Chester University
Charles A. LaJeunesse, College Misericordia
Jerald J. Marshall, University of Central Florida
Patricia Owen, St. Mary's University
Ralph G. Pifer, Sauk Valley Community College
Raymond L. Scott, Whittier College

Special gratitude is extended to the many clients we have known, whose courage and trust have allowed us to share in their journey toward health and well-being. We clearly could not have written this book without them. Clark is especially thankful to Christine, Ashley, and Dan for their love and patience during the writing of this book. And finally, Jocelyn would like to thank her husband, Jo, for supporting her through yet another writing project.

C. R. C.
J. M. S.

Case Studies in
Abnormal Psychology

CHAPTER 1

Adjustment Disorder:
It Could Happen to Anyone

*Show me a sane man and I will cure him
for you.*   CARL JUNG

*Each chapter of this casebook opens with an individual's story. Written in
an informal style, the stories describe the thoughts, feelings, relationships, family history, work patterns, and so on of the people portrayed in
the cases. You will become familiar with not only the symptoms of the
psychological disorder under discussion but also the person who lives
with that disorder. As you read each story, begin to formulate a mental
image of how the person functions, making hypotheses about what's
"normal" behavior and what's not.*

MARIA'S STORY

Maria sat on her bed and let the tears roll down her cheeks. It was a Friday
night in mid-October, and she was alone in her dorm room again with a pile
of unopened books on her desk and a box of chocolate chip cookies from her
mother to keep her company. Her mind drifted to her family in California,
imagining what they were doing. Her mother was probably helping her
younger brother carve a pumpkin for Halloween. It saddened Maria to think
that this would be the first Halloween she would miss. Aunt Lourdes would
be there, too, criticizing her mother and bossing her brother around, and
maybe Maria's cousin would also be there. Her father would be out in the
garage, doing whatever he does there; Maria never knew for sure. And her
younger sister would be on the phone, clicking from one call waiting to another. When Maria lived at home before moving away for college, her sister
annoyed her, but tonight Maria missed her terribly.

What's wrong with me, Maria wondered. For the past two weeks she had
been crying for no good reason, feeling sorry for herself. She was more irritable
than usual, and the smallest things set her off. Her usual strategies for shaking
off a bad mood—listening to music, eating chocolate, calling her friends—

weren't working. Yesterday, she dropped by Professor Wilson's office during office hours to pick up the handout from the class she missed. When he asked her how her first semester of college was going, she burst into tears, and all Maria had wanted at that moment was to melt into the linoleum under her feet. She was horrified that she had let him see her like that. She made up some excuse of a relative dying, and she flew out of the office before he could reply.

He must think I'm crazy, Maria thought. If she had been truthful, she would have told him, "The semester is going horribly. I feel lonely, and I miss my boyfriend and my family. The women in my dorm are stuck up, and the guys are worse. Nobody cares about anybody; they all walk around campus like they've got it all together. I'm scared to say a word in class because I'm sure I'll sound stupid. I hate this place, and I want to go home to my family, who understands me."

What prevented Maria from returning home was that she didn't want to disappoint her parents. She was the first person on either side of her large, extended family to attend college. Maria wanted to go away to college more than anything in the world, and when she got a scholarship to a college on the East Coast, she begged her parents to let her go. Her mother worked especially hard to convince her father that it would be acceptable and valuable for his daughter to leave home and live on her own before getting married. Aunt Lourdes and Uncle Victor criticized her father severely for giving in, but her mother stood by Maria. Maria felt guilty for the overtime her father worked to save enough to send her away. Calling her family to complain was definitely not an option, Maria decided, so she wept privately and felt herself slowly sinking into a dark and lonely place.

This was the first time in her eighteen years that Maria had felt depressed. Her childhood was happy, and she grew up in a boisterous, loving Mexican American household in California. Her parents weren't perfect, of course: Her father was restrictive and unemotional, and her mother was critical at times, but Maria had no doubt her parents loved her. Since both her parents worked, she was charged with a good deal of responsibility for her two younger siblings, whom she cherished. She didn't mind taking care of them, but she did mind that her family struggled financially. She had decided as a young girl that she was going to be different from the others in her family. She was not going to drop out of school, and she was going to make money so her parents would not have to work so hard in their old age.

I'm failing at the first step toward my goal, Maria thought. I can't even make it in college. She was worrying about her grades because she had missed some classes these past two weeks. She had 8:30 classes twice a week, and normally she would jump out of bed when the alarm rang, but lately she had turned it off and then dozed off, waking up an hour later. By then she had missed her class. She was procrastinating more than usual, and she looked at the stack of books, thinking about the unfinished reading and two papers she had to write for English class.

Her roommate, Tiffany, noticed the changes in Maria, but Maria ignored her offers to talk and help. She liked Tiffany, but she was intimidated by her confidence and independence. Maria admired Tiffany's self-assurance. Tiffany didn't seem to need anyone, least of all her family, whom she called occasionally but rarely talked about. Maria was very dependent on her parents, and if calls hadn't been so expensive, she would have telephoned her mother every day. They were quite different people, Maria decided: Tiffany fit in, and Maria was out of place at the college.

When Maria walked around campus, she was afraid to make eye contact with the other students, afraid of their mocking glares, so she kept her eyes pinned to the ground. She began to dislike her curly black hair, and she wished that her legs were longer. Her clothes weren't right either, and she stopped wearing the outfits her mother had bought for her before leaving. She even looked different from the other students.

Maria was particularly self-conscious at dinner time, when the other students in the dorm walked down to the cafeteria in pairs and small groups. Maria had no one to eat with her, so she usually waited in her room until most of the students had returned from dinner before going down to the dorm cafeteria. It didn't look so odd then that she ate by herself. No one asked her to join them, except Tiffany, and Maria was almost certain Tiffany had invited her just to be nice.

Maria regretted her decision to leave home and attend college in another part of the country. If she had taken Aunt Lourdes's advice to attend the local university, her life would be happy now, and she could be near her boyfriend, Brian, and her friends. Maria had always been shy and studious, unlike her younger sister, whose beauty and easygoing personality drew others to her like a magnet. Nonetheless, Maria had developed a close circle of friends, and although she wasn't as popular as her sister, she was never lonely.

She and Brian had met their senior year, and they had dated steadily until she left for college. Brian also was shy, and Maria appreciated his gentleness. Brian admired Maria's dedication to school, and he liked the fact she was serious, with plans for the future. Brian had made plans to attend the local university, but he never tried to stop her from leaving. "I'll e-mail you every day, and I'll call you as often as I can. We'll make it," he had promised, and Maria believed their love could last. At first, the messages arrived daily, long and flowery proclamations of his love, which cheered Maria, helping her through her initial homesickness. Lately, they had become briefer, less romantic, and less frequent.

Maria logged on to her computer, hoping for a message from Brian. Her excitement quickly turned to dread, however, as she began reading the message she found. "I won't be coming for Thanksgiving. I didn't plan on it, but I met this woman. I'm confused. I still love you, but I need some time. It's so hard being away from you." Maria began sobbing, and Tiffany became concerned when she found Maria that way after returning from her date. She fixed Maria a cup of tea and coaxed her to tell her what was going on. They talked into the night and the next morning, Tiffany accompanied Maria to the college counseling center, where she arranged for an emergency appointment with a psychologist.

> *Before continuing with the case history, take a minute to think about the following questions, designed to direct your thinking further about the signs and symptoms, possible causes, and contributing factors of the problem. Some of the questions may be obvious to you, but others may raise points you had not considered. The questions also preview some of the information addressed later in the Assessment and Case Conceptualization sections that follow.*

▰▰▰   *WHAT DO YOU THINK?*   ▰▰▰

1. Would you characterize Maria's close relationship with her family as healthy or not? Explain your answer.
2. Maria felt that she did not "fit in" at the East Coast college. What are the psychological and environmental factors contributing to that feeling?
3. Evaluate Maria's level of distress, and make a prediction regarding her recovery.

> *The Assessment section presents actual data collected by the treating psychologist. Such data include the results of objective and projective psychological tests (such as the Rorschach or the MMPI-2), structured clinical interviews, mental status examinations, self-report checklists, clinician observations, family interviews, and histories. You will probably note that the style of writing is more formal in this part of the chapter to reflect the technical nature of assessment. In many cases the rationale for choosing a particular form of assessment will be provided, and occasionally the clinician's preliminary hypotheses regarding the client will be given, but generally speaking the Assessment section presents information in an objective fashion without analysis or interpretation. As you read the Assessment section, be aware of how that information may confirm or dispute your own hypotheses about the client.*

Assessment

Recognizing that Maria was in crisis, the psychologist immediately assessed Maria for suicidal thoughts. Maria denied that she had any thoughts of hurting herself. The psychologist then conducted a brief mental status examination to assess orientation, presentation, and intellectual functioning. The psychologist noted that Maria was well groomed and appropriately dressed. She had difficulty making eye contact and was tearful during the interview, but she was cooperative. She was oriented to time and place and seemed to have above-average intelligence. Her rate of responding to the questions was slightly slower than might be expected but not severely so. She denied having any hallucinations or delusions and appeared to have adequate reality testing.

The psychologist then conducted a structured interview to assess for a mood disorder. Maria's symptoms included tearfulness during the past two weeks, a diminished interest in her schoolwork, increased irritability, and difficulty waking early in the morning. She did not report any changes in her weight or her appetite or an increase in feelings of worthlessness or guilt. She maintained that she had become increasingly self-conscious since she started college but that she had always been shy around strangers. She did not report excessive worry, although she was concerned about her schoolwork and missing classes.

Maria had not suffered any physical or sexual trauma. She had been taken to the emergency room at age six when she hit her head after falling off the climbing bars at school. The family history did not point to any psychiatric problems. Her mother had some medical problems from a car accident she had had five years ago, and her father had had his gallbladder removed. No substance abuse was reported in her immediate family, although Maria admitted that her maternal grandfather died of cirrhosis of the liver.

Maria described her family relations as excellent. She was a timid child and stayed very close to her mother as a young girl. She had initial difficulty separating from her mother when she first started going to school but quickly adapted and soon loved school. She was an excellent student and reported being well adjusted. She described herself as second-generation Mexican American with strong ties to her cultural identity.

As was customary for all students who visited the college counseling center, Maria completed the Minnesota Multiphasic Personality Inventory (MMPI-2) and the Millon Clinical Multiaxial Inventory II (MCMI-2), two widely used objective personality inventories. Her responses on both revealed that she did not have any gross pathology. On the MMPI-2, her scores for Scale 2 (Depression) and Scale 7 (Psychasthenia) were slightly elevated but were not clinically significant. Her scores on the MCMI-2, which assesses more pervasive characterologic traits of the individual, were slightly more elevated on the dependent and avoidant scales but again were not clinically significant. This pattern suggests that Maria tends to be dependent on others, assuming a more passive stance in her interpersonal relations. She is likely to underestimate her own value and may place others in greater value than herself. Currently, she is experiencing some sadness and worry over her life situation.

The Case Conceptualization section draws on the details of the case history and the findings from the assessment phase to understand the dynamics of the person and the disorder. It is rare that a disorder has one cause or affects only one aspect of a person's life. More likely, a number of factors interact in a complex way. Thus, the cases in this book have been conceptualized from a biopsychosocial perspective, which means that the biological, psychological (cognitive and emotional), and social (environmental and cultural) correlates are examined whenever pertinent. As you read this part of the chapter, note how the research you have examined and information you have learned from your class lectures and textbook are applied to an actual case.

Case Conceptualization

At the time of her crisis, Maria was involved in sorting out her identity, an appropriate developmental task of late adolescence. She had been plucked from a safe and nurturing home and dropped into an environment that resembled her home very little. With a tenuous understanding of her own identity and a lack of supportive, familiar people in her surroundings, Maria became overwhelmed. The "Dear Jane" letter from her boyfriend added insult to injury, and her situation quickly took a turn for the worse.

What factors paved the way for this transitory crisis? Maria was a healthy and happy individual before she left for college, so how did she become overwhelmed so quickly? One piece in the puzzle is her temperament. Jerome Kagan and his colleagues (Kagan, Reznik & Snidman, 1988) have completed research that suggests that shyness is present at birth and that some infants have a "shy gene." Despite efforts to alter this personality trait, timidity tends to prevail in such individuals. Maria likely counts among this group. In a safe and familiar environment such as her home or social group, her timidity was not a serious impairment; however, when she found herself in a foreign environment, the insecurities and self-consciousness rose to the surface. She could not make new friends because she felt awkward and out of place. She sensed that others were more at ease at the college than she, and she began to evaluate her physical appearance negatively. These attitudes and behaviors prevented her from reaching out to others, resulting in social isolation and loneliness.

Some of Maria's self-consciousness was probably a distortion of her external world and the product of her inborn timidity. However, given that Maria was Latina, there may have been a reality base to her experience. She felt that she looked different from the other students, and she probably did, since the student body was largely Caucasian. At home she also was a minority, but Latinos were a larger presence in her state of California, and she was surrounded by her extended family a good deal of the time. Despite her high level of acculturation, Maria still considered herself Latina, and she was proud of the Mexican values and beliefs to which she adhered. Maria did not fully trust Tiffany, whom she viewed as quite distinct from herself, and this distance was likely exacerbated by their cultural differences.

An additional consideration in Maria's case is the developmental challenge of adolescent separation and individuation, traditionally thought to be essential to a healthy development (A. Freud, 1958). The primary task of this stage is for adolescents to disengage from their parents by severing ties and "shedding dependencies." By doing this, they are able to consolidate their own ego identities and establish other intimate relations. Failure to complete this stage of development adequately is hypothesized to result in psychopathology. Popular literature has referred to this transition as an "identity crisis."

According to these principles, one might conclude that Maria was abnormally attached to her family and that her enmeshment with them prevented her from developing her own identity. However, more recent research (Ainsworth, 1972, 1989; Grotevant & Cooper, 1985; Josselson, 1988) has questioned traditional theory and found that secure attachments serve to enhance, not impede, the breaking-away process. As long as Maria maintained a connection with her parents, she felt safer in negotiating her individuation process of forming her own identity. It was when she abruptly separated from them and failed to remain engaged that she began to experience adjustment problems.

Maria was unprepared for these challenges because her home life had been happy and she had been shielded from adversity by a protective family. She had a foundation from which to draw, but she lacked the maturity and experience to know how to pull herself out of a difficult situation. In some ways Maria's brush with distress was responsible for teaching her how to handle her emotional problems and prevent subsequent ones.

The Diagnosis section formalizes a diagnosis using the criteria set out in the Diagnostic and Statistical Manual of Mental Disorders, *Fourth Edition, commonly referred to throughout the text as* DSM-IV. *When appropriate, additional and competing diagnoses are given or ruled out, and a rationale is provided for doing so.*

Diagnosis

Maria was diagnosed with an adjustment disorder with depressed mood, acute duration. To qualify for this diagnosis, the individual must (1) have developed emotional or behavioral symptoms in response to a discrete psychosocial stressor that is considered within the realm of normal experience, (2) have greater distress than expected from exposure to the stressor or have social or occupational impairment, (3) not qualify for another Axis I disorder, such as major depression, and (4) not have the symptoms beyond a six-month period once the stressor is no longer present.

There were two identifiable stressors in Maria's case. First of all, she left the safety of her extended family and friends for a college far from home that differed culturally from her previous environment. Maria developed a depressed mood in response to this stressor, which then impaired her academic functioning. She missed classes and fell behind in her assignments, atypical of Maria's previous functioning. In addition, her boyfriend had begun dating another woman, intimating that there would be a rupture in the relationship.

The main question facing the psychologist was whether Maria qualified for a diagnosis of major depression; if so, that diagnosis would supersede a diagnosis of adjustment disorder. The results of the assessment phase did not point to previous bouts of depression in Maria's life, so Maria's current depressed state was not considered to be an exacerbation of a preexisting mood disorder. Further, her symptoms were not severe enough to satisfy a diagnosis of major depression, which requires at least five of a possible seven symptoms. (See Chapter 5 for a detailed discussion of major depressive disorder.) Maria had only three depressive symptoms that were diagnostically significant: sadness/tearfulness, diminished interest in everyday activities, and sleep disturbance. Posttraumatic stress disorder (PTSD), which is a severe stress reaction to an abnormal event, was ruled out for Maria, since a new school and romantic breakup are within the realm of normal experience and her symptoms were not typical of PTSD (for example, flashbacks). People with personality disorders (PD) can respond to stress in severe ways, and these people usually demonstrate impairment in interpersonal functioning. The clinician's observations and Maria's test results did not point to the presence of a personality disorder, however.

Adjustment disorders are quite common, occurring in approximately 10 to 15 percent of the population (Kaplan & Sadock, 1985), and most are accompanied by depressed mood (Maxmen, 1986). Children and adolescents frequently are diagnosed with this disorder (Newcorn & Strain, 1992) due to the rapid developmental changes and succession of challenges facing them. Of particular concern in diagnosing adjustment disorder for adolescents and young adults is the danger in overlooking a more severe psychiatric problem and attributing their emotional and behavioral dysfunction to a "phase."

The clinician concluded that Maria had had a stable upbringing and that her interpersonal and family relations were healthy prior to her recent emotional distress. The emergence of a depressed mood in response to the stress of a new school and separation from loved ones was understood as a maladaptive reaction to a normal challenge of life. It was expected that Maria would recover swiftly with effective interventions, since she appeared to have the necessary psychological resources. It was not expected that she would later develop a psychiatric disorder because recent research (Kovacs, Gatsonis, Pollock & Parrone, 1994) has shown that adjustment disorders have a short-term prognosis and do not predict later dysfunction.

> *The Treatment and Outlook portion of the chapter outlines the most effective treatment for the disorder. A more detailed explanation of the treatment used in the actual case is then given, along with the prognosis for the client. It is important to note that clinicians employ a variety of treatment modalities, the selection of which is based on the theoretical orientation of the clinician and the research supporting its use. Clearly, a number of other forms of treatment may be appropriate for many of the cases presented here, and the inclusion of one form over another does not necessarily imply its superiority.*

Treatment and Outlook

People with adjustment disorder usually respond well to brief psychotherapy. Maria engaged in eight weeks of supportive psychotherapy offered by the college counseling center to help her manage the distress of her breakup with Brian and to help her integrate into her new college environment. First, the therapist explored Maria's reaction to her new environment, helping to normalize the difficulty of leaving her family and friends for the first time. He encouraged Maria to reach out to other students with whom she felt comfortable. Maria attended a few meetings of the Latino Student Union, where she talked to several students she recognized from her classes. She no longer rejected Tiffany's invitations to socialize. Tiffany's help during Maria's crisis convinced Maria that Tiffany did care about Maria's well-being, and she began to trust her roommate more. The therapist also helped Maria to recognize that even though culturally she was a minority on campus, many students shared her self-consciousness and feelings of inadequacy. The therapist encouraged Maria to accept her shy nature but to guard against isolation in new situations.

Maria explored her relationship with her family, and she began to recognize the pressure she placed on herself to succeed. She decided to let her parents know about some of her difficulties and allow them to provide emotional support, which helped Maria tremendously. The therapist did not find Maria's reliance on her parents' support to be maladaptive; on the contrary, he believed that a continued closeness with her parents would provide her with the anchor she needed to develop her own identity and grow more independent.

With the therapist's guidance, Maria was able to recover from her breakup with Brian. She recognized that the geographic distance made it difficult to sustain a relationship and that it was important for her to focus her attention on her current life. She became more hopeful about having a romantic relationship in the future.

Finally, the therapist recommended that Maria develop a stress-reduction program for herself that included some form of physical activity and relaxation. Maria's level of distress, although serious enough to impair aspects of her functioning, was not sufficient to require psychopharmacologic treatment.

The prognosis for Maria was excellent. She finished her eight counseling sessions before going home for semester break. By then she had recovered from her depressed mood, had completed her academic assignments satisfactorily, and had made two new friends. She expressed apprehension about returning home and seeing Brian, but she felt confident that she would not fall into crisis again. If she did, however, she assured the therapist that she would seek counseling again.

> *The chapter concludes with a few questions to spark your thoughts and develop critical thinking. Some questions refer directly to the case presented, and others use the disorder as a springboard for further reflection. You may find it helpful to record your responses in a journal.*

▬ *THINKING CRITICALLY* ▬
QUESTIONS FOR DISCUSSION OR WRITING

1. Many people still view seeking psychological treatment with suspicion and are afraid that they will be labeled as "crazy" for the rest of their lives. Consider a scenario in which Maria is reluctant to seek treatment. What argument could you present to her to convince her that counseling would be beneficial to her?

2. Did you agree with the treatment that Maria was given? Why or why not? Do you think that Maria would have had the same results if she had been given medication (for example, an antidepressant)?

3. Explore the impact of culture in Maria's case. How, if at all, would Maria's case have been different if she had been Caucasian from the East Coast?

4. The title of this book is *Case Studies in Abnormal Psychology*. How abnormal was Maria?

CHAPTER 2

Panic Disorder:
Terror in the Cereal Aisle

*Do not look upon this world with fear
and loathing. Bravely face whatever the
gods offer.* MORIHEI UESHIBA, The Art of Peace

JEFF'S STORY

Jeff cranked up the volume on the car radio, singing along with Whitney Houston. Jeff was in a good mood this morning because he had finally taken a step in realizing his lifelong dream of becoming a performer by the age of thirty. He had an audition the next day for a role in a local musical production. Finally, after ten years of putting it off, he was going to get up on a stage and act and sing. It wasn't Broadway, but he had to start somewhere, or at least that's what Richard, his lover of eleven years, had convinced him to believe.

Jeff parked the car and zipped in to the grocery store to pick up a few items for breakfast, pausing in the cereal section to select a new brand. As he scanned the shelves, he realized for the first time just how many choices there were. Suddenly, out of nowhere, a crushing pressure pushed on his chest, and his throat tightened, as if he were choking. His heart raced, and within seconds his palms were clammy. The cereal boxes, which had been straight-edged and three-dimensional only a split second before, faded into the background like a fuzzy backdrop in a movie. Jeff was filled with sheer terror, and his breathing became short and rapid. "This is it. I'm having a heart attack, and I'm going to die," Jeff thought in horror. He experienced a very strong impulse to escape, so he dropped his shopping basket and rushed out of the grocery store to the safety of his car. He was gasping for air, frightened that he would die.

By the time he reached the parking lot, the pressure on his chest had eased up somewhat, and his breathing had begun to return to normal, enough for Jeff to believe that he had survived. He sat in his car for a long time—Jeff couldn't say precisely how long—before attempting to drive. "What the hell was that?" he wondered. "What is wrong with me?" That happy moment

11

with Whitney Houston seemed light years away, replaced by a growing fear and dread that what had just happened in the grocery store might strike again.

Then Jeff suddenly remembered a similar experience when he was seventeen while driving down the freeway with his father. It had been raining, the roads were slick, and the traffic was quite heavy. Cars were merging and passing him at great speed, and he recalls his father stiffening next to him, his teeth clenched, ordering him in a very stern voice to "get in the other lane." Suddenly, his breathing accelerated and his heart began to pound loudly and furiously, as if it were lodged between his ears. He was completely panicked, and the lights from the cars around him blinded him. He managed to change lanes and pull over on the shoulder of the road, but to this day he is sure that it was a miracle that they were not killed.

Jeff had chalked up that experience to being a new, scared driver, without giving it a second thought, because he never had problems driving again. He had other fears, like riding in elevators or being in high places, but Jeff considered these to be fairly ordinary fears, since he knew lots of people who had them. His strategy to avoid these situations when he could worked well for him so far, but he had never had such a frightening episode as the one at the grocery store.

Once at home, Jeff tried to conceal his panic from Richard. But when Richard started chatting about the audition, Jeff's face froze. There was no way he was going to that audition tomorrow, he thought, and what if he had one of those attacks while he was on stage? The thought of losing control in front of an audience that had come to evaluate him turned Jeff's stomach into a knot. Recognizing the fear in Jeff's body language, Richard coaxed Jeff to tell him what had happened. After hearing about Jeff's grocery store experience, Richard wisely insisted that Jeff consult a physician to make sure nothing was wrong with him physically.

Jeff had come to trust Richard's judgment over the many years they had been together. They had practically grown up together since falling in love at age nineteen. They had both sacrificed a great deal to stay with each other, including relations with their parents. Jeff felt that he had disappointed his father even before he told him that he was gay. His father, a stern, religious man from the Bible belt, could not accept that his only son was gay. Jeff did his best to share his father's interests in sports, playing ball, and cheering at the football games, but he couldn't hide his disinterest from his father, who knew that something was "not normal," as he said, with his son. Jeff was happy staying home, listening to music, and playing the piano. He knew all the words to the Broadway musicals, and he listened to those records over and over, driving his mother crazy.

His mother was a smart woman—Jeff always thought he got his smarts from his Mom and his looks from his Dad—but she was very unhappy. Most of the time she was busy keeping house and parenting her two children, but often she would "take sick" and spend days in bed, complaining of headaches and stomach problems. Jeff worried constantly about his mother, and he tried to cheer her up by singing songs and bringing her tea and toast. He felt responsible for her "spells" at times because his Dad would blame Jeff, saying: "If you were better behaved, then your mother would not be so sick," or "Look what you've done to your mother, now." Jeff prayed that God would not allow his mother to die, because he was petrified of being left with his father.

Jeff tried to act like a "normal" kid while he was in high school, even dating girls, but when he met Richard at age nineteen, he fell instantly in love and decided it was time to come out to his parents. During his last face-to-face conversation with his parents, his father told him, "If you go off with that man, you will never be allowed in this house again. You will no longer be my son." Jeff left his mother, his record collection, his room, and his belongings behind in that house. His younger sister, Tish, managed to keep in touch with Jeff, and eventually he was able to retrieve his favorite records through her.

The first five years of his relationship with Richard were still a blur in Jeff's mind. They were madly in love, traveling, partying, and scrounging for any jobs they could get. Money was tight, but it didn't seem to matter because they had each other. Their carefree approach to life came to an abrupt end when Richard discovered he had a heart defect, and they went into debt to pay for the expensive tests and treatments. Jeff began to monitor Richard's behavior like a hawk; he was so frightened that if Richard exerted himself or experienced too much stress in his life, he would simply drop dead. Jeff did everything he could to lighten Richard's load. Even though Richard was physically stronger, Jeff began to do all the heavy lifting and strenuous tasks at home, he worked more hours and managed the finances, and he did his best to protect Richard from negative thoughts.

Most important, however, Jeff gave up his dream of becoming a performer because he thought the lifestyle would be too stressful for Richard. He never told Richard that he had sacrificed his dream for him because he thought Richard might try to talk him out of it. He simply stuffed his desire away and went to work for a travel agent. Well liked by his colleagues and customers, Jeff did quite well. Meanwhile, Richard had an assortment of odd jobs through the years, but when the work became too stressful, he quit at Jeff's urging.

The two weathered many losses together as they watched a number of their friends die of AIDS. When Jeff's best friend died nine years into their relationship, Jeff did not think he could sustain one more loss. The nightmares started shortly after the funeral, and his everyday fears worsened. If Jeff didn't find Richard sitting at his usual spot in front of the TV when he walked in from work, he would feel a tightening in his gut and a fluttering in his heart.

He began calling Richard three or four times a day at work, just to hear his voice, which annoyed Richard, causing them to argue frequently. Jeff found himself drinking more whiskey in the evenings than usual, and they often had particularly acrimonious fights when he'd had too much to drink. They decided to work through their problems in couples' counseling, and Jeff finally told Richard about his lifelong dream to become a performer, which Richard encouraged him to pursue.

Jeff felt that he had already survived the worst—the family problems, the money problems, Richard's heart problems, the deaths, which was why he couldn't understand why he was having these attacks now. Jeff consulted a medical doctor, and he was relieved that the medical examination didn't reveal any heart problems. However, he was quite dismayed when the physician suggested that he see a psychiatrist because the attacks might be psychological.

Jeff delayed calling the psychiatrist, and he continued to have similar attacks, about one a week. Mostly they struck when Jeff was outside the home at the shopping mall or at a coffee shop, but once he had been awakened by an attack in the middle of the night. The attacks always took him by surprise and were similar in nature: His heart pounded, his throat tightened, and he felt a tingling in his arms. He began to grow terrified of leaving the house—especially of going to work, because he worried constantly that he would have an attack in front of his co-workers and be completely out of control. On several occasions he stayed home from work because his fear was too intense. He also begged out of grocery shopping to avoid returning to the "scene of the crime," as he dubbed the cereal section, and for the first time in their relationship, Richard took over that task. Jeff was ashamed of his inability to control his fear, and although he had always considered himself a strong person who could endure adversity, for the first time he began to see himself as weak and defective. He worried that he was going crazy.

He was able to conceal from Richard that he continued to have the attacks because he didn't want Richard to push him to see the psychiatrist. Six weeks after the first attack, however, when Richard and Jeff were shopping, an attack caught Jeff in the middle of a sentence. He couldn't finish his thought, and his breathing grew shallow. Richard recognized Jeff's fear and urged him to seek some psychiatric help, and Jeff finally agreed.

▦ *WHAT DO YOU THINK?* ▦

1. Jeff's physician ruled out a medical explanation for his "attack," yet Jeff's experience of physical symptoms was real. What are other explanations for his physiologic response and the ensuing fear?

2. What evidence do you have from Jeff's history that he is an anxious person? What may be contributing factors to his anxiety?

3. Jeff wondered why he was having these attacks at a seemingly positive point in his life. How would you answer this question?

Assessment

The clinician Jeff consulted recognized his symptoms as characteristic of panic attacks: the sudden rush of fear, accompanied by a racing heart, sweaty palms, a sensation of choking, and a fear of dying. However, he conducted a thorough psychological history and assessment and gathered medical information before making a final diagnosis, since panic attacks also can mimic other physical and mental disorders.

First, the psychologist obtained Jeff's medical records with his permission. Panic attacks can be associated with a variety of medical conditions, including hyperthyroidism, seizure disorders, vestibular disorders, hypoglycemia, and cardiac conditions such as arrhythmias. Jeff's electrocardiogram (ECG) was normal, and his physician had ruled out a cardiac condition to explain his attacks. The tests performed for thyroid dysfunction and hypoglycemia also were negative. Jeff's medical history did not point to any previous seizure activity, nor was there a history of seizures in his family.

A thorough history of substance use was obtained, since use of amphetamine and related substances, including caffeine, also can contribute to or cause a panic attack. Jeff admitted that he had used marijuana regularly and amphetamines infrequently in high school and during his twenties and that he continues to drink alcohol regularly. However, he had discontinued use of all illegal substances shortly after Richard had developed his heart problem. He consumes approximately four to six cups of coffee per day.

A detailed clinical assessment of his attacks was carried out to identify where and when the attacks occurred, their frequency and duration, the precise symptoms during attacks, and the thoughts and feelings Jeff experienced before, during, and after each attack. Jeff's attacks averaged about one a week, lasting about ten to fifteen minutes. Most of the attacks occurred when Jeff was outside the home. Jeff reported that he was always surprised by an attack and that he was frightened of dying or having a heart attack during the acute phase. Afterward, he feared he was going crazy, and later on he felt shameful that he could not control his fears. The clinician also assessed for the presence of major life changes preceding the initial attack, and Jeff noted that he had plans of realizing a lifelong dream of becoming a performer and that he had had an audition scheduled for the day after the attack. Jeff also attached importance to his impending thirtieth birthday.

Panic attacks often coexist with depression and a more free-floating anxiety (Newman & Bland, 1994), and Jeff's history included symptoms of both. The clinician gathered interview data and administered a number of self-report assessment instruments to evaluate for mood. Jeff's mood had decreased since his attack, accompanied by sleeplessness, feelings of failure and guilt, and increased irritability. He admitted that he worried constantly, that he had done this most of his life, and that he often felt as if bad things were going to happen to him. Jeff's score on the Beck Depression Inventory (BDI-II), a self-report instrument widely used for confirming a diagnosis of depression, indicated that he had a mild level of depression at the time he began therapy. Jeff also completed a Beck Anxiety Inventory (BAI), another self-report instrument to assess for the presence of anxiety. His scores indicated that he experienced a moderate amount of anxiety a good deal of the time.

Jeff was not able to provide detailed information regarding his family's psychological and medical history. He noted that his mother had what appeared to be vague somatic complaints (for example, headaches and stomachaches) and that her moods fluctuated. An uncle on his maternal side of the family had committed suicide, and some alcoholism was present on his father's side of the family.

Case Conceptualization

Jeff's panic attacks appeared to strike "out of the blue" without apparent warning or provocation, a terrifying feature of panic. In fact, Jeff was perplexed that these attacks began at a seemingly happy time in his life, after he had surmounted a number of challenges in his life. Are these attacks purely random, or are there identifiable causes for them? The answer involves a combination of biological, psychological, and environmental factors that contribute to the development of panic disorder in Jeff's particular case.

Once a medical condition has been ruled out, as it was for Jeff, the panic attack may be understood as a physiologic response to perceived danger (McNally & Eke, 1996). This is a rather complex process that will be summarized here in a very cursory way. Jeff's natural "alarm system," which mobilizes energy efficiently and quickly to deal with danger, gets set off when no apparent threat is present, as was the case in the cereal aisle. Jeff's symptoms of panic—racing heart, tightening in his throat, shortness of breath—were caused by the body's "fight or flight" response. The adrenal glands secrete epinephrine (also called *adrenaline*), which in turn causes the heart to race, the respiration to increase, and the muscles to contract. The tightness in Jeff's throat was caused by this constriction.

In individuals without panic attacks, this alarm system functions normally and sets off this physiological response only when there is a clear threat of danger. It remains unclear why people like Jeff have alarm systems that overfunction, but some researchers (Dager, Cowley & Dunner, 1987) believe that such people are biologically different in some way. Other researchers (George & Ballenger, 1992) have suggested that there is increased activity in the hippocampus and locus ceruleus portions of the brain, which monitor and control the brain's response to stimuli. There is also some indication that there is increased activity in the adrenergic system, which modulates heart rate and body temperature.

In addition to potential biological differences, Jeff's cognitive appraisal of his bodily sensations also played a prominent role in the development of his panic attacks (Clark, 1988). The clinician used the following example to clarify how Jeff might have interpreted bodily sensations differently from his partner. If Richard drank too much coffee and experienced an increased heart rate, he would likely attribute it to his coffee consumption and wait for the uncomfortable sensations to pass. Jeff, on the other hand, might interpret his heart palpitations (also caused by too much caffeine) as imminently dangerous, a sign of heart attack or death, thus activating his body's "fight or flight" response and setting off a vicious cycle of panic.

Once Jeff had his first panic attack in the cereal section, his apprehension increased, and he became acutely aware of his bodily sensations, a hypervigilance that made him inordinately sensitive to panic symptoms (for example, changes in breathing, heart rate, body temperature, and so on). It is also interesting to note that after the attack in the grocery store, Jeff was able to identify other situations in his past, once in an airplane and another one at the Grand Canyon, that were similar to panic attacks but which Jeff had attributed to his fears of flying and of heights.

Jeff puzzled over the timing of that first attack in the grocery store: Why then, when his life was seemingly calm and happy? A careful examination of the stressors in Jeff's life indicated that he and Richard had indeed overcome serious obstacles in their lives together. Nonetheless, Jeff was about to embark on his performance career, no doubt a source of excitement but also of anxiety. He had postponed his debut for many years, overtly out of consideration for Richard but also out of his own performance anxieties. In Jeff's mind, the audition was a crucible to assess whether he had "what it took" to pursue an acting career.

An additional consideration was the upcoming milestone of turning thirty, which only accentuated his need to "get going" with his career. The clinician was surprised to learn from Jeff that this birthday was a dreaded one because in his mind Jeff had always planned on being famous as he entered his fourth decade. Clearly, the stakes were high as Jeff approached this date.

Panic attacks in adulthood have been associated with a number of features in the person's early childhood environment, among them critical parents, emotional insecurity and dependency, and the discounting of assertive behavior. Closely attached to his mother, Jeff fretted about losing her because she was often "sick" with vague somatic symptoms, and Jeff felt guilty for her illness as a result of his father's admonitions. Jeff internalized that "making a ruckus" or "causing problems" could have severe consequences and that it is better to suppress these impulses. Later, as an adult, he reenacted this scenario with Richard, feeling overly responsible for Richard's health, suppressing his own desires, fears, and emotions to protect Richard.

Jeff experienced multiple losses in his life. He feared losing his mother and later Richard due to heart problems, he was abandoned by his father, and he lost a number of close friends to AIDS. Already a worrier, these events exacerbated Jeff's belief that the world was a dangerous place.

Diagnosis

Jeff's attacks were consistent with the criteria for panic attacks as outlined in *DSM-IV* as a distinct episode of severe fear or discomfort with at least four of the following symptoms:

1. Racing heart, palpitations
2. Sweating
3. Shaking
4. Shallow breathing, belabored breathing
5. A choking sensation
6. Chest pain
7. Nausea or abdominal discomfort
8. Dizziness, feeling light-headed
9. Derealization or depersonalization
10. Fear of losing control or of going crazy
11. Fear of dying
12. Numbness or tingling
13. Chills or hot flashes

Jeff experienced seven of these symptoms regularly during his attacks. A diagnosis of panic disorder was made because his panic attacks were recurrent: In the two months prior to therapy, he had had weekly panic attacks. Not all individuals with a diagnosis of panic disorder have this pattern of frequency; the panic attacks may be less frequent for a longer period of time, for instance. Generally speaking, the panic attack reaches a peak within ten minutes and then begins to subside. Severe anxiety can follow an attack and last an hour or so.

In order for the diagnosis of panic disorder to be made, at least some of the panic attacks must occur spontaneously, that is, in the absence of specific situational triggers. Although Jeff was able to identify factors in his history that likely contributed to his development of panic disorder, his attacks remained for the most part uncued by situational triggers. For example, the cereal selection was not the precipitating cause of his grocery store attack.

People with panic disorder experience considerable distress over when and where the next attack will strike. Jeff worried constantly about the consequences of his attacks, concerned that he would have an attack while auditioning for his musical and later that he would have one at work.

A final criterion for the diagnosis of panic disorder is a change in behavior as a result of the panic attacks. Jeff found himself avoiding common situations such as grocery shopping in order to evade a potential attack. He handed this task over to his partner, Richard, which was a significant change for the two of them and a "lesser of two evils" for Jeff because he did not trust Richard's ability to select appropriate groceries. Jeff was disturbed by this change and believed that he was "weak" because he couldn't overcome his fear of the grocery store. He viewed his panic attacks as a "character weakness" and wondered if he would ever be able to overcome them.

The clinician did not diagnose Jeff with agoraphobia, which literally means "fear of open spaces." The underlying fear in agoraphobia is the anticipation that a panic attack will strike in a situation for which there is no escape (Clum & Knowles, 1991). Further, people with agoraphobia are also concerned about what other people would think of them if they had a panic attack in public. Thus, to minimize the distress and the embarrassment of panic attacks, people with agoraphobia will avoid situations such as crowded spaces, freeway driving, tunnels, bridges, and so on. When Jeff sought treatment, he was beginning a pattern of avoiding work and the grocery store, but he managed to leave his house nonetheless. The clinician did not find sufficient evidence that Jeff's avoidance had advanced to the stage of agoraphobia.

The clinician noted that prior to this series of panic attacks, Jeff worried more than the average person about his relationship, financial difficulties, and the health of his partner. This more pervasive, chronic anxiety raised the question of a generalized anxiety disorder, which often coexists with panic disorder (Wetzler & Sanderson, 1995). Although the worrying did cause Jeff to exhibit some irritability and restlessness, his social and professional life was not significantly impaired by his worrying, so the clinician ruled out this diagnosis. Since Jeff had used substances in the past and had turned recently to alcohol to manage some of his anxiety, the clinician decided to address Jeff's substance-abuse problem once his panic attacks were under control. (See Chapter 9 for a more detailed discussion of alcohol dependence.)

Treatment and Outlook

The most widely used treatments for panic disorder are cognitive-behavioral (Clark, 1988) and pharmacologic (Ballenger et al., 1988) approaches. The goals of treatment are to reduce the physiologic effects of the panic, eliminate avoidant behavior related to the anxiety, and change the thoughts that maintain the fear of an impending attack. The most common treatment has been a behavioral approach of gradually exposing a patient to the feared situation, thus reducing the phobic avoidance and anticipatory anxiety. For example, to reduce Jeff's avoidance of the grocery store, Jeff asked Richard to assist him in approaching the store progressively over a period of a week. Each day he and Richard got closer to the site where Jeff had had the attack. Once Jeff was able to enter the store, he returned the next day and moved toward the dreaded cereal section. After increasing his tolerance of being there accompanied by Richard, Jeff attempted to enter the store alone, and so on until he was able to drive to and shop in the store on his own. This technique was especially helpful for Jeff, and although he always felt a twinge as he approached the cereal aisle, he was nonetheless able to resume the shopping again.

Cognitive-behavioral therapy (CBT) has been shown to help people with panic disorder to identify, regulate, and restructure their negative thoughts that relate to the danger of their panic attacks. Since panic attacks mimic life-threatening situations, many patients interpret their bodily sensations in a catastrophic way, believing that they are facing a physical or mental emergency (for example, that they are having a heart attack, going to die from choking, or are going crazy).

Jeff's therapist educated him about the physiologic effects of the "fight or flight" stress response, and Jeff was able use this information to mentally challenge the thought that he was having a medical emergency when the attack occurred. CBT also can be used to reduce avoidance behavior by challenging a patient's belief about the danger of entering a situation reminiscent of a previous panic attack.

Jeff kept a diary of his past and subsequent attacks, in which he noted the time of day, the physiologic symptoms accompanying the attack, and his thoughts and feelings before, during, and after the attack. He was able to examine some of the negative interpretations that came up during and after the attack (for example, "I'm a weak person because I can't control these attacks") and, with the help of the psychologist, identify the inaccuracies (for example, "I am having difficulty right now with these attacks, but it doesn't mean that I am weak; I have shown great strength in the past"). Jeff was able to keep a similar diary for his anticipatory anxiety, and he found it very helpful in reducing his fears of attacks.

Other behavioral techniques such as progressive relaxation, yoga, and meditation have been found to reduce overall anxiety in individuals with panic disorder. Jeff practiced deep breathing exercises daily and used these during the course of the day to calm himself when he felt fears about his panic attacks approaching. He was never able to turn to deep breathing during the actual onset of an attack, but he found that the regular practice calmed him considerably. At the clinician's recommendation, Jeff also greatly reduced his caffeine intake, since caffeine is associated with panic-like symptoms in some individuals.

A final treatment for panic disorder is psychopharmacology. Some benzodiazepines have been shown to reduce panic attacks (Ballenger et al., 1988) and are used widely because of their fast-acting properties. However, benzo-diazepines are habit-forming and place patients at risk for drug dependence. Given the presence of substance abuse in Jeff's family and his own reliance on alcohol, Jeff wanted to try the cognitive-behavioral approaches before using medication. Other trials using tricyclic antidepressants (Klein & Fink, 1962) and selected serotonin reuptake inhibitors (Schneier et al., 1990) have shown efficacy in managing panic disorder, and Jeff was told that medications that were not habit-forming were available if necessary.

The prognosis for Jeff was very good. After twelve weeks of treatment, he managed to go through the final eight weeks free of attacks. A six-month follow-up revealed that he had not had another attack. He has resumed his role as the grocery shopper in the family, and he has not missed work as a result of his disorder. Although he maintained that he was calmer, his free-floating anxiety did not remit completely, and he still calls himself a "constant worrier." Unfortunately, Jeff never attended his audition, and to date he has not returned to the stage.

▬ *THINKING CRITICALLY* ▬
QUESTIONS FOR DISCUSSION OR WRITING

1. Some people with panic disorder find it difficult to believe that they do not have a medical condition, even when tests fail to detect one. Suppose a friend of yours felt this way. How might you explain what happens physiologically to help your friend understand the panic attacks?

2. Being gay in a predominantly heterosexual world can be stressful because of the cultural bias against this sexual orientation. Explore the ways in which Jeff's life was affected negatively by these prejudices and the extent to which, if any, this stress was associated with his panic disorder.

CHAPTER **3**

Obsessive-Compulsive Disorder: *Too Much of a Good Thing*

> Doctor. *What is it she does now? Look, how she rubs her hands.*
> Gentleman. *It is an accustomed action with her, to seem thus washing her hands: I have known her continue in this a quarter of an hour.*
> WILLIAM SHAKESPEARE, Macbeth

PHILLIP'S STORY

4:30 a.m. The bedside alarm breaks the stillness of the night. Phillip lunges to shut it off before it wakes Theresa, his girlfriend. He slides out of bed and gazes at her motionless form. Thankfully, she seems to have slept through it. At least maybe they won't fight this morning. Things are bad enough, he thinks, as he shuffles off to the bathroom, rubbing the sleep from his eyes.

Phillip stares at the mirror. He carefully thinks through every step of the elaborate ritual he has devised for shaving. He lays out his razor and shaving cream, puts them back, and then lays them out again. With painstaking diligence, he turns the razor so that it is exactly parallel to the sink. He taps his fingers on the porcelain and hums a Smashing Pumpkins song to himself. Finally, he turns on the water and silently counts, hoping to make it to one hundred before the water gets hot.

"One hundred and five!" he almost shouts out with excitement as the running water begins to steam. Now Phillip turns the faucet that controls the cold water. One-quarter inch he turns it: still too hot. Another quarter inch, then another, until the water is just right. If the water gets too cold, he has to start over again.

Slowly and methodically, Phillip washes his face. Following an exacting procedure, he works his way from his forehead to his chin. He picks up the shaving cream and shakes the can exactly seven times. He lathers his face, careful to distribute the foam evenly. He shaves, rinsing his razor with each stroke. Washing off his face, he then rubs his fingertips over his cheeks and neck. "Not smooth enough," he says to himself and shaves his face once more.

Showering and dressing, Phillip continues to follow his morning routine, paying careful attention not to deviate in the slightest from his self-prescribed rituals. Anticipation of each step in the sequence raises his anxiety; satisfactory completion brings relief. "Please don't wake up, Theresa," Phillip thinks to himself. "You'll throw me off, and I'll never get to work on time."

Phillip enters the kitchen and starts his breakfast ritual as he hears Theresa wake up and turn on the shower. Its now 6:30 a.m. The morning has gone well so far, and he begins to relax a little. He's finishing his breakfast as Theresa comes in.

"What time did you get up this morning?" she asks.

"Oh, about 5:30," Phillip replies, lying in order to avoid a fight. Lately, Theresa has lost patience with him. First, it was her complaint that there was no room to walk around their apartment. Jokes about his being a "pack rat" soon gave way to criticism and disgust because he simply was unable to throw anything away.

This was Phillip's third significant relationship. He had dated several women, usually classmates or co-workers. He wanted to marry Theresa, but their recent conflicts over his hoarding and lateness had caused a significant strain on their relationship. Theresa, who is three years older than he, was a math professor at a local university. She was considering an offer for a tenured position in another state. This offer had precipitated something of a crisis in that they both felt tremendous pressure to make a decision concerning their commitment to each other. While Theresa seemed to share his love, she was afraid that Phillip's problems would interfere in their relationship and in his ability to hold a job.

At 7:45, Phillip left home for work. Despite the tedious and demanding nature of his morning rituals, it was driving that scared him half to death. For the past six months Phillip had developed a fear that he had run over someone anytime he went over a bump or heard an unusual road noise. His fear became so great that he had to drive repeatedly over his route to make sure that there was not a body lying in the road. This new fear consumed so much of his time that he was repeatedly late to work. He had been fired from his last job as a city planner two months ago. Although he had easily found a new job, he had settled for a lesser position and salary in exchange for employment that offered more flexible hours. His fear continued to worsen, and he often required an additional thirty to forty-five minutes to reach his destination. Driving any place besides work was simply out of the question.

As Phillip finally pulled into the parking lot at work, it was 9:15. It had taken an hour and a half to drive what would take anyone else forty-five minutes. Nonetheless, Phillip was relieved. At work he was relatively free of the need to perform compulsive rituals or be consumed by obsessive doubt. He sat in his car and wondered how he had gotten to this point.

At twenty-eight, Phillip was a college graduate with a degree in engineering. Although he often was teased at work about his meticulous grooming and his avoidance of throwing out the trash, he was generally well liked. With the exception of his being late to work, his job performance was impeccable. He had won awards in the past for his design projects and, before being fired, had risen to the rank of supervisor in his department.

Phillip was born and raised in a seaside town in Oregon. His father managed a health food store, and his mother was an artist. She was home much of the time raising Phillip and his younger brother. Phillip fondly thought of his parents as "typical sixties hippies" who had used drugs recreationally in college but who were now more concerned with the environment and health issues. An uncle had been diagnosed with Tourette's disorder, a disorder involving both motor and vocal tics; otherwise, Phillip considered his family to be loving, supportive, and "normal in their own weird way."

Phillip's childhood was largely uneventful. He was a good student and enjoyed spending his free time building models and exploring the sand dunes near his home. He was always neat and well organized, in contrast to his brother, who was sloppy and tended to leave his things lying wherever they fell. Since the two brothers shared a bedroom, this led to endless arguments between them. He remembered his mother eventually being driven to build a partition that separated each brother's side of the room.

As Phillip grew older, he became increasingly more concerned with cleanliness and health. He washed his hands several times a day and surreptitiously blew on his hands if he touched someone else's things. He prided himself on the neatness of his written work and class projects. In college he moved out of the dorm after his freshman year because he couldn't stand the thought of sharing a toilet seat. Despite these concerns, he maintained an active social life, even though he was considered a "nerd" by some.

Phillip's musings were halted abruptly by the sound of a co-worker calling his name. Although his day at work went well, he was later than usual in getting home. Twice he had to add several miles to his trip in order to reassure himself that he had not run over anyone. Theresa was predictably angry and insisted that he get some help or she would leave him. After much pleading and protesting, Phillip agreed to see a therapist.

▭ *WHAT DO YOU THINK?* ▭

1. Being cautious, careful, and orderly can be positive traits. At what point do they become maladaptive?

2. Being a city planner, with its emphasis on detail, organization, and structure, seems well suited to Phillip's personality. What other types of jobs do you think people like him might be drawn to?

3. What is it about a person that could cause ordinarily beneficial traits to become so self-defeating?

Assessment

Theresa drove Phillip to his appointment with a psychologist they had located through her university. The psychologist listened carefully as Phillip related stories of his morning rituals, his hoarding, and his fears about running over someone while driving. He cried as he recounted how his behaviors had affected his relationship with Theresa and with previous girlfriends and how he had lost a promising career in the city planning office. He was glad to be telling someone about his problems, though, and was desperate to find out if he could be helped.

The psychologist reassured Phillip that he thought he could help but that he wanted to obtain additional information first. He asked Phillip about a number of other symptoms, including various phobias, depression, substance abuse, and panic attacks. He also inquired about several historical factors sometimes known to cause or be associated with the symptoms described by Phillip, such as head injury, the use of certain drugs, or various medical conditions.

Phillip admitted that he experienced several symptoms of depression, which had worsened around the time he lost his job as a city planner. He experienced no other phobias besides his fears of contamination and illness. He had not used drugs or alcohol for several years following an incident in which he had become intoxicated and yelled at his then girlfriend. They had broken up as a result, and Phillip had sworn off drinking because he did not want to "lose control" again. He had never experienced a panic attack. Finally, Phillip had never suffered a head injury and had no history of serious health problems. He readily agreed to see a physician and obtain a physical examination prior to the next meeting. The psychologist had insisted that a physical examination be conducted to rule out any underlying medical condition prior to initiating a psychological or psychiatric intervention.

During Phillip's second appointment, the psychologist administered a structured clinical interview designed to clarify the nature and severity of a patient's obsessive thoughts and compulsive behaviors. On this instrument, the Yale-Brown Obsessive Compulsive Scale, or Y-BOCS (Goodman et al., 1989), the clinician rates the patient's responses to ten items concerning how much time is spent on the patient's symptoms, how much interference they cause, how distressful they are, how much of an effort is made by the patient to resist these symptoms, and how much control the patient feels he or she has over the symptoms. Ratings are made on a five-point scale from zero (none) to four (extreme), for a possible maximum score of forty. Any score over twenty is considered to be indicative of obsessive-compulsive disorder (OCD). Some additional test items address specific obsessions and compulsions, levels of insight, indecisiveness, being overly responsible, degree of difficulty starting or finishing tasks, and pathological doubting.

From this comprehensive interview, Phillip admitted spending over six hours a day engaged in obsessive thinking and compulsive behavior. Only when he was at work was he completely free of these intrusive thoughts and behaviors. He felt that the OCD symptoms caused him substantial interference in his work and social life, and he was severely disturbed by this. He made some attempts to resist these obsessions and compulsions but often was unable to. Except at work, he felt that he was rarely successful in controlling his OCD symptoms, no matter what he tried. Based on his responses, Phillip achieved a score of twenty-eight on the Y-BOCS, suggesting that he met the criteria for OCD.

In addition, Phillip displayed fair insight into his condition. He admitted, albeit reluctantly, that some of his thoughts and behaviors were absurd and excessive. He also avoided driving because he did not want to hit anyone, and he disliked going to public places for fear of contamination. He had significant problems making decisions, and he constantly doubted his perceptions and memories. He blamed himself for every problem in his relationship, even those over which he clearly had no control. And he rarely finished any project he started, often becoming distracted or giving in to the need to perform a compulsive behavior.

Case Conceptualization

Obsessions and compulsions are among the oldest recognized symptoms. Once ascribed to possession by the devil, many victims of the Inquisition and Salem witch hunts were likely suffering from OCD. OCD was once thought to be very rare because few people sought treatment for this disorder. Many sufferers kept their problem a shameful secret, confining their rituals to their homes. However, several recent community surveys show a prevalence rate higher than anyone suspected: 2 to 3 percent of the U.S. population will show these symptoms at some time in their lives (Perse, 1988). Similar rates of occurrence have been found in most other countries surveyed except in Taiwan, which for some reason has unusually low rates of all psychiatric disorders.

OCD is the fourth most common psychological disorder (behind alcohol and drug dependence, depression, and phobias), affecting about seven to ten million people. Probably the most famous person to have suffered from OCD is Howard Hughes, the eccentric millionaire aviator. It affects men and women equally, although the age of onset in men is often earlier than in women by about five years. While childhood OCD clearly resembles its adult counterpart, children rarely request help or experience their symptoms as undesirable. When a parent or teacher brings the child to the attention of a mental health professional, the child is often misdiagnosed as having attention-deficit hyperactivity disorder (ADHD).

The onset of OCD symptoms is usually gradual, but acute onsets have been observed. For most sufferers, the severity of the illness waxes and wanes as the symptoms are exacerbated in relationship to stress. A few (15 percent), however, show a progressive deterioration and may become psychotic. The vast majority (80 percent) of those with OCD experience both obsessions and compulsions, although about 15 percent will have obsessions only and 5 percent will display only compulsive behaviors.

Some researchers have identified what they call *obsessive-compulsive spectrum disorders*. These disorders share a number of the same symptoms and respond to some of the same treatments. These include body dysmorphic disorders (a preoccupation with imagined or excessive defects in one's appearance), hypochondriasis (the fear of having a serious disease based on a misinterpretation of a physical symptom), binge eating, onychophagia (nail biting), pyromania (fire setting), repetitive self-mutilation, trichotillomania (hair pulling), and kleptomania.

There are various causes of OCD. The disorder runs in families and probably has a genetic basis. Identical twins are much more highly concordant for OCD than are fraternal twins. Between 10 and 15 percent of the first-degree relatives of someone with OCD are also likely to have the disorder. The incidence of ADHD and tic disorders such as Tourette's disorder is also high in the families of those with OCD.

In the past, psychodynamic theorists believed that OCD arose when unacceptable wishes and impulses were only partially driven out of consciousness. To defend against the awareness of these wishes, those with OCD used the defenses of isolation and undoing. *Isolation* separates an idea or image from the feeling associated with it and prevents the feeling from becoming conscious. It is the energy of the repressed, consciously unacceptable emotion that gives the idea or image its compelling obsessional quality. When the isolation defense is about to fail, the secondary defense of *undoing* (doing the opposite of what one wishes to do) produces a compulsive act. Phillip's fear that he may have run over someone might be said to contain an unconscious wish to kill someone that causes him to feel guilt as if he had actually carried out the deed. According to this theory, he can reassure himself only by returning to see if there is a body on the road.

Psychodynamic theorists associated their defensive pattern with a partial regression to an early stage of development when children are intensely concerned about control over their bodily functions. Regression revives the childhood belief that mere thoughts can cause external events. It is this magical thinking that makes obsessions so disturbing and compulsive actions so strongly effective in bringing relief (Fenichel, 1945).

Behavioral psychologists rejected the psychodynamic concept of repression but agreed about the significant role of anxiety in OCD. They proposed that some people have intense biological responses to stress or have learned early in life to believe that certain thoughts are unclean, immoral, or dangerous. Whenever the person with OCD has the unacceptable thoughts, she or he becomes anxious, so the thought triggers the anxiety. Compulsive rituals are then believed to reduce the anxiety and reestablish a sense of control (Rimm & Masters, 1974).

Recent psychological studies have identified OCD as a malfunction in the neural pathways that link the frontal lobes with the basal ganglia in the brain. Magnetic resonance imaging studies have shown tissue loss in the caudate nucleus, which is part of the basal ganglia. The frontal lobes have been described as the seat of deliberation and judgment, and the basal ganglia serve as a relay station in the planning and execution of movements. In patients with OCD, the caudate nucleus does not seem to be performing its usual function of preventing vagrant thoughts from being translated into action. The neural circuit that includes the caudate cingulate and orbitofrontal cortexes (areas just behind the forehead) and thalamus is hyperactive because the usual inhibitory feedback mechanisms are not working. As a result, obsessional thinking (reflected in positron emission test studies as high frontal lobe activity) persists until a compulsive ritual stops it. As noted earlier, OCD can be caused by head injuries that damage the basal ganglia or by diseases that cause nerve degeneration in that area of the brain (Sergeant, 1994).

Generally speaking, since psychodynamic methods of intervention have not been very successful in treating OCD, these theories generally have fallen out of favor. Increasingly, there is more research support for understanding OCD as a type of neurological disorder that is closely related to other frontal lobe disorders such as ADHD and tic disorders. There is still much to be learned about the causes and bases of these disorders.

Diagnosis

OCD is characterized by recurrent obsessions or compulsions that occupy a significant amount of time or that result in significant distress or impairment (APA, 1994). *Obsessions* are defined as unwelcome and distressing ideas, thoughts, images, or impulses that repeatedly enter the patient's mind against his or her will. These thoughts usually are repugnant to the patient, who may recognize them as senseless. They also may be incongruent with the patient's personality. Common obsessions include fear of harming others; repeated doubts; fears of swearing and of doing something embarrassing; concerns with cleanliness, contamination, or illness; sexual or religious preoccupations; and magical thinking (believing that something bad will happen unless everything is in the right place).

Compulsions, on the other hand, are actions that the patient feels driven to perform despite the recognition that they may be senseless or excessive. The patient may attempt to resist performing the behavior, but his or her anxiety will not diminish until the behavior is completed. Common complaints include those of cleaning or washing, checking, repetition, counting, ordering or arranging, and hoarding.

It is important to recognize that almost everyone has occasional obsessive thoughts and engages in some compulsive behaviors, especially in times of stress. These transitory occurrences would not indicate a diagnosis of OCD, since they must lead to significant interference in one's social or occupational functioning before meeting the criteria for this disorder. Usually, the obsessions or compulsions must take up more than one hour a day, keep someone from functioning normally at work or school, or disrupt the person's social activities or relationships before constituting a problem that requires treatment.

Treatment and Outlook

Phillip was treated by those methods in most common use today for OCD: behavior therapy and medication. He was referred to a psychiatrist for medication and began taking Luvox (fluoxamine), one of the newer medications known as selective serotonin reuptake inhibitors (SSRIs). Although 70 to 80 percent of OCD patients respond to medication, no one really understands why it works. Serotonin is one of many neurotransmitters in the brain that allow the individual neurons to communicate with each other and to act in concert. Interestingly enough, the reuptake of serotonin in the brain for people with OCD seems to be normal. Serotonin is involved in many brain circuits besides those of the frontal cortex or basal ganglia. SSRIs cause an immediate rise in serotonin levels but usually require two months or more to alleviate the symptoms of OCD. Other commonly used SSRIs include Prozac (fluoxetine), Zoloft (sertraline), and Paxil (paroxetine). The tricyclic antidepressant medication Anafranil (clomipramine) was the first drug used to treat OCD, but it is now used rarely because the SSRIs produce less severe side effects (Jenike, 1992).

Since it has been found that most patients relapse quickly if they discontinue the medication unless they also have had behavior therapy, Phillip also was treated with the behavioral techniques of exposure and response prevention. He was first taught relaxation techniques and then asked to rank order situations that provoked distress or anxiety. He was then exposed in his imagination to the obsession-provoking situation, starting with the least distressing, and then prevented from performing his usual ritual until he became habituated to the obsessions and was able to dismiss them. Both imagining the dreaded situation and actual exposure to it were used. He was encouraged to practice these techniques at home, and his girlfriend was involved in the therapy.

For example, in the treatment of Phillip's cleaning rituals, he identified contact with any form of trash as triggering an obsessive fear of contamination and a compulsive need to wash. First, the psychologist demonstrated that he could put his hands in the office trash can and still be safe. He then had Phillip put his hands on the trash for increasing periods of time, gradually increasing the amount of time he had to wait before he could wash his hands. His anxiety about contact with the trash gradually subsided to a manageable level so that he was then able to distract himself from the obsessional thought whenever he took out the trash at home.

As indicated earlier, the vast majority of patients with OCD (70 to 80 percent) can be treated successfully with a combination of medication and behavior therapy. Phillip's symptoms were reduced to tolerable levels that no longer interfered with his work and relationship after about twenty hours of treatment over a two-month period. He and Theresa became engaged and decided to relocate so that she could take a tenured position, with the idea that Phillip could apply for a new job more commensurate with his education and abilities. Phillip agreed that he would continue therapy after he moved.

In rare cases in which nothing else is effective and the OCD symptoms are intolerable, the last resort is brain surgery. The most common operation is stereotactic cingulotomy, which removes part of the cingulate cortex. Another technique is anterior capsulotomy, which severs some connections between the caudate nuclei and the thalamus. About one-third of patients with the most severe forms of OCD obtain relief through surgery. They may take weeks or months to respond, suggesting that the brain needs time to establish new connections and ways of operating. The most serious potential side effects of surgery are seizures and personality changes manifested as poorer judgment and planning ability (Jenike & Rauch, 1994).

▬ *THINKING CRITICALLY* ▬
QUESTIONS FOR DISCUSSION AND WRITING

1. OCD is a good example of a psychological disorder about which our understanding has changed drastically over the past twenty years. Previously conceptualized as an anxiety disorder (and it is indeed still classified as such in *DSM-IV*), its neurological basis is now firmly established. How does this change in the way we understand the biological bases for psychological disorders affect our understanding and treatment of mental illness in general?

2. Why do you think carefully and supportively exposing a patient to the very thing he or she so fears, such as the germs associated with trash, could be effective in resolving their symptoms?

CHAPTER 4

Posttraumatic Stress Disorder: *A Horror That Never Stops*

A heavy burden does not kill on the day it is carried. KENYAN PROVERB

MISHA'S STORY

"You're the best, Misha," his supervisor said when Misha agreed to make a delivery to an unsafe part of town that evening. Misha ran his fingers through his thinning hair and frowned at his boss's compliment, thinking, "I just do my job, whatever it is, I do it. That's just the way it is." But he was grateful to have his job, which took him several months to find after he arrived in this country with his wife and two young sons from a small town in Russia. It seemed no one wanted to employ a 52-year-old immigrant who spoke little English, even though he was a responsible, hard worker. Misha had told the Russian case worker who found him this job, "I'll do anything to support my family. I'll do anything to avoid being on government support." Misha had kept his word, and a year later, he had become the star employee, willing to come in on any shift any day.

That evening, Misha navigated the streets easily because he had come to know the city quite well from his delivery job. He turned down the street bearing the name on his delivery slip and squinted as he tried to discern the numbers on the houses. He found 1564 and 1584, but he couldn't locate 1574. He decided to park the vehicle and walk down the alleyway between the two buildings, carrying the large delivery parcel in his arms. Misha took in his surroundings. It was a quiet, poorly lit street, and the scent of night-flowering jasmine filled the air. As he turned into the alleyway, a large man suddenly emerged from the darkness, and Misha froze, terrorized when he saw the shiny knife the man held in his hand. Misha thrust the box in the face of the man in front of him to free his arms, but by then two more men appeared, grabbing Misha on either side and pushing him down to the sidewalk. Misha was sure that he was going to die, and he felt powerless to defend himself against the knife. Hearing a car approach, the men grabbed the money in Misha's wallet and ran away, disappearing as suddenly as they had appeared.

Misha does not remember how much time passed before he was able to pull himself together to drive back to the store. He was shocked at what had just happened to him, yet he felt numb, as if the incident had happened to someone else. Back at the store, as Misha attempted to reconstruct the story for the store manager in his limited English, he was overcome with embarrassment that he had failed to note important information: He had no recollection of the assailants' facial features, their dress, or even their age. He was certain of only two images, which were indelibly etched into his memory: the first assailant's hand and the size and shape of the knife. Misha had always prided himself on his visual recall and awareness of his surroundings, so when the manager brought Misha's attention for the first time to a bloodied cut on his arm, Misha became quite disturbed. He had no idea how it got there. It must have been the knife, but he had no memory of being knifed.

This incident was so different from the one that occurred less than a month ago, Misha thought, when a young man bearing a gun entered the store and ordered the three workers to get down on the floor while he emptied the cash register. Misha remembers that he was afraid then, of course, but he thought to himself, "If I die here, I will be with the others. I won't die alone." Afterward, he felt a special bond with those co-workers, since they had survived together, and he recovered from that experience quickly. But Misha felt utterly alone and terrified in the alleyway, and he lost his wits. He couldn't defend himself.

That night at home Misha could not stop reliving the event in his mind: the darkness, the sudden appearance of those men, the knife in front of his eyes, his helplessness. "Why didn't I see them coming?" Misha wondered. "How could I have been so caught off guard? Why didn't I at least get a picture of their faces?" Misha was especially ashamed because he had been a prize fighter in his younger days, and he had never lost a fight—he was fearless and agile. He always saw the attacks coming when he was fighting: What happened to him that night?

His wife, Irina, tried to comfort Misha, but he rebuffed her attempts at soothing him. The next morning Misha was determined to go to work and face his fears and go on with his life, but he was jittery and irritable, lashing out at co-workers whom he had previously gotten along with. He jumped whenever the phone rang or the door slammed. He could not stop the thoughts from invading his mind, especially about his failure to respond with courage. He felt that his strength had been sucked out of him. When the manager asked him to deliver a package that evening, he agreed, but as soon as he got into the car, he froze again, unable to start the car. He was gripped with fear just thinking about approaching the scene of the assault. Then he began crying. "My world is crumbling," he thought. "I can't take care of my family anymore. I can't protect my wife and children from danger. I have no more worth."

His manager suggested he take a few weeks off of work, and Misha reluctantly agreed. But instead of improving, Misha's condition worsened day by day: He stopped sleeping, he ate only little and erratically, and he began to experience severe mood swings, irritable and aggressive one minute, passive and crying the next. He had excruciating pains in his neck and legs, and at times his legs would buckle under him. He did not want his children going outside the apartment because he was sure the "hooligans" would come after his family and attack them. He dreaded nightfall because the horrors visited him then, like a nightmare that never ends. He insisted on keeping the lights on in the apartment at all times, and he had three additional locks installed on the door. He paced during the night, and when his wife summoned him to bed, he screamed at her.

He knew what his wife must be thinking: that it would be better to get rid of him because he was only a burden now and of no use to the family. He had begun to think that perhaps she would poison him so she wouldn't have to put up with a weak man who could not protect his family.

Their relationship had not always been that way. Misha met Irina a year after his first wife had died of cancer. Until that point, nothing could take his mind off his loss, but when Irina took pity on him and comforted him, he began to feel more hopeful about his future. They had a romantic courtship, and since he had a good job in Russia, he was able to buy her presents and take her on weekend trips. Both of them loved music, and Irina played the piano for Misha, and they went to concerts in Moscow together. They were married shortly after the acceptable bereavement period and had two children. Irina almost lost her second baby from complications after the birth, and the two were isolated in the hospital for quite some time, away from Misha and their other son.

Their older son began to suffer from respiratory problems and was diagnosed with tuberculosis shortly after the fallout from the Chernobyl incident contaminated their area. At that point, Misha decided to emigrate to the United States to obtain better medical care. Although it was hard for him to leave his daughter by his first wife behind, she had settled into a good marriage and job, so he could not uproot her. And they had quarreled about his marrying Irina so quickly after the death of his first wife. She accused Misha of disrespecting her mother's memory; Misha did not know how to make her understand that Irina had lifted the loneliness he felt, injecting him with a new hope.

Misha had had many sorrows before meeting Irina. His father had died in the war when Misha was a toddler, and he and his two older brothers were raised by his mother and his grandmother. His mother suffered from a series of ailments, including diabetes, asthma, and high blood pressure. But Misha had always secretly believed she suffered from a broken heart, having lost her husband so young. His grandmother was the strong one in the family, and she acted as head of the household. Misha was a sociable child who made friends easily, but after his best friend died in a drowning accident at age fifteen, Misha began to withdraw and turn to music for solace. At twenty Misha lost his mother, and he married his first wife shortly after that. They had been married for twenty years when his wife died after a prolonged and painful illness.

Irina became quite concerned about her husband's behavior after the assault. She had never seen him so lifeless and flat, sitting and staring for most of the day, smoking cigarette after cigarette. All her efforts to help him were useless; even her excellent cooking failed to interest him. When he slouched over and cried, Irina approached him to comfort him, but he only pushed her away, often accusing her of wanting to kill him. When he threatened to end his own life, Irina panicked. After one month, she decided to take him to a doctor, who referred him to a psychiatrist. The psychiatrist prescribed a number of medications for Misha, who was diligent and hopeful about taking them.

Nevertheless, his condition remained unchanged: His appetite did not increase, his sleep was sparing and fitful, and he experienced a number of physical pains throughout his body. His nightmares were becoming increasingly violent, such as his children dying in a pool of blood while he gazed on, helpless. He pushed his family and friends away, too ashamed to let others know how weak he had become following the assault. His boss had been very understanding, but Misha could not perform his usual duties, and eventually he lost his job. Misha retreated to a narrow world in his small apartment and feared for his family's life each time they entered the dangerous world outside those doors. The mere thought of driving toward the street where the assault occurred panicked Misha, and his breath would become short.

Initially, Irina tried reasoning with her husband, explaining that only a small percentage of people on the street would commit an assault, but no words could change Misha's belief that the streets in his city were perilous, especially at night, and that he would never be able to thwart an attack on his safety. Irina found herself tearful and despairing to watch the deterioration of her husband, who only one year ago had been strong and hopeful. She realized that there was nothing she could do and once again insisted that he be reevaluated by a medical professional.

▒▒▒ WHAT DO YOU THINK? ▒▒▒

1. How would you explain the fact that Misha had so little recollection of the assault incident?

2. The assault on Misha was a threat to Misha's safety and his life, which would distress most people, but many would consider the assault to be a less severe act of violence compared with others resulting in grave injury or death. Despite this, Misha was unable to recover from the distress caused by the assault. What are some of the factors that help explain why Misha experienced prolonged and severe distress?

3. Misha emigrated to the United States in search of better medical treatment for his son. How might his immigrant status and expectations of life in this country have interfered with his recovery process?

Assessment

Misha was assessed by an English-speaking psychologist with the assistance of an interpreter. A detailed history of Misha's life events and functioning prior to, during, and after the assault was taken, and this history examined previous psychiatric problems, exposure to prior traumatic experiences, family history, and cultural beliefs. The clinician also reviewed Misha's behavior during the incident, the thoughts and feelings he had immediately after, and the effect of the trauma on Misha and his family. The psychologist consulted with the psychiatrist who had first treated Misha, and Misha's medical records were requested. A structured interview, a mental status examination, and two brief self-report checklists were administered. Misha was not given any objective personality inventories to complete because of his limited English-language proficiency. Misha's wife was interviewed as well.

On the mental status examination, a formal assessment of aspects of a person's behavior, Misha showed good orientation to time and place. His grooming was poor: he was dressed in a crumpled shirt, and the stubble on his face indicated that he had not shaved in at least two days. He walked slowly and slouched over when he was sitting, making little eye contact with the psychologist, rubbing his temple and his legs repeatedly during the interview. His mood was sad, but he showed little expression on his face. He was slow to answer questions that involved concentration, and when the examiner asked Misha to solve simple math problems, he simply shook his head and said, "I used to be able to do those; I can't anymore."

Misha admitted that he was suspicious of other people and often felt that he was being pursued by the assailants. He frequently wondered if his wife were trying to poison him. he denied any homicidal thoughts, but he admitted to wanting to end his life, although he had no specific plan for doing so. Sometimes he heard voices in his head that told him how weak and worthless he was.

The clinician did not doubt that the sudden change in Misha's functioning and the level of emotional distress he experienced were related to the assault experience. Nonetheless, she conducted a thorough history to assess Misha's premorbid functioning, or his state prior to the incident. Misha admitted to periods of depressed mood in his past, usually following the loss of a significant person in his life. After the tragic drowning of his boyhood friend, Misha had become more reclusive and more irritable, and he had many nightmares. The death of his first wife devastated him, and he described a prolonged period of sadness, with a number of symptoms characteristic of depression: sleeplessness, loss of appetite, loss of interest in his job and friends, and a hopelessness about his future. He experienced another "low point" when his wife delivered her new baby and the health of both mother and child was in peril. His reaction to these losses was considerably less severe than his current symptoms, however. He denied any history of psychiatric illness in the family, but he admitted that his mother often was sad and lethargic and that she drank quite a bit of alcohol in the evenings.

The structured interview revealed that subsequent to the incident, Misha experienced the following symptoms: He repeatedly reexperienced the episode in his mind, with distressing images of the knife intruding in his mind's eye, which terrified him. He had nightmares involving helplessness and terror. He avoided leaving his house and refused to drive on any of the streets close to where the incident occurred. He refused to talk about the incident with his family, and he refused to reveal the trauma to friends. He felt isolated and removed from his family, with feelings of worthlessness. He could not play with his children as he had before. He slept little and only during the day, and when he was awake, he was jittery most of the time, unable to concentrate on any activity. He often screamed at his wife aggressively, which he had never done before, and he was suspicious of most people. He cried regularly and had thoughts of killing himself. He had no hope for his future.

Case Conceptualization

Misha's immediate reaction to the assault could be understood as a normal reaction to an abnormal event, since his personal safety was violated. What distinguished Misha from most people, however, was his inability to recover from the trauma, causing him unrelenting torment and impairing virtually all aspects of his daily functioning. This prolonged distress is characteristic of posttraumatic stress disorder (PTSD), which develops in 25 percent or less of assault victims (van der Kolk, McFarlane & van der Hart, 1996). Are there other factors besides exposure to the trauma that help account for the development of PTSD, then? Why did Misha go on to develop PTSD? What are the risk factors?

Perhaps the most evident risk factor is the nature of the trauma itself. Trauma varies tremendously, and Misha's trauma involved violence perpetrated by another person, which is unlike a natural disaster, for instance. This difference can influence how traumatized individuals conceptualize their trauma, which in turn may affect recovery rates. Misha felt that his behavior in some way influenced the outcome of the assault, and part of his cognitive response to his trauma was a belief that he had failed—first in not anticipating the assault and second in not taking appropriate and courageous action to protect himself. People who experience natural disasters believe that their safety is threatened as well, but they rarely believe that they are responsible for the trauma, resulting in less shame and isolation. It is not only the objective severity of the stressor that matters, however; the subjective experience is also equally, if not more, important in its effect on the person, as Misha's case illustrates.

The individual's response at the moment of the trauma also can predict the outcome. It appears that Misha dissociated during the assault, psychologically removing himself from the scene, accompanied by a sense of unreality. He also developed amnesia to a number of the details of the crime, notably the superficial knifing he received. This dissociative response appears to interfere with long-term recovery (Holen, 1993; Marmar et al., 1994). First, dissociation as a coping response to stress prevents traumatized individuals from responding with full awareness during the traumatic event, potentially placing them in greater danger. Further, dissociation fragments memory and prevents subsequent integration of the experience, an essential factor in recovering from traumatic stress.

Dissociated memory is hypothesized (van der Kolk, McFarlane & van der Hart, 1996) to become encoded at a perceptual rather than verbal level. Brain imaging conducted during the evocation of traumatic memories indicates that there is decreased activity in Broca's area, the part of the brain most closely responsible for translating experience into speech, and at the same time increased activity in the right hemisphere, which is associated with the processing of emotions and visual images.

The traumatized person's response immediately following the stressor is critical to the development of PTSD. The importance of seeking out social support at this time is emphasized; note that Misha attempted to go to work and "get back on the horse," but he was unable to perform his regular duties. He experienced shame and isolation quickly following the assault, rejecting his wife's attempts at consoling him and normalizing his experience. Further, Misha did not receive immediate trauma assessment and only sought medical treatment one month after the assault. An individual counseling intervention soon after the assault would likely have helped Misha by educating him about traumatic stress, normalizing his experience, and assisting with a plan for his safety and recovery (Viney, Clark, Bunn & Benjamin, 1980).

Misha's history included a number of pretrauma risks, which are associated with PTSD. Genetic factors (for example, Misha's mother's depression and substance abuse) and biological vulnerabilities such as low cortisol response to stress (Yehuda et al., 1993) have been linked to PTSD. Misha also had previous exposure to trauma, which makes one more, rather than less, vulnerable to psychological complications following another trauma. The untimely and tragic death of his adolescent friend changed Misha from a sociable, easygoing boy to a more reclusive, apprehensive one. Although Misha's response to the robbery at gunpoint just weeks before his assault did not create undue distress, it is possible that the cumulative experiences primed him for a shift in his schema regarding the safety of his world. In sum, given Misha's pretrauma experiences, coupled with his response during and immediately after the trauma, it is not surprising that his recovery was neither swift nor uncomplicated.

Being an immigrant likely complicated Misha's recovery. Ironically, Misha had uprooted his family to resettle in the United States because he wanted his son to have access to better medical care. He trusted that his family would thrive here and overcome the health threats present in his country of origin. This basic trust was shattered because his own safety and health were severely threatened, placing in question the sacrifices Misha and his family had made.

Diagnosis

Misha's history, symptoms, and test results were consistent with a diagnosis of posttraumatic stress disorder (PTSD), which refers to a prolonged (longer than one month) period of extreme distress following exposure to a traumatic event involving real or threatened death or injury that impairs the individual's major spheres of functioning. Distress is normal and expected after exposure to a trauma, and many people experience an acute stress response following a traumatic event, but most people are able to recover from the incident and integrate the event into their consciousness, returning to near-normal functioning within a few weeks. In PTSD, however, the immediate response becomes chronic, and there is an ensuing adaptation to the enduring symptoms.

By the time Misha consulted the psychologist for reevaluation, his symptomatology, present for eight months, had become chronic. In the interim, he had lost his job, withdrawn from his friends, and given up his usual household and child care responsibilities. The fear from the event had been transformed into a sense of threat and horror that had generalized to all spheres of his life.

To qualify for a diagnosis of PTSD, individuals must have symptoms in three categories: intrusive, avoidant/numbing symptoms, and increased arousal. Individuals must respond to the trauma in all three ways, but the degree to which they do may vary. Misha showed symptoms in all three realms.

Intrusive symptoms include distressing thoughts and images of the traumatic incident that enter the mind involuntarily; distressing dreams and/or nightmares related to the event; flashbacks, dissociative experiences, or hallucinations; and intense emotional or physical distress caused by exposure to internal or external triggers related to the trauma. Misha could not push away the disturbing perceptual images of the incident from his mind, which caused him intense torment. Any reminder of the incident caused panic in

Misha: knives on TV, mention of the street, even the scent of night-flowering jasmine, and so on.

Avoidance and numbing symptoms constitute the second category. Misha exerted a great deal of effort avoiding any reminder of the trauma: He avoided speaking about his trauma, he refused to go near the scene of the assault, and he avoided contact with others. Misha could not recall crucial pieces of the incident, he felt estranged from his wife and children, he lost interest in most activities, he had a limited range of emotions, and he stopped thinking about the future.

The third category of symptoms relates to increased arousal patterns; while emotional responses tend to be constricted, autonomic arousal patterns are highly reactive following a trauma. These include sleep disturbances, irritability, concentration problems, excessive attention to surroundings (hypervigilance), and jumpiness to external cues (startle response). Misha had all of these symptoms.

It would seem that Misha was a clear-cut case of PTSD, but "pure" cases of PTSD, uncomplicated by other psychiatric symptoms, are somewhat rare, so the clinician made a number of considerations before the final diagnosis. First, it was necessary to rule out a mood or anxiety disorder predating the traumatic event, since numbing, avoidance, and increased arousal also can be symptomatic of these disorders. Both Misha and his wife described a happy, functioning existence prior to the assault, and the assault interrupted it abruptly. Although she could not ascertain this with certainty, the evaluator suspected that Misha had had episodic depressions during his adolescence and young-adult years, triggered by the deaths in his life. Nonetheless, there was little evidence to suggest that Misha was depressed at the time of the assault; on the contrary, he had secured employment and was beginning to adjust to his life in this country.

The clinician further evaluated Misha for major depression as a concomitant of the traumatic exposure and his inability to recover from the event. Mood and anxiety disorders occur commonly with PTSD (Green, Lindy, Grace & Leonard, 1992). The fatigue, the sleep and appetite disturbances, the suicidal ideation, and the cognitive self-denigration and hopelessness present in Misha were characteristic of major depression. (See Chapter 5 for a more detailed description of major depressive disorder.)

Treatment and Outlook

People with PTSD feel powerless in controlling the intrusive reexperiencing of the trauma, which looms large in their consciousness. They have narrowed their world to manage the overpowering distress and have built external and internal defenses to protect them from the relentless torment. Successful therapy restores a sense of control over these intrusive and avoidant responses. In this way clients are able to tolerate a wider range of more intense emotional responses, which allows them to integrate the traumatic experience into their personal narrative as only one of many challenges in their past that they were able to survive and move beyond.

Clearly, this is no easy task. Many people with PTSD have adapted to the chronicity of their symptoms and have left most traces of their previous life behind, as Misha had. Recovery can be painful, and avoidance of the painful material in their lives has become central to their coping. Furthermore, the personal connection between the client and the therapist is exceedingly delicate for those with PTSD, especially for the victims of violent crimes, for whom trust is difficult. The possibility of the client's symptoms worsening from insensitive or incompetent care is always a concern.

Despite the preponderance of PTSD, there is a dearth of research on effective treatment modalities to inform clinicians working in this area (van der Kolk, McFarlane & van der Hart, 1996). The major approaches to treatment include cognitive-behavioral therapy (Solomon, Gerrity & Muff, 1992), including both exposure therapy (to help clients face the feared stimulus) and anxiety management therapy (Rothbaum & Foa, 1996), and psychopharmacology to reduce emotional numbing, hyperarousal responses, and psychotic or dissociative responses.

The initial treatment Misha received several weeks after the trauma was psychopharmacologic, consisting of a tricyclic antidepressant, sleep medication, and a fast-acting antianxiety agent. It is unclear why Misha's symptoms were not managed by the medication, and in the eight months he followed the medication regimen, his symptoms only worsened. By the time he sought psychological assistance, his responses had become entrenched.

The psychologist used a combination of psychoeducational, cognitive-behavioral, and interpersonal approaches to treatment. She also consulted closely with the psychiatrist managing Misha's medication. The first step in the treatment involved educating Misha about the effects of trauma on the body and the mind. The clinician normalized Misha's experience. Using a metaphor that Misha could embrace from his fighting years, the psychologist emphasized that Misha had lost "his strength" when he got taken by surprise and that the healing process would involve reclaiming that lost part of himself, which had been left in the "ring," the scene of the assault.

In order to accomplish this task, Misha was told that he had to revisit the traumatic experience in his mind and create a narrative to make sense of the perceptual images he had stored in his memory. Traumatized individuals have what Janet (1925) called "a phobia of memory" (Vol. I, p. 661) that severely interferes with the process of integrating the traumatic experience into the individual's life story. It's as if the experience has a visual component without an accompanying script to convey the whole story. The psychologist used the technique of prolonged exposure to the trauma to help Misha put words to his story and integrate the physical, cognitive, and emotional aspects of the experience.

The psychologist had Misha close his eyes and recall the experience moment by moment and report it as if he were narrating a movie. The psychologist then asked Misha to describe his thoughts and feelings during each step of the process. This experience was highly anxiety provoking for Misha, and after the first session, his somatic experiences worsened. The clinician explained that the initial portion of the treatment might be stressful but that if he could "stay in the ring," Misha would eventually triumph over his terrifying memories. With the help of the psychologist, Misha was able to recognize that he had responded to the assault with courage but that he had been taken by surprise, as anyone might have.

Concurrently, Misha learned techniques for managing and reducing his anxiety. He practiced deep breathing and progressive relaxation and received regular massages to reduce muscle tension. He began to take progressively longer walks with his wife, which helped his sleeping and increased his exposure to public places.

The combination of the prolonged imaginal exposure and the anxiety-reduction techniques assisted Misha as he began to synthesize the traumatic experience. With the help of the psychologist, whom Misha had come to trust, Misha recognized that he could evoke a memory related to the traumatic experience in the therapy office and tolerate the associated emotions without being overwhelmed. The psychologist also addressed the changes in Misha's cognitive schema that were brought on by the trauma and in particular his lack of self-efficacy in protecting himself or his family, his generalization that the world is unsafe, and his sense of futility in the family system. They worked collaboratively to challenge these beliefs.

Since music had been restorative for Misha after the loss of his boyhood friend, the therapist asked him to bring in music that had had special meaning for him in the past. Initially reluctant and skeptical about the place of music in a doctor's office, Misha eventually began to trust the psychologist's judgment and brought in tapes of jazz musicians he had admired before. The therapist coincidentally shared a similar taste for music, so this sharing of music strengthened the therapeutic bond and provided some relief for the client.

The third aspect of the treatment addressed Misha's social isolation and loss of trust in his close personal ties. Misha believed that he was a burden to his family and that he contributed nothing to the family system. The therapist encouraged Misha to engage in enjoyable activities with his wife (such as walking together); at the same time, she encouraged Misha's wife to resume her own social and professional activities gradually to provide her with support and relief from the stress of caring for an individual with PTSD. Both responded well, and their marital relations improved somewhat.

The prognosis for Misha was fair. The prolonged exposure to the traumatic memory was successful in relieving some of Misha's somatic and arousal symptoms: His sleep improved, his appetite increased, and his concentration improved. However, the emotional numbing and avoidance responses were more entrenched and resistant to treatment. Misha continued to withdraw from his friends, although his involvement with his wife and sons increased somewhat. After six months of treatment, he began working part time as a handyman at a church down the street from his house, which increased his subjective feelings of value and renewed a bit of hope in his ability to once again provide for his family.

▄▄ *THINKING CRITICALLY* ▄▄
QUESTIONS FOR DISCUSSION OR WRITING

1. It is quite common for other psychological disorders (for example, major depression and panic disorder) to co-occur with PTSD. Provide an argument that Misha's various symptoms are not a separate disorder (PTSD) but part of a mood, anxiety, or somatization disorder.

2. Misha had suicidal ideation and very poor appetite and sleep patterns. Would Misha have benefited from hospitalization? Why or why not?

3. Most researchers of PTSD recognize that the nature of the traumatic event influences how and if a person develops PTSD. Explain how Misha's experience might have been different if his trauma had been a natural disaster (for example, an earthquake) or if he had experienced severe childhood physical abuse.

CHAPTER 5

Major Depressive Disorder:
A Flat and Frozen World

For those who have dwelt in depression's dark wood, and known its inexplicable agony, their return from the abyss is not unlike the ascent of the poet, trudging upward and upward out of hell's black depths and at last emerging into what he saw as "the shining world." WILLIAM STYRON, Darkness Visible

JENNIFER'S STORY

Jennifer blinked back the tears that formed so quickly and easily recently, dabbing at the corners of her eyes to keep her mascara from smudging. She mustered all her energy this morning to put on makeup and dress up for the lunch with her mother. She hadn't been out of her house in days, and just as soon as she arrived at the restaurant, she wanted to turn around and crawl back into bed. As she walked in, her mother smiled at her broadly, as she always did, and Jennifer forced a smile, too. The smile belied her feelings, however. Jennifer took a deep breath and began to tell her mother what she had concealed from her over the past three months: that she was not doing well, that she felt lost and confused.

Even as she was recounting this to her attentive mother, she felt defeated. "What good can come of this? I've made a terrible mistake asking Mom to lunch and burdening her with my screwed up life," she thought. "And what can she do to help me out of this? She has her own problems." Then Jennifer felt the walls closing in on her again. They were white and flat, and they shut out the lively noise around her. She pushed herself to continue talking, but that curious feeling of being removed washed over her, as if her ears were stuffed with cotton balls, muffling voices. What she didn't tell her mother was that lately she had begun to think she might be better off dead. Not that she'd ever do it, but she was frightened the other day when she found herself staring at the shiny blade of the kitchen knife, which she had grabbed to cut up some vegetables.

Her mother kept up a string of encouraging words: "This will pass." "You can overcome this." "You need to get away from Mark." And so on.

None of her mother's assurances seemed to make a difference to Jennifer, but her mother persevered. As she looked at Jennifer's fair skin and strawberry blond hair, her mother was once again struck by how little Jennifer resembled her Filipino side of the family and how much she looked like her deceased husband, Jennifer's father.

Jennifer's mother recognized the pain she saw in her daughter's face because she had been there herself. In fact, she was Jennifer's very age—twenty-five—when her first husband, Brian, died of a brain tumor. Her son, Jack, was four years old, and Jennifer was barely two at the time. She recalled the cold chill that set in right after the funeral and wouldn't go away. It was like her veins were ice, and she was frozen to the world around her. She could not tolerate Jack's rambunctious behavior or Jennifer's crying. She retreated to her bed whenever she could and stared at the ceiling or cried. Alarmed by this behavior, her sister arranged for Jennifer and Jack to stay with their maternal grandparents while their mother visited her brother in the Philippines.

When she returned home six months later, she clung very tightly to Jennifer, whose appearance reminded her the most of her deceased husband, "the Irishman," as her Filipino family dubbed him. She pampered Jennifer and protected her; Jennifer seemed so much more fragile than her son, Jack, who was physically active and seemingly fearless. She probably gave in too often when Jennifer cried and pleaded with her mother to let her stay home from school, but she had been afraid to let her daughter out of her sight. It pained her to think that her daughter would cry when her teachers reprimanded her or that she would be alone on the playground. She could comfort Jennifer and take her to her workplace. Her boss and colleagues didn't mind, and in fact, they showered Jennifer with attention, too.

Her second husband, whom she married when Jennifer was five, worked hard to set limits with Jennifer. He complained persistently about the attention and money his wife lavished on Jennifer and accused her of spoiling Jennifer. Jennifer's mother did buy her daughter beautiful things, because she wanted to give her what she had not had as a girl. Her mother never fought back or crossed her husband, but she didn't change her behavior either. She began to lie about her purchases for the children. She felt that her husband could never understand what it was like to fear losing your own, and little by little, she began to push him away.

He was an excellent provider and an active stepfather to the children. As far as Jennifer was concerned, he was her father, since she had no recollection of her biological father. She called him "Daddy," and no one questioned their relationship because in many ways she looked more like her Caucasian stepfather than her Filipino mother. He played ball with his son and accompanied Jennifer to her ballet classes. He tried very hard to take his place as parent.

But in Jennifer's mind she knew her stepfather was "an outsider." He wasn't invited to her mother's family reunions, where the Filipino clan gathered twice a year. Her last name was different from his. She didn't have the kind of relationship with him that she shared with her mother. Later, as an adult, Jennifer was able to articulate the connection she felt with her mother as a child: "We're one person, my mother and I." There were times, however, when the safety of that bond gave way to fear. Jennifer often discovered her mother crying at her vanity, her makeup spread out in front of her in disarray. Jennifer panicked at these moments because she knew something must be terribly wrong for her mother to cry. She knew that she had to do something, but she didn't know what. Then her mother began to drink. First, it was after dinner, but by the time Jennifer was in junior high school, she would return from school in the afternoon and her mother would already have a glass of wine in her hand.

By ninth grade, Jennifer was developing physically and turning into a striking teenager. Boys eyed her and sent her notes, but she played cool and aloof. Inside she was terrified of boys, certain that she would end up like all her cousins on her mother's side. At every family reunion Jennifer noticed that one more of her teenage cousins had gotten pregnant and that her aunts talked anxiously about their children's involvement with gangs or drugs. Jennifer made a pact with herself that she was not going to turn out like her Filipino family and that nothing would stand in her way of becoming a successful graphic artist with plenty of money to travel and own a home. Even though there were a number of Filipino boys at her school, she ignored them because she was certain that getting involved with them would signal the end of her dream.

In high school her stepfather's behavior began to change, as he spent less time at home, and when he was home, he was highly critical of Jennifer and her brother. His relationship with Jennifer's brother was explosive, the two frequently screaming and slamming doors. Jennifer stayed out of the way during these altercations, and she managed to avoid her stepfather's ire. One afternoon he flew into a rage when Jennifer talked back in a smart way. Jennifer knew she was treading on thin ice, but she didn't expect what happened next: He pinned her against the wall as if he were going to strangle her. Jennifer felt terror at that moment, and in her mind, her life began to unravel at that point.

Once reliable and attentive, her mother became unpredictable. Some of the time she would come right home after work, but other times she would stay out late and stumble in drunk after midnight. Her parents fought bitterly, at times physically, and her brother started using drugs. Jennifer felt adrift and confused by this turn of events. When Jeremy entered her life at this low point, Jennifer was grateful to have someone to turn to and rely on. He was two years older, and to Jennifer he seemed confident and wise. She began to spend weekends at his house, and they started a sexual relationship after a few months. Jennifer was sure she was in love.

There was only one snag. Jeremy had a "dark side" that emerged when he was drinking, which he did often. Sometimes he brooded over the worthlessness of his life and threatened suicide. Other times he would break out into a rage and throw things at Jennifer. Later in the relationship he began to push and hit Jennifer. She pleaded with him to stop drinking, which he promised, but after a few weeks he would break his promise, and the violence would start again.

Jennifer found it difficult to leave Jeremy because she believed he was her only source of support. He was not always abusive; he could be loving and console her when she was scared. He often planned surprises for her, and he bought her gifts. She could sometimes bring him out of his funk, and this made her feel strong and needed.

Besides, her family was quickly disintegrating. Her stepfather was absent most of the time, and her mother had begun a series of affairs with unsavory men. She pulled Jennifer into her intrigues and made her promise that she would never breathe a word to her stepfather. Jennifer covered for her and lied to her brother and stepfather. Finally, her stepfather discovered his wife's affairs and threw her out, filing for divorce.

Jennifer stayed with her stepfather and brother briefly, until her mother found a one-bedroom apartment. Jennifer tried living with her mother, but she was horrified by her mother's behavior. Jennifer was relegated to the living room couch because her mother brought home drunken, abusive men that Jennifer despised. Her mother pleaded with her to stay, which she did until she finished her two-year degree at the community college. She finally found the courage to leave both her mother and Jeremy when she was twenty, and she moved out of town to go to a graphic design school, which her mother agreed to pay for.

School was like the calm after the storm, and Jennifer immersed herself in her schoolwork. She was determined to do well, and she put herself on a rigorous schedule of schoolwork, exercise, and part-time work. She got excellent grades and got herself in shape. She deliberately avoided making friends or dating. Her plan worked well for a year, but soon she began feeling lonely and estranged from her family and friends. Jennifer befriended a man she met at a party, and they soon began dating.

Jennifer was attracted to Mark's small, lean body, which was in excellent physical shape from regular workouts at the gym. He also was financially secure, employed by a large company as a software engineer. Initially, Mark was generous, showering Jennifer with gifts and treating her to expensive dinners and trips. They quickly rented an apartment together and set up house. They both worked, and Jennifer was happy to assume the bulk of the housekeeping. How different Mark was from Jeremy, even his small size contrasted with Jeremy's bulky body, and Mark was quiet and controlled, a welcome change after Jeremy's fury. They socialized with Mark's friends regularly, and Mark introduced Jennifer to his family.

Soon, however, Mark buried himself in his work, working late hours and traveling frequently for his job. He'd return from work and immediately turn on the TV, paying little attention to Jennifer, who had looked forward to their evenings together. She wanted more from him, and when he shut her out, she became quite angry, her temper flaring. She began to resent all the housework and cooking she did for him, but her outbursts to him seemed to fall on deaf ears. She also resented the time they spent with his family, whose forwardness and exuberance frightened her. Jennifer was sure that she was being judged by them and that she didn't measure up.

Things took a turn for the worse when Jennifer lost her job at the advertising firm where she had been employed in an entry-level position. Mark began badgering her to look for work, but as the weeks rolled by, Jennifer lost interest in most things. She used to work out at the gym faithfully, but it became increasingly difficult for her to mobilize enough energy to drive there. She stopped seeing her friends from work, and when they left messages on the answering machine, she would neglect to return them. She hardly ever left the house, and fears set in about being around people, about looking for work, even about reading the classified ads. She was afraid of what was happening to her, but she thought it would pass. If she could only get a job; if only Mark could be more patient and attentive.

Mark complained about having to shoulder all the finances, so Jennifer worked even harder at keeping house to even things out. Mark began criticizing her for "doing nothing" with her life, and she began to feel useless and incompetent. It seemed that the worse Jennifer felt, the more critical of her Mark became. When Mark went away on business trips, Jennifer panicked, and the night before every trip, she become enraged, blaming him for all her problems. Deep down, she knew it wasn't his fault, but she didn't know what else to do, for she felt she couldn't spend one more day by herself, going over and over in her mind her dismal life with Mark, her resentments, her failures. Lately she had begun crying constantly. She often didn't get dressed until Mark came home, staying in her bedroom and staring at the ceiling for most of the day. She was frozen inside, as if her veins were ice. The world felt so dark and cold that she longed to crawl into something warm and soothing and just stay there. It had gotten to the point where she wasn't sure she could bear the pain of those endless days any longer. That's when she began thinking about ending her life.

Jennifer decided to seek her mother's help at that point. By then her mother had begun to pick up the pieces of her own life, and she came willingly to her daughter's rescue. She called her daughter two or three times a day, and she stayed with her when Mark went away on business trips. She took her shopping, to dinner, and to the movies. She gave her spending money so that Jennifer wouldn't have to ask Mark for it. She bought her a car. She suggested that she leave Mark and come back to live with her.

Jennifer's mother arranged for her daughter to talk to a priest from a local church about couples' counseling to work out the problems she and Mark were having in their relationship. The priest suggested that Jennifer seek counseling herself, since she seemed very unhappy in her life. Jennifer agreed.

▬▬▬   *WHAT DO YOU THINK?*   ▬▬▬

1. Identify the behavioral, cognitive, and affective symptoms of Jennifer's emotional distress. What do you see as the major factors contributing to this distress?

2. Jennifer grew up in a biracial, bicultural household. What role, if any, do you suppose this played in her identity development? How might this environment have exacerbated her difficulties?

3. What concerns, if any, did Jennifer's case raise for you regarding her health and safety?

Assessment

The psychologist that Jennifer consulted entertained a number of hypotheses concerning Jennifer's case. He identified symptoms that were likely related to disturbances in mood and anxiety, so he conducted the Structured Clinical Interview for DSM-III-R (SCID) and administered the Minnesota Multiphasic Personality Inventory (MMPI-2) and the Beck Depression Inventory II (BDI-II; Beck & Steer, 1996). On the MMPI-2 Jennifer obtained significant T-scores for the Depression scale (T-score = 70) and the Psychasthenia scale (T-score = 65), a common profile among people seeking psychiatric treatment that is associated with depressed mood, rumination, tension, excessive guilt, and low self-worth. It is important to note that an elevated score on the Depression scale does not confirm a diagnosis of depression. Jennifer's score on the BDI-II was 35, which indicates a severe depression in people who are already diagnosed with depression. The SCID indicated that Jennifer had difficulty sleeping and woke up early, cried excessively for no reason, had a diminished interest in socializing, worried constantly about other people's opinions of her, and had a lack of interest in most things. She did not hear voices or have persecutory thoughts, homicidal ideation, obsessive-intrusive thoughts, or flashbacks of past traumatic experiences. She denied having mood swings and had never, to her knowledge, had an elevated mood in which she experienced racing thoughts or euphoria. She reported increased irritability during premenstrual days.

Jennifer's suicidal ideation raised a red flag, and the psychologist questioned its severity. Jennifer denied having a plan of action to carry out her suicide, and the suicide-related questions on the MMPI-2 were not positive, but she admitted to passive, transitory thoughts of suicide. The clinician also wondered about the residual effects of earlier trauma and loss, so he administered the Trauma Symptom Inventory (TSI; Briere, Elliott, Harris & Cotman, 1995), which is a 100-item self-report scale to assess the frequency of symptoms associated with trauma. Jennifer had high scores on the scales of depression and anger/irritability but not on the remaining eight scales assessing such symptoms as intrusive thoughts, impaired self-reference, dissociation, dysfunctional sexual behavior, and so on.

The psychologist questioned Jennifer's use of alcohol and drugs given the extent of substance abuse in her family. Jennifer reported that she had used alcohol in her late teens but that she was currently abstinent. She denied ever using illicit drugs. The psychologist assessed for the presence of psychiatric disorders in relatives on both sides of her family. Although no relatives had sought psychiatric treatment to her knowledge, Jennifer did describe a number of relatives who were moody, who had alcohol and drug abuse problems, or who had migraine headaches, insomnia, and nervousness. Jennifer's mother, brought in for a family consultation, described a "breakdown" after her first husband died. Finally, the psychologist referred Jennifer for a complete medical examination to rule out a medical explanation for her mood state. Jennifer was in excellent health, and no physical disorders were identified.

Case Conceptualization

At the time that Jennifer decided to seek psychological treatment, she had been experiencing a number of symptoms for a period of months that most people would associate with "the blues." These symptoms included sadness, crying, loss of interest in usual activities, social isolation, irritability, and sleep disturbances. The friends from work whose calls Jennifer had not returned might be forgiving and believe that she was feeling down because of her job loss. Most people who have had a brief period or two in their own lives when things didn't go well and who have felt a bit depressed can sympathize when others are feeling low.

However, such an identification with a mild depressed mood can be a double-edged sword when a severe depression strikes. Depression is far more painful, producing much more hopelessness than a brush with the blues, which most of us can "snap out of." Jennifer's descent was not a fleeting dip from which she could easily bounce back. It was a severe slide into a dark and frightening chasm, with no certain way out.

She had a lot going for her, so how did she fall into this place? Why now? Why didn't she do something to prevent it? Why couldn't she pull herself out? These are common questions people have when a friend or loved one experiences a severe depression. Formulating the answers requires a juggling act of the many contributing factors, some of which are common to most depressed people and others of which are unique to a specific individual.

Jennifer seemed to sink after she lost her job, but it would be simplistic to think that this event "caused" her depression. People lose their jobs daily and yet manage to remain hopeful and move forward in their lives. Her job loss could be viewed as the immediate, identifiable trigger that set off the episode, the proverbial straw that broke the camel's back. Beyond this specific stressor, however, Jennifer's distress emerged out of a context that included the interaction of biological, psychological, cultural, and historical factors.

One important piece of information from Jennifer's history is that her mother had a similar experience when she was Jennifer's age, triggered by her husband's death. Overcome by a debilitating grief, she was unable to care for her children, whom she loved very much, and she was "sent away" to recover. Although she was able to return to her family six months later, there were indications that the depression lingered: She was unduly anxious about losing her children, she cried often, and she abused alcohol.

The presence of what appears to be complicated bereavement in Jennifer's mother is important because depression tends to run in families. That her mother was depressed increases Jennifer's risk of developing the disorder herself. Part of this may be because a depressed parent cannot manage the parenting role adequately and consistently, and Jennifer's mother vacillated between being overly protective and neglectful of her children. Other explanations point to the genetic components of depression (e.g., Kendler et al., 1993).

A genetic vulnerability to a disorder does not necessarily mean the person will develop that disorder, however. In Jennifer's case, this vulnerability met up with a number of environmental pressures, perhaps the most prominent of which was the amount of interpersonal violence she witnessed and experienced as a girl and teenager. Maria Root (1992) has said that "the wounds of trauma wear many masks" (p. 229). Jennifer's fears and despair were likely cloaking these early, traumatic threats to her safety and sanity. It must have been frightening and confusing to feel protected and pampered in her mother's embrace one minute and later to watch her stepfather and mother lose control and have physical fights.

Later, Jennifer was herself the victim of verbal and physical abuse in her relationship with Jeremy, and she kept this shameful fact a secret, even from her mother, with whom she had shared most intimate thoughts and feelings. Jennifer already felt estranged from her family at the time, and she had stopped socializing with her friends, so she had few people to turn to when the violence in her relationship emerged. She endured the trauma in an isolated context, which heightened her sense that something was uniquely wrong with her and confirmed in her mind her inability to have a healthy relationship with a man. When Jennifer finally extricated herself from that destructive relationship, she made a conscious decision to stay away from relationships for self-preservation. "They only bring me trouble," she stated to the psychologist.

Other external events exerted pressure in Jennifer's life as well, which intersected with her vulnerability to depression. Of course, the early and tragic death of her father left a hollow in Jennifer's life and created ripples in her environment. Not only had her father vanished, but her mother became withdrawn and eventually left her children for six months, all of this occurring when Jennifer was two years old, an important developmental stage for parental attachment. The loss of her father also had financial repercussions and increased the pressures on her mother. At the critical developmental point of puberty and adolescence, Jennifer's mother began drinking and having affairs. Jennifer found herself adrift and assuming increased responsibility in caring for the family, not an uncommon experience for children of alcoholic parents (Brown, 1988).

The psychologist treating Jennifer was curious about the role that culture played in Jennifer's life. Jennifer straddled the two cultural worlds of her mother and father. Her mother's experience was that of a poor, immigrant Filipino who married a middle-class Caucasian man. By belonging to the dominant group in this country, Jennifer's father had greater access to work and money. Jennifer identified with her father's world and, because of her Caucasian features and skin color, gained acceptance there. She admits to rejecting her Filipino side because, as she told her psychologist, "They are all crazy on that side of the family." In her quest for a more financially secure future, Jennifer abandoned a potential source of social and emotional support in the large, extended side of her mother's family, who lived close by. Ironically, Jennifer had become the daughter her mother hoped for by rejecting her mother's culture and social status.

These stressful and traumatic events occurred in Jennifer's life at the same time that she was developing notions about herself and her world. Her beliefs about her value, about the dangerousness of the world around her, about her ability to function independently and establish intimate ties with others—all these were influenced by her environment and interactions with early caretakers. Jennifer's thoughts and interpretations of herself and her world, what Aaron Beck (1967, 1979) has called a "cognitive schema," serve as the basis for her processing of information. Jennifer filtered her experiences through this lens, sifting and sorting according to the framework she had constructed.

Many of the beliefs of her schema were not accurate and led to subsequent psychological distress. For example, Jennifer believed that she could not take care of herself and that she needed another person physically present to protect her. Thus, when Mark had to leave on business trips, Jennifer felt panic, for she was afraid that she could not manage alone. Even though Jennifer had managed on her own on numerous occasions, this fear arose from a distorted belief that "something bad will happen and I won't be able to function."

Many of the other beliefs that Jennifer had were negative and pessimistic. Her thinking was black and white. "If it isn't perfect, then it's a failure." "If Mark watches TV and doesn't pay attention to me, then it means he doesn't love me." And so on. She made assumptions about what others thought of her, and those assumptions usually were negative. Jennifer was convinced that Mark's family hated her, despite Mark's repeated assurances that they did not. Even when presented with contradictory information, Jennifer was able to discount favorable appraisals: "They are just saying that because they want to be nice." Her appraisal of future events was often hopeless: "People always leave me" or "No one can help me."

Jennifer's cognitive assessment of her value, her life, and her future had become severely pessimistic when she sought treatment. Further, her response to that state likely exacerbated an already existing depressed mood. She abandoned some of her usual activities such as exercise and social contact that have been shown to lift mood, and instead, she isolated herself from her friends, assuming what Nolen-Hoeksema (1990) has called a "ruminative response" to her depressed mood, dwelling on her failures, her lack of a job, and her resentments toward Mark. She focused her attention on her deficits, which increased her despair and hopelessness and decreased her sense of self-efficacy.

She could not "snap out of it," and her distorted thinking impaired her ability to identify viable and functional solutions to her predicament. She had begun to think that suicide was an answer. Although her thoughts were passive ones, Jennifer believed that she "would be better off dead."

Diagnosis

The *DSM-IV* characterizes a major depressive episode by the presence of sadness and/or loss of pleasure and interest in most things for at least a two-week period, accompanied by a constellation of other symptoms including changes in sleep, appetite, weight, and energy level. Depressed individuals may feel worthless and guilty and think passively or actively about suicide. Many may believe that others would be better off if they were dead, while other depressed people may desire to end their lives because they can no longer bear the pain of living. Their ability to concentrate may be compromised, and they may complain of severe difficulties in making decisions, even small ones.

Was Jennifer experiencing a major depression? Many of her symptoms matched those of a major depressive disorder. She experienced increased sadness, decreased energy and motivation, insomnia, negative assessments of herself and her future, and passive suicidal thoughts. She also reported a diminished interest in sex, irritability, ruminative thinking, and extensive crying—all associated with major depression. Her depressed state interfered with her normal functioning, such that she was unable to continue her job search or socialize with friends and Mark's family. The duration of depressive symptoms is an important criterion in the diagnosis of major depression and can help clinicians differentiate between milder and more severe episodes of depression. Jennifer had been experiencing these symptoms for well over a month, underscoring the severity of her depression. The clinician also considered whether Jennifer had dysthymic disorder, which involves a chronic depressed mood present for at least two years, more days than not. Clearly, Jennifer had experienced dysphoric episodes in the past, but in the year preceding this most recent episode, Jennifer had experienced a stable mood, with adequate professional and interpersonal functioning.

Jennifer's history and presenting symptoms raise the question of an anxiety disorder as well. She described being fearful as a child, of not wanting to separate from her mother, of experiencing panic when Mark went away, and a nagging sense that something bad was going to happen. Jennifer's retrospective descriptions of her childhood distress around separation, along with her mother's corroborating depiction, made the clinician wonder about a diagnosis of separation anxiety. He considered this diagnosis with caution, however, since notions about familial interdependence can vary among cultures. An independent consult with a Filipino therapist would help the clinician disentangle healthy interdependence from a pathologic enmeshment.

Anxiety and depressed mood often occur together (Angst, 1993), making it quite difficult for a clinician to determine whether one state predominates or whether the anxiety is part of an anxious depression. Although Jennifer's psychological test results also indicated some symptoms of anxiety, such self-report instruments distinguish poorly between the two (Dobson, 1985). Jennifer's psychologist decided to treat Jennifer for depression, since she clearly met the criteria for a major depression, and to reconsider the treatment plan if her anxiety persisted once the depression remitted.

Treatment and Outlook

Fortunately for Jennifer, clinicians working with depressed clients have a number of treatment options that have been relatively well supported by research. The choice of treatment would depend, of course, on the clinician's theoretical perspective as well as on the client in question. Some studies (Hollon, Shelton & Loosen, 1981) suggest that a combination of drug therapy and talk therapy, especially if the latter is interpersonal or cognitive therapy, is the most effective approach to treatment for depression. The medication is effective in treating the *vegetative* symptoms (for example, sleep and appetite disturbance), while psychotherapy improves adjustment (for example, mood, suicidal ideation, occupational and interpersonal functioning).

The most common type of treatment for depression is perhaps psychopharmacology. Psychiatrists often prescribe antidepressants for depression, including the newer selected serotonin reuptake inhibitors (SSRIs), such as Prozac, Luvox, and Paxil, as well as a host of older medications. Psychiatrists base their decision to prescribe a particular antidepressant on a number of considerations, which may include specific side effects and cost for the patient. Antidepressants alter the chemistry of the brain to regulate the flow of certain neurotransmitters that are hypothesized to play a role in the regulation of mood. Many depressed people experience more energy and less depressed mood after they take medications.

Interpersonal therapy (IPT) is a brief form of therapy that focuses on how a person relates interpersonally. The underlying assumption of IPT is that interpersonal processes play an important role in the initiation and maintenance of a depression (Klerman, Weissman, Rounsaville & Chevron, 1984).

Cognitive behavioral treatment (CBT) is a structured, collaborative approach to therapy that challenges the distorted thinking of depressed people and assists them in coming up with healthier, more accurate assessments of their situation (Beck, Rush, Shaw & Emery, 1979). This type of therapy typically does not explore earlier causes for current emotional states but instead focuses on the client's present state and in particular on the maladaptive thinking that interferes with healthy functioning.

The clinician working with Jennifer chose a treatment combination of psychopharmacology and talk therapy, and Jennifer was referred to a psychiatrist early in treatment. Although some clinicians might argue that Jennifer did not require antidepressant medication because she had a number of strengths that would likely see her through her depression (for example, college education, above-average intelligence, a career), her sleep and appetite were sufficiently impaired to cause concern for both the psychologist and the psychiatrist, and a course of SSRIs was prescribed.

The psychologist made the decision to treat Jennifer with cognitive therapy, given Jennifer's verbal ability and compliance with homework assignments and his own expertise in this form of therapy. Jennifer was able to identify and learn to rework some of her black-and-white thinking and to ease up on her perfectionistic demands of herself and others. In particular, the clinician helped Jennifer to recognize that some of her dissatisfaction in her relationship was due to the effects of depressed mood on her thinking, which magnified Mark's negative features and discounted his efforts at being supportive in the face of her illness. Previously, Jennifer valued Mark's reserve and his ability to make and save money. However, as her depression set in, these attributes were transformed negatively: Mark then lacked empathy and feeling for her, and she found him to be selfish and withholding.

Jennifer's psychologist also explored with her the ways in which depression can strain a relationship, even those previously on solid ground. Jennifer's dependency on Mark and her need for support were intensified by her depressed mood, and at the same time, Mark's efforts at satisfying those needs were discounted, creating a cycle of disorder and dysfunction in the relationship that exacerbated their conflict. Concurrently, Mark, who expressed inadequacy and discomfort around her intense moods and irritation, became overwhelmed by Jennifer's depression and resorted to his coping mechanism of withdrawing further.

Depressed mood also can negatively influence appraisals of self-worth, self-efficacy, and competence. The clinician challenged some of Jennifer's beliefs that she was incapable of taking care of herself and helped her to recognize that her depressed mood had shaken her confidence but that previously she had functioned well, even in the face of adversity.

The prognosis for Jennifer was quite good. With a combination of cognitive therapy and psychopharmacology, she was able to improve her mood and her energy enough to make the changes she needed to make. She managed to get a part-time job in her field, and she decided to move out of Mark's apartment but continue to date him. Although she continues to rely on her mother for financial assistance, she has gained some confidence in her ability to manage her finances and her work on her own. She is more hopeful about her future, but she remains cautious about relationships with men.

Depression can be a debilitating experience. Left untreated, it can impair relationships and work performance and, in severe cases, lead to suicide. Depression also can be "contagious," affecting those who live with depressed people. Fortunately, most depressed people who seek treatment respond favorably to a combination of antidepressant and talk therapy, providing them with relief and hope for their future.

▦ *THINKING CRITICALLY* ▦
QUESTIONS FOR DISCUSSION OR WRITING

1. Women are twice as likely as men to be depressed during their lifetimes (Nolen-Hoeksema, 1990). Current research has not clarified the precise reasons for this discrepancy, although most researchers agree that it is due to a combination of social, developmental, and biological factors. What is it in our culture that might have placed Jennifer at risk for depression due to her gender?

2. Jennifer's boyfriend told the psychologist that he thought Jennifer was depressed because her mother spoiled her and she was used to getting whatever she wanted. How would you respond to this?

3. Jennifer's psychologist recommended both talk therapy and psychopharmacology to treat her depression. Given Jennifer's personal assets (for example, above-average intelligence, education, ambition), how likely is it that Jennifer would have responded equally well without the medications?

CHAPTER **6**

Bipolar Disorder:
A Seductive Madness

*For me insanity is super-sanity. The normal is
psychotic—a collective psychosis. Normal
means lack of imagination, lack of creativity.*
JEAN DUBUFFET, in The New Yorker

SUZANNE'S STORY

It was 2:00 a.m., the third night that Suzanne had gone without sleep. She sat
alone by a statue in the middle of campus, writing furiously in her notebook.
The words poured out of her. Her thoughts raced so fast that her pen could
hardly keep up. As her hand began to cramp, she shouted an expletive that
echoed from the library across the quad. Suzanne cursed her body, since it always seemed to let her down at times like this. "How am I ever going to finish my book," she thought, "if my damn hand gets tired out?"

Suddenly, Suzanne had a flash of insight. Her mother was a secretary for
a large medical corporation. Suzanne could dictate her novel, and her mother
could type it. Brilliant! Off she scrambled to a pay phone to tell her mother
about her idea.

Suzanne's mother was startled from a deep sleep by the ringing of her
phone. Suspecting it was her daughter, she picked up the receiver and listened
as Suzanne prattled on unintelligibly, something about a book, what happened in sociology class yesterday, and the reason so many kids do drugs.

"I've got it all figured out, Mom," Suzanne was saying. "Don't you see?"

With the pause in her daughter's stream of consciousness, her mother
glanced at the clock and said, "It's two fifteen in the morning. What are you
doing up?"

Suzanne rambled on about her parents not appreciating her talents, how
they never supported her, and how eating lettuce made her brain work better.
She finally pleaded with her mother to get up and take shorthand while she
dictated.

"No, Suzanne," said her mother, "Go to bed and get some sleep."

Enraged, Suzanne slammed down the phone. She stormed across campus,
screaming out about her mother's insensitivity and how much more intelli-

59

gent dolphins are than humans. A sleepy voice from one of the dormitories yelled for her to shut up. Suzanne threw her notebook in his direction, called him "pig," and proceeded on toward the football stadium.

Squeezing through a gap in the fence, Suzanne made her way onto the field and sprawled across the fifty-yard line. She stared at the stars and calmed herself by thinking about her prodigious talent as a writer and how rich and well known she would be once her book was published.

Her thoughts raced on. Suddenly, Suzanne remembered Brian, who was still asleep in her dorm room. Although she barely knew him from class, she had seem him at lunch two days ago and had invited him to a movie that night. They had snorted a few lines of his cocaine and made love six times. Brian had come back to her room a few hours ago, but by then Suzanne had become engrossed in the idea of writing a book. He had fallen asleep waiting for her to come to bed.

Her thoughts continued to wander. Relaxed for a moment, Suzanne began to worry that she would fall asleep before she could finish her book. As she got up and looked around, she noticed a small group of mushrooms growing on the field. "These will keep me awake and help me see things clearer," she thought, as she gobbled down sixteen of the white-capped domes.

Suzanne began to walk back toward the main campus, suddenly afraid that she had lost her notebook. As she recalled all the notes she had carefully written down for her book, she reached a state of near panic. Frantically, she began searching for her notebook. When she could not find it, she collapsed on the ground and began to cry uncontrollably. To add to her misery, the mushrooms began to wreak havoc with her stomach, and she felt extremely ill. She threw up, imagining that the mushrooms were draining all her ideas, indeed her life, from her. Picking up a piece of broken glass, she cut her wrists several times before passing out.

Suzanne awoke two days later in the university hospital. She learned from the nurse that she had been found by a security guard lying unconscious on campus. Her stomach had been pumped, and the cuts on her wrist had been bandaged. Suzanne wondered how the cuts had gotten there. Her head ached, and she felt miserable. The nurse told her that she was being transferred up to "psych" because of her suicide attempt.

Suicide! Suzanne bolted out of bed, yelling at the nurse and pulling out the intravenous line attached to her arm. It took four orderlies to restrain her while she was sedated with Haldol, a major tranquilizer. She was taken to the inpatient psychiatric unit while she slept.

Over the next few days, Suzanne learned a lot about psychiatric units. She learned that some of the nurses and therapists seemed to care and were very helpful, while others were patronizing or authoritarian. Some of the other patients seemed normal, while others were clearly crazy, but even the crazy ones could be friendly and interesting. Most of the other patients were on medication. She was invited to attend groups on cognitive therapy, relapse prevention, communication skills, and art therapy, but mostly Suzanne slept or watched television. Her doctor came to see her every day and asked her all kinds of questions about her life, her family, and school.

Suzanne told her doctor about growing up in a small southern town and how her family had moved to Atlanta when she was in junior high school. Her father was a pediatrician. She described him as a moody man who drank heavily, was always critical of her, and never seemed to be around. Her mother, the secretary, raised her and her younger brother. She was very close to her mother. Leaving home to go away to college had been difficult for both of them.

Suzanne had always excelled in school. She had taken three honors courses in high school and had gone to college on a full scholarship. She had been senior class president, captain of the swim team, and a member of the National Honor Society. One summer she had gone with her father to work in a refugee camp in Thailand, while last summer she had cycled through France with her mother for four weeks as a graduation present for being class valedictorian.

Always busy and on the go, Suzanne had never even thought about seeing a therapist. She knew some friends that did, but during the rare times that she had felt "low," she had dealt with it by forcing herself to get even busier. The low periods would pass eventually, usually without incident. However, there had been one time while with her father on the Thailand trip that had been different.

During the day while her father saw a seemingly endless stream of crying babies and somber older children, Suzanne worked for the camp administrator. She typed, ran errands, delivered food and medicine, and helped out in a variety of other ways. One day near the end of her stay she had ridden her bicycle into town to pick up some medical supplies her father had ordered. On the ride back, one of the packages must have fallen from her pack because it was missing when she arrived at her father's tent. As usual, he was sarcastic and criticized her irresponsibility. Suzanne began crying, feeling ashamed and angered. This incident led to several days of moodiness and sulking on her part. Eventually, she asked to leave the camp a week early and flew home. Uncharacteristically, she lay around her room until her mother was able to coax her back to life. While this time in her life was troubling, Suzanne had written it off to her difficulty getting along with her father and had mostly forgotten about it until her doctor expressed interest.

Suzanne's parents flew up to visit, and her doctor asked them questions, too. She learned that there was a history of alcoholism and depression on her father's side of the family and that a great-uncle had spent much of his life in a state hospital for manic-depressive illness. She was also surprised to learn that her parents had been in marital counseling off and on over the years. Despite her difficulty getting along with her father, Suzanne had always thought there was nothing wrong with her family. Now she learned that her parents had nearly divorced several times and that her mother had attended Al-Anon groups for support in dealing with her father's drinking.

Despite her objections, the doctor and her parents agreed that Suzanne should drop out of school for the semester, return home, and begin treatment with a psychologist. While she had refused to take any medication in the hospital, the doctor spoke with her about the possible benefits of taking mood stabilizers. The day before she was to leave the hospital to go home, she became severely agitated and irritable. She accused her parents and doctors of trying to ruin her life, was verbally abusive to other staff and patients, and finally had to be sedated once again, delaying her release.

When she came out of the sedation, Suzanne became the life of the unit. She attended all the groups and kept everyone amused with her constant jokes and puns. She seemed to have boundless energy and organized card games and contests and even led the other patients in exercises. While she seemed somewhat like her old self, her mother noticed that she was more confident than usual. They discussed all her plans—how she was going to graduate in three years, live in France, and be a writer. The way her daughter jumped from one train of thought to another so quickly reminded her mother of the late-night phone call a few days ago. Eventually Suzanne agreed to go home with the understanding that she would return to the university in a few months for the fall semester.

▓▓ WHAT DO YOU THINK? ▓▓

1. Suzanne seemed surprised to learn about the problems in her family, since she believed there was nothing wrong with them. Have you ever learned anything about your family that surprised you or made you think about your family or yourself differently?

2. Suzanne seemed like a person who had everything going for her. What impact on her life do you think her experience will have?

Assessment

A few days after Suzanne returned home with her parents, she went to her first appointment with a psychologist. In addition to reviewing in detail the episode that led to her hospitalization, the therapist also focused on the events in Thailand that had resulted in behaviors so uncharacteristic of her. She had Suzanne tell her all about her life and family and also asked a number of questions about substance abuse, attention-deficit hyperactivity disorder, and her medical history.

Suzanne admitted that she had "gotten drunk a few times in high school" but said that she no longer drank because she did not like how alcohol made her feel. Reluctantly, she confessed that she did use "speed" and other "uppers" to help her study at night. She denied that these were a problem because they helped her "be more productive" and stated that she could "live without them." Her history was inconsistent with that of someone with attention-deficit hyperactivity disorder (see Chapter 14). A complete medical examination conducted in the hospital revealed that Suzanne enjoyed excellent physical health, had no history of significant illness, and was taking no medication.

The psychologist paid careful attention to the way that Suzanne behaved in her office. She noticed that Suzanne spoke rapidly and with great determination no matter the topic. She sometimes changed from one subject to another abruptly. Highly distractible, Suzanne got up to look out the window whenever a car with a loud engine drove by. She seemed unusually cheerful and optimistic for a bright young woman who had just been forced to leave college, and her self-esteem was boundless and grandiose.

When asked, Suzanne admitted that she sometimes went on shopping sprees when she really couldn't afford to. She also confessed to driving recklessly, blaming "all the other stupid drivers" who "forced" her to speed excessively. Finally, she admitted that there had been three other occasions in which she had engaged in sexual behavior with someone she did not know very well. While she admitted this was unusual for her, she minimized its significance because "nothing bad had ever happened."

Case Conceptualization

Suzanne's history and presenting symptoms are all consistent with an impression of bipolar disorder. Also known as *manic-depressive illness,* it is characterized by the extreme moods of mania and depression that are polar opposites of one another. A syndrome that consists of depressive episodes only is sometimes referred to as a unipolar disorder. Manic episodes are thought to hardly ever occur without accompanying depressive periods.

Bipolar disorder has been recognized for centuries as the most dramatic of all mood disorders. Many creative people such as writers (for example, Fyodor Dostoyevski) and actors (for example, Patty Duke) have suffered from mania, fueling speculation about the connection between this illness and creativity. It affects nearly one in every hundred people, with men and women being equally affected. Interestingly, while the first episode in males is more likely to be a manic episode, the first episode in females is likely to be a depressive one.

Mean age of onset lies between fifteen and twenty-four. A five- to ten-year interval between onset of illness and age at first treatment or hospitalization is not uncommon. Onset prior to age twelve is rare. Onset after age sixty is most likely associated with a medical condition, such as stroke (Tohen et al., 1994). The course of bipolar disorder is extremely variable. Untreated patients may have more than ten full-blown episodes of mania and depression in their lifetime interspersed by periods of hypomania and normality. Five years or more may elapse between the first and second manic episodes, but the time periods between subsequent episodes may narrow.

Evidence of epidemiologic and twin studies strongly indicates that bipolar disorder is an inheritable illness. A child with one bipolar parent has a 30 percent risk of developing a mood disorder, while a child with two bipolar parents has a 75 percent risk. Identical twins show a much higher concordance rate than do fraternal twins. However, the means of inheritance remains unknown, and the role played by environmental stressors also remains uncertain (APA, 1994).

Bipolar disorder can wreak havoc on a patient's life. Divorce rates are two to three times higher than in a normal population, and the occupational status of patients with bipolar disorder is twice as likely to deteriorate as that of comparison subjects (Coryell et al., 1993). Patients are also at high risk for suicide, especially males during a depressive episode. Comorbid substance abuse, especially drugs such as cocaine and "speed," is often a factor.

Diagnosis

Because depressive disorders are covered elsewhere in this book (see Chapter 5), attention here will be devoted to the diagnosis of manic episodes. Mania is an abnormally and persistently elevated, euphoric, or expansive mood. The mood can have an infectious quality to those around the person, but it is recognized as excessive by those who know the person well. This elevation in mood can quickly turn to irritability, however, especially if the person's wishes are thwarted.

Other prominent features of a manic episode can include an inflated sense of self-esteem, a decreased need for sleep, rapid or pressured speech, racing thoughts, and distractibility. The patient often starts several projects at once or jumps from one interest to another without regard for risk or the need to complete what was started. The patient may become extremely restless and agitated. In extreme cases, a full-blown psychotic state may occur that can be difficult to distinguish from schizophrenia. Poor judgment often results in spending sprees, reckless driving, foolish financial decisions, and indiscriminant sexual behavior, sometimes with disastrous consequences.

Manic-like symptoms also can be induced by antidepressant medication, certain medical conditions (such as multiple sclerosis, brain tumors, or Cushing's syndrome), and substance abuse (such as with cocaine or amphetamines). Treatment or removal of these conditions often results in a cessation of symptoms. Hypomanic episodes, which are similar to manic episodes but not as severe, also may occur. Such periods are often cherished by the patient as times of increased efficiency, productivity, or creativity.

Treatment and Outlook

Following her assessment, Suzanne and her family were informed about her diagnosis and encouraged to learn all they could about it. Suzanne was referred to a psychiatrist, who started her on lithium. She also was encouraged to participate in individual psychotherapy with the understanding that bipolar disorder is a long-term illness that can manifest itself in different ways at different times.

Suzanne made rapid initial progress in treatment. Within a period of a few weeks she devoured several books and articles on manic-depressive illness and stabilized her mood through the consistent use of lithium. Soon, however, she began to complain of boredom. Thinking her ennui related to being away from school, she enrolled in two classes at a neighboring community college. Against the advice of her therapist, she began working two part-time jobs. She began to feel that the lithium slowed her down, and she stopped taking it in order to have enough energy for work and studying.

A month before she was to return to the university, Suzanne experienced another manic episode. She bought several thousand dollars' worth of computer equipment with her father's credit card and stayed out all night drinking with a friend. When she came home the next morning, her parents threatened to hospitalize her again if she did not come in for an emergency appointment and begin taking her medication again, with their supervision.

Suzanne was firmly confronted by her therapist, who explained how denial is such an integral and confounding part of being bipolar. The psychologist also discussed the importance of establishing regular patterns of sleeping, eating, and physical activity. Suzanne had to come to grips with the fact that while not being manic was less exciting and productive than normality, it also was better than facing the consequences of her manic judgment and the severe depression that so often followed her periods of euphoria.

Suzanne was able to return to the university as planned. She took a light load that first semester, as had been agreed on during a meeting with her parents, psychologist, and psychiatrist. Over the next few years, she continued to struggle with denial, her reluctance to give up the manic experience, and the sometimes irritating side effects of her medication. Gradually she learned to trust her therapist when she pointed out behaviors that were likely to negatively influence her mood. Eventually, she learned to identify prodromal symptoms that signaled the onset of a new episode. During periods of symptom remission, she was able to take a maintenance dose of lithium and thus reduce the medication side effects she abhorred, such as nausea and drowsiness.

Suzanne's case is fairly typical. She is fortunate that she did not become psychotic during her manic episodes and that she is one of the roughly 80 percent of patients who display medical manic symptoms in response to lithium treatment (Goodwin & Ebert, 1973). For patients who do not respond to lithium, or for those who display one of the variations of classic mania (rapid cycling or dysphoric mania), there is also valproate (Depakote) and carbamazepine (Tegritol). Antidepressant medication also can be used to treat the depressive episodes that inevitably accompany the manic periods, although care must be taken lest a manic episode be unintentionally induced. Electroconvulsive therapy also has been found to be effective in the treatment of acute mania.

Medication alone is insufficient to treat any disorder of mood. Psychotherapy is important to reduce distress, improve functioning between episodes, and decrease the frequency of future episodes. It is often important for patients with bipolar disorder to discuss the emotional consequences of having a diagnosis of major mental illness, the problems associated with stigmatization, problems with self-esteem, interpersonal problems, marriage and childbearing issues, academic and occupational problems, and the consequences of the reckless, violent, or bizarre behavior that may occur during manic episodes. Developing and maintaining a trusted therapeutic alliance is often the key to producing the most successful outcome possible.

THINKING CRITICALLY
QUESTIONS FOR DISCUSSION OR WRITING

1. Suzanne experienced certain aspects of her illness as positive. Why would anyone want to give up these periods of increased energy, euphoria, and productivity?

2. Despite our increased knowledge about the biological bases for most mental illnesses, there continues to be an enormous stigma in some parts of our society about seeking treatment. Why do you think that is so?

CHAPTER 7

Schizophrenia:
An Endless, Private Nightmare

Realizing I was crazy didn't make the crazy stuff stop happening. MARK VONNEGUT, The Eden Express

JAMIE'S STORY

Jamie sat alone in the hospital cafeteria, her leg shaking furiously under the table. She was careful to sit with her back to the wall so that she could keep her eyes on everyone. She carefully examined her beef stroganoff, searching for physical evidence of the poison her voices had warned her it contained. Finding none and feeling hungry, she took a bite and then repeated her search on the next morsel. She thought she heard someone from the next table say, "They tricked her this time; she's gonna get it," causing her to intensify her scrutiny. She looked over at the food server, wondering if he had been able to locate a poison that was devoid of taste or color.

Two other women from Jamie's psychiatric unit walked up to her table with their food trays and asked if they could join her. Scowling, Jamie hissed, "No!" and covered the table with her hands as best she could. The women walked away, and Jamie thought she heard them say they were going to get her tonight while she slept.

Quickly, Jamie pushed away that thought and tried to focus. Her legs continued to shake. "I've got bigger fish to fry," she thought to herself. "If the Colombian drug lords find me here, they'll surely kill me. They're everywhere, and they can pay off anyone."

With that, Jamie quickly scanned the dining room. Her eyes fell on the Hispanic janitors eating lunch together at the other end of the room. "They must be the hit men," she thought, "I've got to get out of here." Leaving her food tray on the table and her lunch half-eaten, Jamie snuck out the side entrance of the cafeteria. She thought she heard her voices say "There she is; we've got her now" in heavy Spanish accents, but she was not sure. She went back to her room and curled into a ball under her blankets, trying to calm herself by repeating a nonsense phrase over and over: "Sodemojo, sodemojo, sodemojo."

When the group therapist came in a few minutes later to announce that process group was starting, he found Jamie asleep. "Come on, Jamie, time for group," the therapist gently prodded.

"No, I'm tired," Jamie said.

"Come on, Jamie. Its just your meds making you sleepy. Your doctor said you should try to come to at least this group every day."

Reluctantly, Jamie followed the therapist out of her room, failing to notice that she had not put on her shoes, combed her hair, or straightened out her rumpled clothing.

In group, Jamie sat quietly with her eyes downcast. "I don't belong in here," she thought to herself. Yet, oddly, being in the hospital was the first time she had felt relatively safe in a long time. When she had called Dr. Thomas, her psychiatrist, yesterday and told him she was hiding in an abandoned warehouse and hadn't eaten or taken her medication for five days, she had readily agreed to his proposal for hospitalization. It had taken her a while to call for help because her voices had tried to convince her that her doctor was part of the Colombian drug cartel. When she heard his reassuring voice, however, she told him right where she was and didn't mind when the police came to pick her up.

Interrupted from her thoughts by another group member, Jamie kept her head down and just said, "I don't know." She wished she could pay better attention to what was going on, but between her voices and the feeling of sticky goo like cotton candy in her head, she could hardly focus on anything. She hoped she would feel better soon from the medicine her doctor had given her. Her voices said, "*He's trying to poison you with that stuff.*" She tried to ignore them by humming to herself.

Later that afternoon Jamie lay on her bed. She was startled to open her eyes and see an Hispanic man dressed in a suit standing at the foot of her bed. He was carrying a rifle and wore dark glasses. His thick moustache and wide-brimmed hat obscured his face. She screamed and ran out in the hall, calling for help.

A nurse came over, asking what was the matter. "In my room, in my room" was all that Jamie, shaken, could eke out. The nurse took Jamie back to her room and looked inside.

"There's nothing in your room, Jamie," the nurse said reassuringly. Jamie peered in.

"He must have snuck out the window," she said, ignoring the fact that her windows were sealed shut and barred from the outside.

The nurse redirected Jamie by inviting her to the day room for some hot chocolate and a game of cards. Jamie went along, for the moment forgetting about her voices and the elusive intruder in her room.

Jamie enjoyed playing cards. She could focus on the game, one of the few things she found she could concentrate on. No one really asked her any questions when they played either. It was just small talk, and no one seemed to mind if she just kept quiet. She was a little disappointed when her doctor stuck his head in the day room and asked if she would join him in his office.

Once they were both seated, Dr. Thomas offered Jamie a glass of water and asked how she was doing. Jamie sat quietly, fiddling with her blouse, and began to slowly rock back and forth. Dr. Thomas moved a little closer to her and spoke softly but firmly: "Jamie, look at me." Jamie looked up, her rocking becoming slightly more rapid. "I need to you to listen," the doctor said. "How are your voices?" Jamie muttered that they were still there. "I'm going to change your medication, Jamie," the doctor said. "I'm hoping a new one will help you feel better and make it easier for you to deal with the voices. I also hope it will make you less agitated."

Jamie said "OK" and wondered if the drug lords had put her doctor up to this. She had known him several months, however, and her trust in him tended to win out over her paranoia most of the time.

That night Jamie made a telephone call home to her husband, Mike. She told him about the man in her room and about her doctor changing her medications. She told him that her doctor thought she would be discharged from the hospital and start a day treatment program in a few days. Mike was distant and seemed put off by the notion that she might be coming home soon. Jamie asked how he was doing. Mike started to complain about how tired he was from working all day and then having to come home, cook, and clean house. She hung up on him when he started screaming about the "vacation" she was getting at the hospital. He called back a few minutes later, apologizing and telling her to come home as soon as she could. They hung up on agreeable, if not quite friendly, terms. Jamie joined the other patients at the nurse's station to receive her nightly medications: one for her voices, one for her anxiety, and one to help her sleep. As she swallowed the pills under the nurse's watchful eye, Jamie couldn't help but wonder if they were poisoned.

Walking back to her room, Jaime noticed a cool breeze blowing in from the back patio. In a moment of unusual clarity, she thought to herself, "How did I end up here?"

Jamie's recent problems had started a few months ago when she was twenty-three. Always a quiet, shy child while growing up, she had been an average student who was never a behavior problem. She always had a few friends but was content mostly to stay at home and help her mother with her younger siblings. After high school, she had gotten a job as a bank teller and continued to live at home. It was at work that she had met her husband, one of the security guards. They had married after a year's courtship and seemed happy together. Jamie's family was relieved that she had found someone to care for her, since they used to joke that their daughter "wouldn't find a husband unless he dropped in her lap."

Things were fine until Jamie suffered a miscarriage with the couple's first child. She became acutely depressed after this loss and was unable to be consoled by her husband or family. She became more isolative and soon stopped going out of the house. Her husband took her to see a psychiatrist, Dr. Thomas, who had been recommended by their pediatrician. She was diagnosed with depression and started on antidepressant medication. Her husband was told to be patient with her and that she would likely get better in a little while.

Instead of getting better, however, Jamie's symptoms worsened. She started to believe that she was being punished for past "sins" and began a series of ritualistic behaviors designed to "atone" for her guilt. Her husband went along with her at first, hoping that by honoring her unusual requests he might help her feel better and return to her old self. One day he came home to find her in the bathroom sitting in a pool of blood, having cut herself repeatedly with a razor blade. Later she explained that she had been trying to get rid of all the "evil" in her and thought that she could do so by letting out blood. Her husband rushed her to the emergency room, and after being stabilized medically, Jamie was admitted for her first psychiatric hospitalization.

▨▨▨ *WHAT DO YOU THINK?* ▨▨▨

1. Jamie seems to have difficulty distinguishing between the voices in her head and what is going on around her. What kinds of problems would this lead to?
2. Despite her paranoia, Jamie seems able to trust her doctor. How might you account for her ability to do so?

Assessment

At first the doctors and therapists working with Jamie were confused about her diagnosis. She appeared to be severely depressed, yet she behaved bizarrely. She sat in her room, never changed her clothes, and answered in one-word utterances or grunts when spoken to. She seemed unresponsive to any attempt at communication, until her mother visited almost a week after her admission. Initially unresponsive, when her mother got up to leave, Jamie began crying and screaming uncontrollably. It required several attendants to restrain her, and her psychiatrist ordered that she be sedated with Haldol.

Following this episode, Jamie became more active, but at the same time she began to exhibit more bizarre behaviors. Observers on the hospital ward noted that at times she seemed as if she were talking to someone when she was by herself, and she seemed frightened to be around other people. She began to complain to the staff about her roommate: a frail, elderly woman, who Jamie believed was attempting to sexually assault her. The psychiatrist ordered psychological testing to assist in determining her diagnosis and to help in developing a treatment plan.

During the initial interview with Jamie, the psychologist asked a number of questions about her life. Jamie spoke in a low voice, sometimes being very dramatic in her gestures, at other times more subdued. She spoke in a way that sometimes did not make sense to the psychologist, jumping from one idea to the next in a seemingly random manner. One time she said the word "poo-poo" and started laughing hysterically. When she spoke about the miscarriage, she seemed to have no emotion but indicated that she knew who had caused her misfortune. Jamie was very suspicious of the psychologist and required a great deal of reassurance to participate in the assessment.

When asked, Jamie admitted that she heard voices and that she had heard them for several months, beginning around the time of her miscarriage. She reported that she had cut herself in response to a command from one of her voices, which she identified as "Satan's boss." She said that this voice had told her that if she ever wanted to have a baby, she had to purify herself. She believed that she had lived an evil life, despite there being every indication from her parents and husband that she was in fact quite reserved, honest, and responsible. She believed that other people could read her thoughts, which was why she was quiet sometimes: "If I don't think anything, they won't be able to know what I'm thinking about." She denied any suicidal ideation, and she stated that she had no intention of killing herself when she cut herself in the bathroom.

Jamie was administered several psychological tests. On the Wechsler Adult Intelligence Scale–Revised (Wechsler, 1981), she scored in the average range of intelligence. Her worst performance was on tests of attention and concentration; she complained that she couldn't do these tasks and gave up without trying very hard. On a test of verbal, abstract thought, she demonstrated a concrete, simplistic attitude in her thinking. Instead of giving definitions to some words on a vocabulary test, she offered associational responses or other words that rhymed with the word she was asked to define. When asked to say what was missing from some pictures, she said some bizarre things, like it was the bowl that was missing from the picture of a goldfish.

On the Minnesota Multiphasic Personality Inventory 2 (Hathaway & McKinley, 1989), a self-report measure of personality functioning, Jamie's answers matched a pattern indicative of a person in acute turmoil experiencing a thought disorder. Although she reported feeling depressed, worried, and tense, she also admitted to thinking that was autistic, fragmented, and tangential with unusual content. She admitted to delusions of persecution and feelings of unreality. She seemed to lack self-confidence and felt intense guilt about what she perceived as her failures. She seemed to be suspicious and distrustful of others, deficient in social skills, and most comfortable when by herself.

Finally, Jamie was given the Rorschach, a series of ten inkblots presented with the simple instructions: "Tell me what this looks like to you." Her responses suggested that she was preoccupied with maintaining a sense of control, especially in dealing with other people. Her aggressive impulses tended to be denied and projected onto others. Her psychological defenses were fragile, primitive, and easily overwhelmed. She seemed to regress easily from a reliance on obsessive-compulsive coping strategies to paranoid patterns of denial, rationalization, and projection. Her perception of reality was distorted, and she tended to view the world in a highly idiosyncratic manner. For example, to a card that most people see as either a bat or butterfly, Jamie responded, "It looks like a fingernail with dirt under it." Her thinking was confused and illogical, and she perceived her environment as dangerous and threatening. Self-absorbed, she felt alienated from others and seemed especially frightened of men.

From this evaluation the psychologist concluded that Jamie had experienced an acute psychotic episode following a period of relatively rapid decompensation beginning four months prior to admission, precipitated by the stress of her miscarriage. Jamie's psychiatrist began treating her with Risperidol, one of the newer antipsychotic medications. Her condition improved, and she was able to return home three weeks after being hospitalized.

Case Conceptualization

Schizophrenia was one of the first psychiatric disorders to receive attention from the medical field, beginning with its initial conceptualization by Emil Kraepelin in the last century. Called at that time *dementia praecox,* he and later Eugen Bleuler identified several different subtypes of the disorder, depending on the predominant manifestation the disease took on in a given individual. Later, schizophrenia was distinguished by a distinction between positive and negative symptoms, based on Hughlings-Jackson's (1931) classification of neurological disorders. Here, negative symptoms were viewed as the result of a loss of function due to structural brain damage, whereas positive symptoms represented the release of functions formerly inhibited by higher cortical areas (the frontal lobes) that are now dysfunctional. In schizophrenia, the positive symptoms include hallucinations, delusions, and disorganized speech and behavior. Negative symptoms include blunted or restricted affect, social withdrawal, and poverty of speech.

Jamie's case is typical in that her schizophrenia developed between her late teens and mid-thirties. Childhood schizophrenia is rare and is a difficult diagnosis to make. Schizophrenia also can begin later in life and is similar to earlier-onset schizophrenia except that it occurs more frequently in women. The disorder affects roughly 1 percent of the population, with similar rates of prevalence reported throughout the world. It affects women and men about equally, although women are more likely to have a later onset, more prominent mood symptoms, and a better prognosis.

The course of schizophrenia varies markedly from person to person. In Jamie's case, she had gradually developed symptoms such as social withdrawal, loss of interest in her usual activities, unusual behavior, and irritability that preceded her miscarriage. She was so habitually shy and quiet that initially her idiosyncracies were overlooked by those around her. Eventually, Jamie experienced an active phase of the illness precipitated by the stress of a miscarriage and marked by psychotic symptoms: hallucinations, delusions, and loss of contact with reality. Over time, she experienced periods of exacerbation and remission in her disorder. Others with schizophrenia remain chronically ill. Positive symptoms tend to respond well to treatment with medication, while the negative symptoms tend to worsen over the course of many schizophrenic's lives. Some schizophrenics manage to remain fairly stable, with some exceptional patients able to complete graduate degrees and function as attorneys and psychologists. Numerous studies have found that the following factors are associated with a better prognosis: good premorbid adjustment, abrupt onset of symptoms, later age of onset, being female, an identifiable precipitating event, disturbance of mood, active-phase symptoms of brief duration, good functioning in between active phases, absence of structural brain abnormalities, normal neurological functioning, a family history of mood disorders, and no family history of schizophrenia (APA, 1994). Based on these factors, Jamie's prognosis was mixed.

Schizophrenia is a multidetermined disorder that involves genetic, psychological, and environmental factors that interact with one another to produce the disorder in ways that are not yet understood. It is now indisputable that genetic factors are involved in the transmission of the disorder (Gottesman, 1991). Consistent findings across numerous twin studies in which the concordance rates for the disease are significantly higher for monozygotic twins as compared with dizygotic pairs, especially when adoption studies are included, provide a compelling argument for this fact. Exactly how the genetic transmission occurs remains a mystery, as does the way in which genetic factors interact with the environment to produce schizophrenia (Fowles, 1992). At the present time, several possible environmental triggers are being researched, including the role of nutrition, exposure to viral infection in utero, and family dynamics. In Jamie's case, although there is no evidence that anyone in her family ever suffered from schizophrenia, there was a strong family history of depression. As we saw earlier, schizophrenia is more common in families with a history of affective disorder, but these patients carry a better prognosis than do those whose family history is positive for schizophrenia.

Many early studies of the families of schizophrenics focused on the pathological behavior of the mother that might have caused the schizophrenic symptoms. These studies, some of which concluded that there existed a "schizophrenogenic mother" whose "double binds" placed the child in a lose-lose situation that in essence drove them crazy, were fraught with methodological problems. Current research tends to focus on the family's response to the schizophrenic family member and how that response influences the course of the disorder. Not too surprisingly, it has been observed that schizophrenics suffer lower rates of relapse and remain out of the hospital longer if they have families who are supportive and not critical of them. Even the presence of one family member who views the patient as "lazy" or "stupid" can undermine the patient's stability (Brown, Birley & Wing, 1972; Mueser et al., 1993). Jamie's stability was greatly aided by her close relationship with her parents. These findings have led therapists to place a higher premium on educating family members about the illness and increasing their involvement in treatment efforts. At the same time, groups such as the Alliance for the Mentally Ill provide tremendous support for family members of the mentally ill while at the same time lobbying state and national legislators to provide a voice for this largely apolitical group.

Over the years, social critics point to the insanity of our society as a cause of schizophrenia. R. D. Laing (1967) was one of the more articulate exponents of this position. These writers, overlooking or minimizing the genetic basis of the disease, call schizophrenia a "sane response to an insane society," suggesting that our modern, industrialized world creates such a degree of alienation from the environment, other people, and oneself that the only way one could reasonably cope is to become psychotic. These writers at the same time romanticize schizophrenia, finding it as a source of insight, creativity, and, in some cases, spiritual renewal. Anyone who has ever spent much time with someone who is schizophrenic knows that far from being enlightened and creative, most of the time these patients suffer tremendously. They are largely frightened and confused. Like anyone, they may be insightful occasionally, but this does not appear to be the result of their schizophrenia. Jamie spent much of her life in fear of being discovered and murdered. While her delusions may seem irrational and silly to an observer, they were as real to her as this book is to you. One possible explanation for why these social critics reached the conclusions they did may lie in the poor diagnostic distinctions that were made before schizophrenia was more narrowly defined in recent years. Patients with bipolar disorder are often creative and crave the hypomanic state. Since these patients are also often psychotic, they may have been misdiagnosed as schizophrenic.

Diagnosis

Jamie met the criteria for schizophrenia by displaying the mixture of the characteristic positive and negative symptoms described earlier. To meet criteria for the diagnosis, her symptoms must have been present for at least one month, and some signs of the disorder must have been evidenced for at least six months. Her symptoms also must have been accompanied by a marked disturbance in either her social or occupational functioning and not be caused by the direct physiologic effects of a drug or medical condition (APA, 1994).

The characteristic symptoms of schizophrenia incorporate a wide variety of both cognitive and emotional dysfunctions. These include perception, such as with hallucinations, inferential thinking, language and communication, behavioral monitoring, affect, fluency and productivity of thought, volition, and attention. No single symptom is diagnostic of the disorder; the challenge for the clinician is to be able to recognize the individual presentation of signs and symptoms that are impairing the patient's social and occupational functioning. This challenge was apparent in Jamie's case when her initial presentation appeared to be more like a mood disorder, and it was only when she began to talk about her active symptoms and the presence of a thought disorder was confirmed through psychological assessment that her diagnosis was able to be clarified. Her mood disorder was understood as Jamie's response to her growing awareness that she was becoming ill.

The timelines in the schizophrenic diagnosis are important. If the active schizophrenic symptoms have persisted for less than a month, a diagnosis of brief psychotic disorder would be made. If the disorder has been in evidence for more than one month but less than six months, a diagnosis of schizophreniform disorder would be appropriate. The distinction is important because one-third of all sufferers recover from a schizophreniform disorder, whereas the remainder go on to develop schizophrenia. It is important not to jump to conclusions about the individual's prognosis prematurely. Jamie was given an initial diagnosis of schizophreniform disorder because at the time of her initial assessment she had only displayed symptoms for four months. Other diagnostic distinctions include schizoaffective disorder, in which a mood disorder also has been present in the absence of hallucinations or delusions, and delusional disorder, in which the primary symptom is that of a nonbizarre delusion in the absence of a thought or mood disorder.

Schizophrenia has been organized into subtypes since the inception of the diagnosis, with a wide variety of subtypes identified over the years. *DSM-IV* recognizes five subtypes, and during Jamie's initial evaluation, each of the subtypes was considered. The *disorganized,* or *hebephrenic, type* displays prominent evidence of behavioral disorganization along with flat or inappropriate affective expression. While Jamie's affect was flat, her behavior was not grossly disorganized. The *catatonic type* is often associated with a mental picture of a person standing in awkward positions like a statue, but this type also involves excessive, purposeless activity, extreme negativism, and oddities of speech such as echolalia, when the person simply "echoes" everything said to him or her. Jamie evidenced neither postural rigidity nor hyperactivity. The *paranoid type* meets the criteria for schizophrenia and also demonstrates a preoccupation with one or more delusions. Auditory hallucinations are also common. The prognosis for this subtype may be somewhat better than for other subtypes. Jamie best fit the criteria for this subtype, given her delusions of persecution. The *undifferentiated type* is simply reserved for the schizophrenic who fails to meet criteria for any of the other three types, whereas the *residual type* refers to the schizophrenic who, while no longer demonstrating the positive symptoms of the disease, continues to display the negative symptoms. Jamie occasionally met the criteria for this subtype when her symptoms were said to be in remission.

Treatment and Outlook

While there is no cure for schizophrenia, much effort has gone into treating its symptoms and helping the patient remain stable while continuing to function at the most independent level possible. With the advent of antipsychotic medication in the 1950s, psychiatry finally had a means to reduce the active psychotic symptoms in many patients. These medications do not help every patient, however, and it is impossible to determine who will respond to the medications prior to trying them out. These medications often produce side effects that are at best unpleasant and at worst permanently incapacitating. The primary side effects are those of sedation and extraneous motor movements. In some patients, long-term use of the drugs can result in a condition known as *tardive dyskinesia*, where the patient develops involuntary choreiform movements of the mouth, tongue, lips, and/or upper extremities that may not dissipate even after cessation of the medication. These side effects, or the fear of them, results in much noncompliance with treatment efforts. Not surprisingly, these patients tend to relapse when off their medication and end up back in the hospital.

Jamie often stopped taking her medication during the early years of her illness because she did not like the sedation associated with the drugs. When her psychiatrist tried other antipsychotic medications that were less sedating, she developed symptoms of restlessness and agitation that she also found intolerable. It was not until recently, with the advent of a new class of antipsychotic medications, that some of the side-effect problems have been eliminated. In addition, some of these new medications, such as Risperdal (risperidone) and Clozaril (clozapine) have proven successful with patients who previously did not respond to the older medications, perhaps in part because the newer drugs target different neurotransmitter systems (Ayd, 1995).

Traditional psychotherapy is not very helpful with schizophrenics, but supportive therapy can be very useful in monitoring symptoms, preventing relapse, and improving socialization skills. Some of the most effective interventions can be directed at the patient's family, where education and coping skills development can be useful in decreasing stress for the patient and thus decreasing the chances of relapse (Bellack & Mueser, 1993).

Jamie's condition did not remain stable. Over the years, she had experienced other episodes of active psychosis in which she heard voices, saw things that were not there, and experienced delusions of persecution and grandeur. During the intervening periods when she was not grossly disorganized and psychotic, her social skills and ability to care for herself declined so that she was unable to work and became housebound, going out only to see members of her family. Her husband eventually became fed up with her and filed for divorce. Jamie moved back in with her parents, becoming increasingly dependent on them. She met her current boyfriend, Luke, during one of her many hospitalizations. They moved in together against the wishes of her family, but despite the many difficulties they endured, they mostly got along and were happy with one another. Luke was eleven years her junior. Jamie liked the feeling of belonging that she derived from taking care of him, and he understood her because he suffered from similar problems. Their fights were frequent but brief and never very serious. Their combined disability payments from the government allowed them to live simply but more comfortably than either of them could have on their own.

Over the years, Jamie's paranoid delusions continued to center around being the target of hit men employed by the Colombian drug lords. Although she had never taken drugs herself, she believed that she was the one responsible whenever she read or heard about the U.S. government seizing another shipment of cocaine, marijuana, or heroin. She believed that all information about drug trafficking was somehow embedded in her brain and that the government simply monitored her thoughts in order to determine when and where to intercept the illegal shipments. Although this information was not available to her on a conscious level, Jamie was convinced that the drug cartels knew it was she who was responsible for their losses. She believed the hit men were constantly trying to track her down and that once located, she would be killed. As a result, she had to remain constantly vigilant in order to outwit her pursuers. This preoccupation consumed a great deal of her attention and resulted in much bizarre and inappropriate behavior, such as the time she threw a soda on a Mexican man while at the movies, believing he was a hit man she had to escape.

With the help of a therapist, Jamie's family eventually was able to accept that she wanted to live with Luke, despite the family's concerns about her living with another schizophrenic. As they became more accepting of her choice, she was once again able to enjoy spending time at home, especially with her mother. Her condition stabilized, and she spent less time in the hospital. For the most part, her active psychotic symptoms returned only when she stopped taking her medication, which she did periodically for no discernible reason. Switching to one of the newer medications with fewer side effects was helpful but did not prevent this from happening.

Although we have come a long way in our understanding of schizophrenia in the last century, we continue to know less than we don't know about this disorder. We know that there are structural brain abnormalities, abnormal cerebral blood flow in the frontal regions, and frequent neuropsychological findings such as slowed reaction times and abnormalities in eye tracking, but we do not know why these changes occur or why these abnormalities vary from individual to individual. Much continued research in this area is necessary to improve our understanding so that we can help people like Jamie, tragically struck down in their youth with this chronic, debilitating disease that has been referred to as "the disease that robs the victim of their soul."

THINKING CRITICALLY
QUESTIONS FOR DISCUSSION OR WRITING

1. Until psychology understood the neurological basis for schizophrenia, the disorder often was blamed indirectly on dysfunctional parenting. What difference do you think this new way of thinking about schizophrenia has made on family involvement in treatment?

2. Many "alternative" treatments for schizophrenia have been proposed, including megavitamin therapy, acupuncture, and others. Why do you think these types of treatments are appealing to schizophrenics and their families?

CHAPTER 8

Stress-Related Disorder:
It's All in Her Head

Of course, the concept of stress is an abstraction;
but so is that of life, which could hardly be
rejected as irrelevant to the study of biology.
HANS SELYE, The Stress of Life

SALLY'S STORY

Sally rested her head rest against the high-backed chair, sighing deeply. It had been a hectic week at the office, and she was happy to be with friends at her favorite restaurant, sipping red wine, and trying to relax. The tension in her neck loosened as she began to unwind from the sixty-hour work week she had just completed. Sally squinted slightly at the light glaring from the fixture overhead, and when she returned her gaze to her circle of friends, zigzag patterns formed in her field of vision. The warm, soothing feeling from the wine quickly turned into dismay because Sally recognized these signs well: They often preceded one of her headache attacks.

She fumbled through her purse to locate her Tylenol bottle and downed four tablets. Sally prayed that this time it would not turn into a full-fledged attack, but she recognized that her head was preparing for the battle to be waged there, and she was powerless to avert it. She decided that she had better leave the restaurant early. The lights from the oncoming cars nearly blinded her on the drive home. Halfway there, the nausea began, and tentacles of pain emanated from the throbbing in her right temple, which reached behind her eyes, down her face, and as far as her neck. An invisible cord connected her abdomen and her right temple, sending messages of pain back and forth. Sally massaged the area between her temple and her ear. The pain was unendurable, and she had difficulty concentrating on the road.

Once at her house, she sought her only refuge—a dark room, ice packs on her face, and a pile of blankets to keep her warm. Sally lay immobile on her bed, for even the slightest physical movement increased the throbbing. Mercifully, she fell asleep within an hour, and when she awoke the next morning, the throbbing and nausea had subsided. Yet she felt drained from the experience, as if recovering from a major illness.

79

Sally had experienced these headache attacks for almost half of her thirty years. As a teenager, they occurred about two to three times a month, becoming more frequent in her late twenties. Her mother, herself a headache sufferer, took her to a physician when she was sixteen, the beginning of the long search for an effective medication to relieve the pain. Although a number of them, notably Nardil, a monoamine oxidase (MAO) inhibitor, provided some relief initially, eventually the headaches won out, and Sally learned to sequester herself in a dark room with an ice pack until the siege had passed.

It is hard for Sally to remember what life was like before the headaches or even to imagine her current life without the threat of another attack hovering over her, following her absolutely everywhere she goes, including her prom night. At seventeen she was madly in love with Richard, who took her to the senior prom. Her mother had eased up on her usual strict rules to let her stay out until midnight, and she had saved up enough money for her prom dress. Richard had arranged for a romantic dinner at an expensive restaurant, and just as the main entree arrived, the nausea and throbbing began. As much as she tried, she could not ignore the pain, and Richard escorted her home at 9 p.m., her evening ruined.

The prom night was just the beginning of many spoiled evenings and vacations. A cruel prankster, the headache often struck when Sally was planning to enjoy herself. Sally's mother, a protective and caring individual, fretted over her daughter's condition and tried to prevent her from doing too much in her life. "You need your rest," she often told Sally. Perhaps out of defiance, Sally worked harder to achieve to prove that she could lead a normal life despite the headaches. She was the valedictorian of her high school graduating class, and she was awarded a full scholarship to the best college in the area.

Sally excelled in college and managed her studying around her headache attacks, which continued to strike about once a week. She consulted the physician at the student health center, who prescribed a low dose of the antidepressant amitriptyline to be taken daily. Concerned that the physician had diagnosed her with depression, Sally refused to take the medication and continued her own remedy of sleeping in a dark room. After completing her second-semester exams, Sally experienced the worst headache of her life, and she drove herself to the emergency room of the hospital, where she was given injections and narcotic pain relief. The attending physician insisted that Sally try the amitriptyline regimen, which required that she take low doses on a regular basis. Sally complied with this program for a brief period, but she experienced no relief and soon abandoned the medications.

Shortly after graduation from college, Sally met her husband, a quiet, serious dental student, whom she married when she was twenty-five. Bart empathized with Sally's headache episodes, comparing them to his unpredictable bouts of moodiness. Despite his understanding, however, the marriage faltered. The couple fought considerably about the long hours Sally devoted to her real estate work to become the top seller at the agency. She only stopped her frenetic pace when a headache attack forced her to stay in bed for a day. Bart became jealous of her professional success, even though his dental practice was a healthy one. Sally became impatient with his sudden mood shifts. Three years into their marriage Bart fell into one of his dark moods and killed himself on the evening of her twenty-eighth birthday.

Surprisingly, Sally's headaches did not worsen after the suicide of her husband. Sally turned to her Catholic faith to help her make sense of her husband's action and for some spiritual support. She blamed herself for working so hard and not being available to help her troubled husband, even though her family and friends assured her that his suicide was not her fault. She gave up her real estate job and moved to another town, where she quickly secured a position as human resources manager for a large corporation, hoping that the change would erase the painful memories. Before long, Sally resumed her previous work behavior, putting in long hours and taking on a great deal of responsibility. Part of Sally's job involved mediating interpersonal conflicts at work, which Sally found emotionally challenging. She was unable to stop thinking about them after work, and she discovered that a few glasses of wine took her mind off her problems.

Sally had only a few social ties in her new town, none of them close. She was afraid to start dating again, and her colleagues at work were busy with their own families and relationships. Sally experienced bouts of loneliness and tended to isolate a good deal of the time. After six months at her new job, Sally began to have more frequent and debilitating headaches. They occurred about twice a week, and they were so excruciating at times that Sally could not function at work. Her previous measures failed to provide relief, and Sally began to despair that she would not be able to live a normal life. Her boss noticed the changes in Sally's attendance and performance at work, and he set up a meeting to discuss his concerns. When Sally described the severity of her headaches, he recommended that she consult a neurologist. Despite her compliance, Sally was certain that there was no treatment for her and that she would simply have to tough it out as she always had. The neurologist persuaded Sally to consult a health psychologist, who could help her manage the pain and reduce the stress in her life.

▬ *WHAT DO YOU THINK?* ▬

1. Sally believed that the headaches struck randomly. After reading her story, would you agree with this assessment? Why or why not?

2. Identify any behaviors that Sally engaged in that might have contributed to her headaches.

3. How do you explain that Sally's headaches increased in frequency after she moved to a new town?

Assessment

The health psychologist Sally consulted conducted a thorough assessment of Sally's condition. With Sally's permission, she obtained the medical records from Sally's physician and neurologist. Of note in these records were the following: Sally had no history of head trauma or use of prescription medication other than that prescribed in conjunction with the headaches, although she had taken oral contraceptives during her three-year marriage. Her blood pressure was within the normal to low range. The blood tests for thyroid disease, anemia, or infections related to headaches were negative. Magnetic resonance imaging (MRI) ruled out the possibility of a brain tumor. Sally also was referred to an ophthalmologist for an eye examination to check for weakness in the eye muscle or unequal pupil size, which are symptomatic of an aneurysm. Sally demonstrated no weakness in this area.

The neurologist treating Sally concluded that her headaches were not due to another medical condition and diagnosed her with migraine headache. The psychologist then assessed Sally's lifestyle behavior, stress level, coping strategies, and beliefs about her condition. Sally worked approximately sixty to seventy hours a week, with a thirty-minute break midday. She seldom ate breakfast or lunch but ate a substantial dinner, which she usually ordered through take-out. She consumed two glasses of wine in the evening to relax and help her sleep, but she rarely drank more than this and infrequently drank on weekends. She had never experimented with illegal drugs. She rarely exercised and admitted that she disliked physical activity.

Sally believed that her life was more stressful than most because of her demanding job and the conflicts between staff that she dealt with regularly. She identified her husband's suicide, her move to a new town, and her headaches as the major stresses in her life. She admitted that she regularly used alcohol to relieve her tension and that she occasionally went to a movie to relax. When she had personal problems, Sally immersed herself in her work to forget them. She could not identify any other forms of stress management. Sally's social network had always been slim, consisting of her parents, her younger sister, and two close friends from college. When Sally moved to her new city, she was often alone and she did not make new friends easily.

Sally believed that her headaches struck randomly and that there was no discernible pattern for their occurrence. She also believed that she was more or less powerless to manage the headaches, since nothing she had done so far had helped. She had resigned herself to living with and around them.

Sally believed that she derived most of her self-worth from her professional achievements, adding that she had always been highly praised and valued as an employee. Her family had no history of psychiatric problems, but her father drank quite heavily. Her mother suffered from migraine headaches as well, which began when she was twenty years old. They had tapered off somewhat after she retired as a schoolteacher and following menopause.

Sally's sister had no history of headaches. The psychologist administered the Minnesota Multiphasic Personality Inventory 2 (MMPI-2), a widely used objective personality inventory, to assess Sally's psychological functioning. Sally's responses indicated that she was within normal range in all areas and did not point to psychopathology, although scale 1 (Hypochondriasis), scale 2 (Depression), and scale 7 (Psychasthenia) were more elevated than her other scores.

Sally's history of headache pain is outlined in her story: Beginning at age sixteen, she experienced severe headaches on one side of her head, which usually lasted about one day and on rare occasions two days. The headaches were accompanied by nausea, loss of concentration, sensitivity to light, and coldness, especially in her extremities. Physical movement exacerbated the throbbing. The headaches occurred approximately three times a month for about fourteen years, and then they increased in frequency to twice a week after that. Often Sally would have warning signals, called *auras*, that would occur shortly before the onset of the headache. These included visual disturbances such as zigzag patterns and tunnel vision, as well as sensitivity to light. Sally denied having *prodromes*, or warnings, hours before, of an impending attack. Sally could not identify any precise triggers for the headaches, although she noted that they regularly occurred after periods of stress.

Case Conceptualization

Sally is among the estimated 45 million Americans who experience chronic headaches. Sally suffers from migraine headaches, which are distinct from tension headaches, and are so debilitating that over 157 million workdays a year are lost because of this disorder (Stewart et al., 1992). These headaches not only cause aches and throbbing in the head area but also are accompanied by other symptoms, notably nausea or vomiting.

Researchers are unclear about the exact causes of migraine headaches, but most agree that it is a disorder of cerebral blood flow. People who experience migraine headaches seem to have blood vessels that overreact to a number of triggers. One theory suggests that the nervous system reacts to the trigger by constricting arteries, including the scalp and neck arteries, that supply blood to the brain, thus reducing the amount of blood flow to the brain. At the same time, blood-clotting particles clump together and release serotonin, which is itself a constrictor of arteries.

To offset the reduced oxygen supply caused by this constriction, other arteries dilate, and this causes the release of pain-producing substances. In addition, other chemicals that produce swelling and sensitivity to pain circulate, which activate the pain-sensitive noriceptors. The end result is the throbbing in the head that migraine sufferers experience.

Clearly, migraine headaches are largely physiologic in origin, but they are exacerbated by a number of triggers, some of which are emotional. In Sally's case, a complex interplay between environment, physiology, and psychology was at work, and the psychologist worked carefully with Sally to unveil potential triggers. Some triggers were discrete: Sally was a regular consumer of red wine, a common trigger for migraines. Another trigger for Sally seemed to be strong lights, especially fluorescent lights, not unusual among migraine sufferers.

Other factors were more complex and involved Sally's response to environmental stressors. Sally had had a greater than average amount of change in her life in the year that her migraines worsened. She had lost a spouse to a tragic and violent suicide. Even though Sally desired the geographic move, the lack of social support and the demands of her new job were sources of distress in her life. She found the interpersonal conflicts at work disturbing, and she was unable to unwind from her job once the workday ended.

Sally was on overload, and she lacked the psychological resources to manage the excessive demands these changes made. She began to believe that she could not handle the conflicts at work, and as her headaches worsened, she concluded that she could not manage those either. Her appraisal of her situation, coupled with the challenges presented by her new life, exacerbated her migraine headaches. And like many migraine sufferers, Sally lacked effective coping strategies for managing her stress level. Exercise, meditation, social support, and more leisure time were not among Sally's repertoire of coping techniques. Her only outlet was alcohol, which, as it turns out, was a trigger for her headaches. When she experienced emotional distress, she tended to bury herself in her work, and the physical and psychological demands exhausted her. She also believed that she had no control over her migraines, which she believed struck randomly. As a result, she began to despair that the only hope she had was to resign herself to their existence.

Diagnosis

Sally consulted a neurologist who, after taking a detailed history and completing a number of medical tests, ruled out other medical conditions of which headache is a symptom, such as brain tumor, high blood pressure, and thyroid disease. Sally was diagnosed with migraine headache, classic type. Classic migraines are accompanied by auras, while common migraines are not. The third type of migraines, cluster headaches, are more painful and occur daily for weeks, followed by pain-free periods. Migraines tend to localize on one side of the head, usually with throbbing at the temple. Tension headaches, on the other hand, cause pain in the back of the head, near the neck area. Migraines typically last from hours to days and vary in their frequency from daily to weekly. The average frequency is one to three attacks per month.

Since migraine headaches are a medical condition, only physicians can diagnose them. Despite the fact that migraines are considered a medical condition, they belong to a category of illnesses that are influenced by psychological factors, notably stress. Other illnesses that fall into this category include heart disease, cancer, ulcers, and irritable bowel syndrome, among others. It is important to note that these illnesses are not psychological in origin, as somatic disorders are. However, the interplay between stress and disease has become increasingly more evident since Hans Selye popularized the word *stress* in the 1950s and underscored the physiologic effects of stress.

Thus, in the case of migraine, external triggers can set off the physiologic process that causes the blood vessels in the brain to expand. These include substances (such as alcohol, foods, caffeine, and smoke), sensory inputs (such as lights and loud noises), hormonal changes, diet and sleep alterations, and certain medications. Psychological stress also can set this cycle in motion, which can be due to excess change in a person's life or can be caused by an individual's ineffective response to the various stressors in his or her life. In the latter case, migraine sufferers are likely to perceive greater stress in their lives than others and to lack appropriate and effective techniques for managing the stress they do have, as Sally did.

Migraines often have their onset in adolescence, but they can begin at any age. They are far more likely to affect women than men: 75 percent of those afflicted are female. Migraine headaches run in families, with approximately 70 percent of sufferers having family members who also experience migraines. Recent research (Merikangas et al., 1997) has indicated that individuals who have migraine with aura are at a greater risk for stroke than those who are migraine-free. Preliminary research indicates that the risk of stroke for nonmigraine sufferers between thirty-five and forty-five years of age is 3.6 in 100,000, compared with a 22 in 100,000 risk for migraine sufferers. It is important to note that exact risk figures have yet to be established and that these risks in otherwise healthy women are quite small, however.

DSM-IV does not have a diagnostic category for migraine headache, but Sally's multiaxial assessment would include a mention of her headaches on Axis III, which identifies medical conditions, with mention in Axis IV of the psychosocial stressors that exacerbated her migraines.

Treatment and Outlook

The primary treatment for migraine headache is pharmacologic, prescribed by a physician. In many cases these medications provide only partial relief, and many migraine sufferers seek nondrug forms of treatment, including psychological interventions. Sally's neurologist and psychologist worked closely together to provide her with a complete treatment program aimed at pain relief and anxiety and stress reduction.

Sally participated in a lifestyle class, which incorporated a psychoeducational approach to understanding and managing stress. Sally learned about the stress response and assessed her own behavior, targeting areas for change. In particular, she cut down on the red wine she consumed and introduced exercise into her daily routine, starting by walking and eventually graduating to more aerobic activity. She found that the exercise helped her to unwind from the day's hassles, so she usually completed her routine after her workday.

Sally was encouraged to practice some form of deep breathing to increase the relaxation response in her body. Sally found it difficult to quiet the chatter in her mind, and she began to realize how noisy her inner world had become. The psychologist used biofeedback, which charts body temperature and heart rate visually on a computer screen, to teach Sally to regulate her own relaxation response. She was amazed at the physiologic changes that quiet meditation and progressive relaxation exercises could produce. As her ability to relax increased, Sally began to sharpen her awareness of the effect of stress on her body, something that she had not known before.

Sally's belief that her migraines were completely out of her control did not provide her with a great sense of control, and the psychologist used cognitive therapy to challenge some of her all-or-none thinking. This, coupled with the behavioral techniques described earlier, was helpful in restoring a sense of control over her life again and a bit more optimism about managing the headaches. This personal responsibility also helped Sally to follow her medication regime for the first time in her life.

Once Sally's headache episodes relented somewhat, the psychologist encouraged Sally to explore the guilt and anger she still felt from her husband's suicide. She helped her to finally grieve over her loss, which freed her to consider dating again. The psychologist confronted Sally on using work to avoid her feelings.

The prognosis for Sally was fair to good. She was able to reduce the number of severe headaches by recognizing the more subtle effects of stress in her life and by taking her medication regularly. She admits to feeling much healthier and happier since she implemented the exercise and meditation into her life, although she continues to have migraines at least once monthly. Nonetheless, Sally believes that her work with the psychologist was extremely valuable. It helped her to process her emotions better and to gain more personal control over her situation. She no longer considers herself a victim of the headaches.

THINKING CRITICALLY

QUESTIONS FOR DISCUSSION OR WRITING

1. How might you respond to someone who told Sally that her headaches were all "in her head"?

2. Imagine that Sally is resistant to the behavioral interventions of lifestyle change, meditation, and biofeedback, claiming that it is all flaky "New Age" practices. Formulate an argument that might convince her of the value of this in helping her manage her stress and prevent headaches.

CHAPTER 9

Alcohol Dependence:
The Web That Denial Weaves

*No animal ever invented anything so bad as
drunkenness—or so good as drink.*   LORD CHESTERTON

FRANK'S STORY

As soon as Frank walked into his house that evening, he knew that something was wrong because his wife, Jeannie, and his eight-year-old daughter, Jessica, did not get up from watching TV to greet him as they usually did. Then it came back to him: He had forgotten to attend Jessica's parent-teacher meeting that night, which he had promised to do that morning. It was the last thing Jeannie had said to him as he left for work, "Don't forget. The meeting's at 6:00, and Jessie wants both of us to be there."

Frank went to hug his daughter, who recoiled from him, his breath reeking of alcohol. "I'm sorry, honey, I wanted to be there. I had to work late," Frank said.

Jeannie sent Jessica off to bed, and then she started in on Frank. "How could you forget? Jessie was counting on you being there. You know her teachers are worried about her being so aggressive with the other kids. What is wrong with you?"

Frank wanted to apologize to his wife. He loved his daughter so much and he felt awful letting her down, but the words that came out of his mouth were far from contrite. It was as if something just snapped inside of him, and he lost control. He screamed at Jeannie, "Stop telling me what to do. You just can't stand it when I go out with my friends after work. You want me right here, by your side, at every moment, so you can boss me around. You don't know what it's like to go out there and face that world every day."

"I don't know what it's like? Give me a break! Who keeps this place together while you decide to get drunk and stumble in whenever you please?"

"Shut up," Frank screamed, and then he grabbed Jeannie's favorite antique china lamp, which her mother had given her before she died, and hurled it across the room, where it shattered on the tile floor. His ruddy complexion was even redder now as his temper flared, and Jeannie pulled back in fear. Jeannie could hear the children stirring upstairs, and she worried that they were listening to the two of them fighting again. This was worse than usual, Jeannie thought, and she suddenly feared that he would throw her across the room, just as he had that lamp. In a moment of courage, Jeannie looked at Frank and said firmly, but quietly, "Frank, I'm taking the children to my sister's house. I need some time to think things over." She gathered up Jessica and her five-year-old brother Nathan, and together they drove off. Frank watched the car disappear down the street, and fixed himself a drink, downed it quickly, and freshened it up. He began to calm down after the fourth drink, and he vaguely remembers the phone ringing before passing out in front of the TV.

The next morning Frank called in sick to work. He tried to piece the events of last evening together, but there were gaps. He cringed when he saw the broken fragments of the lamp and remembered his angry outburst. "I'm like my father," he thought in horror.

All his life Frank had tried to be different—strong and decisive—because his father was weak and passive, henpecked by his wife. Yet when Frank's father drank, which was mostly on the weekends, his temper flared, and he turned into a monster. Frank hated the weekends as a child because his father would come home drunk and go after his mother, screaming about this and that, about his "rotten kids." Frank felt particularly helpless when his father hit her. Once in awhile his father would get angry at something Frank had done, and then he'd beat Frank. Frank didn't get beat more than the other five kids, but they never knew who was "going to get it."

Frank always prided himself on the fact that he was different from his father. He never hit his wife and kids because he didn't want his kids to go through what he and his four brothers had experienced. He tried not to play favorites with his children the way his mother had favored Frank's baby brother. And he did his best to stay in the same town. His father had had difficulty holding down a job, so the family moved frequently during Frank's childhood. Between the ages of five and eighteen, Frank attended seven different schools and lived in five towns. Mostly Frank brushes over the tough parts of his childhood because, as he says to his wife, "What's done is done."

When Frank was eighteen, he left home and got his first job as a busboy in an upscale restaurant in a nearby city. Frank recalls how determined and hopeful he was at that point. He wanted to be successful, and he didn't want to be dependent on anyone, especially on a woman. At first, Frank did very well in the restaurant business, moving up from busboy to head waiter in a very brisk period of time. He was handsome and likable, and his customers praised him regularly to the management of the restaurant.

He began to socialize with the other waiters at nightclubs and bars after work, staying out late, dancing and drinking. Frank boasted that he could "drink anyone under the table" then. He often had hangovers the next day and began requesting last-minute shift changes at work. Initially, the other waiters were sympathetic and willing to oblige, but as his requests became more frequent, his colleagues began to complain to management. Two years after starting at the restaurant, he was fired for absenteeism and poor work habits.

It was about this time that Frank began to experience memory blanks after bouts of drinking. One event in particular frightened him. He had taken his date to a restaurant in a town about seventy miles away. They were enjoying themselves, having a fine dinner on a balmy summer evening on the patio under the stars. Frank remembers that they drank two bottles of wine at dinner. After dinner, they went dancing, and he continued drinking cocktails. The last thing he remembers is dancing to the Doors' "Light My Fire." He woke up the next morning in his bedroom, and he was horrified to realize that he could not remember the remainder of the evening. He did not know how he got home. He called his date from the previous evening, who filled in some of the blanks. They had driven forty miles to another club, and finally, she had urged him to drive her home at 4 a.m., but not before he started a fight with the bartender. He felt ashamed of his behavior and humiliated in front of his date.

After that incident, Frank tried to control his drinking. He stopped hard liquor and only drank beer and wine. He never drank on weekdays. He was able to find a sales job with a restaurant supply company, and he did quite well. He met his first wife at this job when he was twenty-three. They fell in love and impulsively got married on a trip to Las Vegas after only six months. The marriage quickly turned sour, however, as his wife spent their money foolishly and Frank lost his temper with her. They were divorced within the year, and Frank plunged himself into his work.

After his divorce, Frank began to have problems. His friends from the restaurant no longer spoke to him, and his colleagues at his current job began avoiding him. He blamed it on his success in selling—he was the top salesperson—but he began to feel lonely and depressed. He began drinking more, and he broke his promise to himself to stay off the hard stuff. He dabbled a little with cocaine. His work suffered, and it wasn't long before he was fired from the restaurant supply job.

During the next ten years, Frank got fired from many jobs. Bosses told him he was difficult to be around and that he responded poorly to direction. Co-workers told him he was moody and belligerent. Even his friends began avoiding him because he borrowed money and never repaid it. Then he met his second wife on a sales call, and he vowed to turn his life around. They dated steadily and got married a year later. Frank was thirty-five, he knew he wanted to have a family, and he was convinced that Jeannie was the perfect partner for him. She understood him, and she didn't care that he didn't have the best job. Frank regards those early years nostalgically when he remembers the fun they had together.

After two years, they had their first child, Jessica. Motivated by providing for his family, Frank found a position as a sales representative for a major food distributor to restaurants. Skillful and knowledgeable, Frank was able to capture some of the most important accounts in the town. At this point, Frank was sure he had made it: He had money and independence, and he was the head of his family. Two years later, Jeannie and he had their second child, Nathan.

Frank wonders how he and his family slid down from that peak during the past five years. Perhaps they were paying the price for a demanding job, which required that he steal time from his family to fulfill the requirements of the job. He knows that he struggled with the pressures himself, drinking more than usual to manage the stress. His wife never complained at first, and she took care of all the household chores. Gradually, though, they began to argue about his business dinners and the after-dinner socializing with associates.

When Jeannie decided to see a counselor about her "depression," their lives changed. Frank was sure that the counselor was blaming him for her problems, and he's fairly certain that the counselor planted the idea of leaving him into her head, too. Frank couldn't fathom why his wife would abandon him at the very point he needed her support the most. His ego took quite a bruising from losing his job last year, and his current job wasn't bringing in nearly the same income.

Frank decided to call his wife at her sister's and plead with her to return home. Jeannie reluctantly came to the phone and stood firm in her position: "Get some help, or I'm not coming back. You drink too much, and you are abusive. I won't live like this, and I won't expose the kids to this kind of treatment." Frank was astounded to hear those words from her mouth, and because he loved her, he decided to make an appointment with a counselor, for her sake.

▨▨▨ *WHAT DO YOU THINK?* ▨▨▨

1. What are the key factors involved in the marital conflict between Frank and his wife?

2. Alcoholics use denial to minimize the problems associated with their substance abuse. Identify the ways in which Frank used denial and the consequences of that defense mechanism on his relationships, work, and family life.

Assessment

The psychologist Frank consulted about his marriage problems formulated a number of preliminary hypotheses regarding Frank's case, which included substance abuse problems, depression, as well as relationship issues. The clinician conducted a thorough interview and administered a number of self-report assessment instruments, notably the Substance Abuse Subtle Screening Inventory 2 (SASSI-2) (Miller, 1994). The SASSI-2 is a screening instrument for substance abuse that assesses personality and behavior traits associated with chemically dependent individuals, with a reported screening accuracy rate of 90 to 92 percent. Frank scored high on the scale that measures a personal predisposition to developing chemical dependency and which is resistant to efforts at concealing problems. His score on the defensiveness scale, which can indicate either conscious concealment or unconscious denial of substance abuse problems, also was elevated. These scores were sufficiently above the cutoff of a T-score of 70 to classify Frank as chemically dependent.

The clinician reviewed Frank's substance abuse history in detail, including the following areas: age at which he began drinking, his family history of substance abuse, his work history, his relationship history, legal history, the role alcohol has played in his life, and his past and current drinking patterns. The psychologist approached the process as a fact-finding mission with Frank, and as they explored his alcohol use, Frank began to see the wide web that alcohol had spun around him.

He first began drinking at the age of thirteen. He and his neighborhood friend stole a bottle of gin from his father's supply and drank it in the woods near their home. Frank remembered that he felt light-headed and enjoyed the feeling, and he recalled that he was able to drink more than his friend. He became quite sick from the experience and didn't touch alcohol again until he began working in the restaurant at age eighteen.

His early drinking days were fun, and he used alcohol to cut loose from the dreary life that he had led as a child. He liked being the "life of the party," and it seemed that women flirted with him more after he'd had a couple of drinks. He boasted that he could drink any of his friends "under the table," and he was often the one who drove his drunk friends home. He didn't worry about his alcohol use because he wasn't like his father: "I became fun when I drank, not like my father. He just got mean."

There was a great deal of substance abuse in Frank's extended family, which is a clear risk factor for the development of alcoholism. In addition to his father, his maternal grandfather also was an alcoholic, who died of liver disease. His mother had taken Valium regularly when Frank was a teenager, and two of his brothers had entered drug rehabilitation programs in the early 1980s for cocaine addiction.

Frank admitted that during his adult life he had had periods of extensive alcohol use, followed by attempts at controlling his use after an incident that alarmed him. His efforts at limiting his alcohol consumption included only drinking on the weekends, switching to beer and wine, and brief periods of abstinence. Inevitably, Frank would return to his previous level. At the time that Frank entered therapy, he was drinking large quantities of alcohol daily. He found himself drinking earlier and earlier in the day "to take the edge off," and he hid bottles of gin in his office and car to have alcohol readily available. He tried to conceal the extent of his drinking from his wife, but she had found a half-empty bottle of gin in the glove compartment and confronted him on it.

Alcohol had interfered with many facets of his life. He had difficulty holding onto jobs because of erratic work performance and excessive absenteeism. More recently, drinking made him moody and belligerent, and he would strike up heated arguments with co-workers and clients, who had spoken to management about his behavior. He had fewer friends than before, and they were reluctant to go out with him. Many had criticized his drinking and even suggested he "go on the wagon."

Like many alcoholics, Frank believed that his drinking was his own business, but his behavior chiseled away at the solidity of his family system. His children were frightened of his unpredictable behavior, and they began acting out at school. His wife was quite dissatisfied in the relationship and had sought treatment for her depression. She had lost the patience she had for him at the beginning and began spending more time apart from him. She was contemplating a separation.

In a separate interview, Jeannie described the changes taking place. "About a year ago Frank started staying out late and coming home pretty drunk. It seems like his personality changed then, too. He started lashing out at us more and losing his temper. I got pretty scared. That's when I went to see a therapist. At first I thought it might be me or the stress of his jobs, but now I realize he just can't control his drinking. When I broached the subject, he flatly denied that he had a problem. I felt pretty powerless. Then I realized that if he didn't do something, our family would go to pieces."

Frank had not been cited for driving while intoxicated, although he had been stopped and warned a number of times by the highway patrol. He had been thrown out of several bars for initiating brawls and behaving inappropriately toward women.

The results of the test battery that Frank completed during the assessment phase pointed to the presence of a depressed mood, not uncommon in alcohol abusers. Frank admitted that he had experienced depression on and off in his life, usually triggered by stressful events such as his divorce, job loss, and so on. He reported that he tended to drink more during these stressful times and that the alcohol masked his depressed feelings.

Since alcoholism is a psychological as well as physiologic disorder, the effects of alcohol on Frank's physical well-being were evaluated. He admitted to high blood pressure and an ulcer, common concomitants of alcoholism. A complete physical examination was recommended to rule out other potential medical problems.

Case Conceptualization

There is a strong familial and genetic component to the development of alcoholism. In addition to his parents, both sides of Frank's family included relatives with serious substance abuse problems. Children of alcoholic parents are at greater risk for developing alcoholism (Cotton, 1979), with some evidence that this is due to hereditary factors (Devor & Cloninger, 1989; Shuckit, 1994). Some research (McGue, Pickins & Svikis, 1992) suggests that these genetic risks are greater for males than for females and are more prominent the earlier the onset of alcoholism. Frank's father was a so-called type II alcoholic, that is, one whose occupational, marital, and social life was severely impaired by alcohol use. Sons of type II alcoholics are at a much greater risk of becoming alcoholic themselves than are sons of nonalcoholics or type I alcoholics, that is, alcoholics with poor health but no severe disruptions in other parts of their lives (Cloninger, 1987).

Studies (Martin, Cloninger & Guze, 1985; Shuckit & Smith, 1996) support the notion that certain individuals are at risk from a biologic standpoint for developing an alcohol disorder. They have a lower level of response to alcohol consumption, which means that they require greater amounts of alcohol to experience intoxication, and this is linked to the subsequent development of alcoholism. Frank's history indicated that he "could drink everyone under the table" at an early stage of his drinking and that he consumed large quantities early on.

Environmental factors also can place individuals at risk, such as early family environment, learned behavior, and extreme social stress. Regardless of his genetic vulnerability, Frank had continued the family tradition of using substances to cope: His father used alcohol to deal with his passivity, and his mother used tranquilizers to relax and manage a chaotic home. When Frank faced difficulties, he increased his drinking, which soon became a central feature of his life.

Frank's early childhood was not nourishing. The physical abuse he received was associated with feelings of shame and worthlessness, which Frank carried with him throughout his life. When relationships splintered or he was fired from a job, Frank tended to blame himself and felt like a failure, and his father's words—"You rotten kid"—would surface. Frank used alcohol at such times to dull the pain and ignore the wounds.

By the time Frank entered treatment, he had direct indicators of his alcoholism: drinking early in the day, withdrawal symptoms (for example, trembling) within six hours of abstinence, the need for greater amounts of alcohol, and job loss due to alcohol-related absences. There also were indirect indicators as well: Frank's alcohol use interfered with his family's ability to function as a secure unit, and his daughter began acting aggressively at school. His wife had lost patience with his behavior and sought treatment for herself, and Frank had begun to pin their problems on her. He also had mounting financial problems.

Frank's faulty belief system also was an indicator that alcohol was a severe problem in his life. Although Frank's occupational and interpersonal difficulties were clearly related to his alcohol use, Frank severely discounted the extent to which alcohol had impaired his life, a common defense mechanism among the chemically dependent. Frank's denial was bolstered by a set of mistaken beliefs about his drinking despite evidence pointing to its deleterious effects. For example, Frank believed that his drinking was a question of choice, not one of dependence. He firmly held to the notion that he could stop when he wanted to. He also believed that his drinking was not the cause of his occupational and marital problems but that work stress and his wife's depression led him to drink more. In this way Frank constructed an elaborate system of rationalizations and fantasies in the face of a growing addiction in order to allow continued alcohol use. As the edifice of his world began to deteriorate around him, he continued to believe that he did not have a problem and that others were creating problems for him.

Diagnosis

Frank's current pattern of drinking and his history point to a diagnosis of alcohol dependence. According to *DSM-IV*, alcohol dependence is characterized by a cluster of cognitive, behavioral, and physiologic symptoms such that an individual continues to drink despite a series of problems brought on by the use of the alcohol. Extensive use of alcohol results in compulsive use, tolerance, and withdrawal.

The key feature of alcohol dependence is compulsive use of the substance, which Frank demonstrated clearly. He had made many unsuccessful attempts to control his drinking, he repeatedly found himself drinking more than he had intended, and his life activities were centered around alcohol consumption, to the detriment of his work, marriage, and family. Frank's tolerance of alcohol, another hallmark of an alcohol disorder, increased, as evidenced by his need to drink greater quantities earlier in the day to maintain the desired effect.

A third criteria of alcohol dependence is the presence of withdrawal symptoms when drinking is stopped after prolonged or excessive use. These symptoms can range from the more common, such as insomnia and nausea, to the more severe, such as hallucinations and grand mal seizures. Frank's withdrawal symptoms remained on the less severe side. He often experienced nausea and vomiting after drinking, and his hands shook in the morning.

DSM-IV distinguishes between alcohol dependence and alcohol abuse. Alcohol abuse is diagnosed when two or more of the following apply: The use of alcohol has significantly interfered with a person's major role obligations, alcohol is consumed when it would be dangerous to do so (for example, while driving), legal problems ensue from alcohol use (for example, arrests for driving while intoxicated), and continued use of alcohol even though it has caused or exacerbated interpersonal interactions. A diagnosis of alcohol dependence is more severe and in Frank's case would supersede that of alcohol abuse.

Frank also was diagnosed with dysthymic disorder, a chronic form of depressed mood that is present for an extended period of time, characterized by feelings of low self-worth. It was expected that Frank's depression would remit once the drinking ceased and he was able to work through thoughts and feelings about his value as a human being. Thus, Frank was given a dual diagnosis of a substance abuse disorder and a mood disorder.

Generally speaking, a dual diagnosis refers to the co-occurrence of a substance abuse disorder and a psychiatric disorder. Of the 14 percent of Americans with alcohol-related disorders, 37 percent also will have a psychiatric disorder. These two disorders may be related in a number of ways. A psychiatric disorder (for example, bipolar disorder) may present a risk for developing subsequent substance abuse, or the use of a substance can trigger a relapse (as in drug use and schizophrenia). In other cases, the substance abuse may not be directly related to the psychiatric disorder at all. Diagnosing additional psychiatric disorders, whether primary or secondary to the substance abuse, is important in preventing relapses. Depression, anxiety, posttraumatic stress disorder, and certain personality disorders such as borderline personality disorder and antisocial personality disorder are commonly associated with alcoholism.

Treatment and Outlook

The initial phase of treatment for Frank was the assessment process, during which the clinician explored Frank's relationship with alcohol. Frank's goal in entering treatment was to get his wife to return home to him, but the clinician quickly recognized that Frank's marriage had little chance of survival if he continued drinking. By examining how alcohol had affected almost every aspect of his life in a negative way, and particularly his relationships, Frank was able to break through some of the denial that discounted the deleterious consequences of alcohol.

Nonetheless, he still believed that he could control his alcohol use, so the psychologist suggested that he test out his hypothesis and limit his alcohol consumption to one drink a day. When this test proved unsuccessful, the clinician suggested that Frank try attending an Alcoholics Anonymous (AA) meeting. The self-help program of AA is perhaps the most widely known treatment for alcoholism and is based on the disease model of alcoholism. Membership in AA is free and voluntary. Members follow a twelve-step program of recovery that acknowledges a lack of control over their drinking and the need to yield to a higher power in order to have recovery from the disease of alcoholism. AA endorses abstinence from alcohol and believes that an alcoholic can never take another drink without a relapse into the disease.

Despite the popularity and visibility of AA, the results of some research into the effectiveness of this type of treatment for alcoholism (Galaif & Sussman, 1995) have indicated that only between 5 and 13 percent of its members maintain sobriety, while a vast majority drop out entirely (Brandsma, Maultsby & Welsh, 1980). One controlled study, however, found AA to be as effective as other forms of treatment (Timko, Moos, Finney & Moos, 1994).

Critics of AA as a form of treatment for alcoholism point to its reliance on a spiritual base for recovery and its insistence on total abstinence from drinking. Rational Recovery, a cognitively based program, also recommends abstinence but relies on cognitive-behavioral techniques for changing the thinking patterns that lead to drinking.

Others advocate an approach to treatment that teaches controlled drinking. This approach does not emphasize the disease concept of alcoholism but rather maintains that drinking is a learned behavior that can be managed by cognitive and behavioral techniques. Clients learn to monitor the physical and behavioral effects of alcohol and to identify triggers to excessive drinking. Proponents of this treatment believe that controlling alcohol intake increases alcoholics' self-efficacy and avoids the shame and sense of failure following relapse from an abstinence program.

Stephanie Brown (1995) encourages a developmental approach to recovery whereby alcoholics are guided through various stages with the help of both outpatient psychotherapy and self-help groups like AA. This was the approach taken with Frank, which yielded good results. After the initial phase of breaking through Frank's denial regarding the damage caused by his drinking, he began to work through a transitional stage emphasizing abstinence, relapse prevention, and restoration of his physical well-being. Frank continued attending AA meetings, which he found quite helpful in maintaining his abstinence. The psychologist worked with Frank on identifying triggers for drinking and developing behavioral and cognitive solutions to these problem situations. Frank began working out and socializing with nondrinking friends. Later work focused on his family and marriage, as well as his low self-esteem.

The prognosis for Frank was good. Six months into his treatment, he once again lost his job due to downsizing of his company. As in the past, Frank turned to drinking to deal with his deep sense of failure as a provider for his family. Fortunately, he did not abandon his treatment, and he was able to turn to his AA sponsor and his individual therapy to help him understand his relapse and work to prevent a similar response in the future.

Frank's wife remained with him while he went through his first year of recovery. After a number of sessions of marital therapy, however, it became apparent that she could not forgive him for the damage he caused during his drinking periods. Eighteen months after Frank stopped drinking, Jeannie filed for divorce. Frank managed to get through the divorce without relapse, and he recently celebrated his two-year anniversary of sobriety.

▬ *THINKING CRITICALLY* ▬
QUESTIONS FOR DISCUSSION OR WRITING

1. Mental health professionals often disagree about whether alcohol abuse is the result of a larger problem (that is, a symptom of an underlying problem) or whether it is the primary problem in a person's life. What are the arguments for both points of view in Frank's case? Which perspective would you endorse, and why?

2. Recent research has linked consuming a moderate number of drinks with prevention of heart disease. Some alcohol counselors endorse teaching "moderated drinking" to people with alcohol dependence by having them limit the number of drinks they consume. Do you think that Frank could learn such an approach? Why or why not? If you were his psychologist, would you endorse such an approach? If you were a public health worker, would you support controlled drinking?

3. Alcohol is viewed in diverse ways, depending on the culture. In what ways does American society contribute to the maintenance of alcohol problems? Explore the role of alcohol in your family and your culture.

CHAPTER 10

Premature Ejaculation: *Under Pressure to Perform*

If your life at night is good, you think you have everything. EURIPIDES

MIKE'S STORY

Mike didn't call Heather, his live-in girlfriend, to tell her he was coming home early. "It'll be a nice surprise for her," he thought as he approached their apartment. "We haven't had enough time together lately." As soon as he opened the door, he quickly regretted his action: Heather was passionately embracing one of their mutual friends. Mike felt his face burning with shame, and he heard Heather pleading with him as he turned around and walked out the door. Mike was not angry at Heather; he blamed himself. "It's my fault," he told himself. "I can't satisfy her. She's too experienced for me. I just wasn't enough."

Mike had been very much in love with Heather for the year that they had been together, finding her exciting and beautiful. Mike believed that Heather was enamored of him. But there was the issue of their sexual intimacy, which had been a problem from the start.

Mike thinks back to their first sexual encounter, which he initiated with some insistence. On their third date, Heather had invited Mike back to her apartment for a drink after dinner and a movie. He had been aroused all evening by her trim body and soft skin; the mere touch of her leg against his increased his desire. At the same time, he felt his shoulders tensing and a knot forming in his stomach, for he feared that he would fail again tonight as he often had in the past. It seemed the more he desired a woman, the more quickly he reached orgasm once inside her. Part of him feared having sex with Heather, but the other part just wanted to get the first experience over with. He'd be more relaxed after that.

Once Mike and Heather were settled on the couch that night, Mike reached for Heather's breast under her shirt, touching it roughly. Heather looked at Mike, bewildered, but he continued the foreplay, intent on performing well this time and maintaining control. In fact, Mike had the feeling he had split off from his body, floating somewhere near the ceiling, watching his performance, assessing his every move. He'd often had this sensation during sexual

101

encounters. He was completely aroused by the foreplay, and he thought Heather might be too, so he entered her. Within seconds, he lost control, ejaculated, and the act was over.

Heather said to Mike gently, "Perhaps we rushed things a little." But Mike could tell that she was disappointed that he wasn't more of a man, that he couldn't fully satisfy her. He pushed the comment aside and pretended it was nothing, hoping that he would have a second chance to rectify things next time. They continued to date and their affection for each other grew, but their sexual intimacy improved little. Mike had no difficulty with arousal, but as soon as he penetrated Heather, he would climax almost immediately. Mike worried constantly that he would lose Heather, especially since she alluded to having sexual adventures with her previous boyfriends. Despite his concerns, he avoided talking about them directly with her.

In the end, it was Heather who initiated a dialogue about their sex life after about four months of dating. She expressed concern about Mike's rough foreplay and his apparent interest in his own pleasure only without consideration of her sexual needs. Mike was very embarrassed during this conversation, and to this day he can recall little of what was said. He remembers responding defensively but promising to be more sensitive to her in the future.

Although they spent longer periods touching and kissing during foreplay, the sexual act itself was often a disappointment for Mike. Heather did not raise the topic again, but in retrospect, Mike recognizes that shortly after that she began to spend more time away on "business trips" and out with her girlfriends until late at night. Not a naturally jealous person, Mike didn't question her behavior. Now he wished he had.

Sex had always been complicated for Mike. He's certain that his religious upbringing didn't help him. He was the third of seven children in a devoutly Christian family. He had one uncle who was a minister and a cousin who had entered the seminary. It was not uncommon for his parents to invite preachers for dinner, and his father was an active member in the church. They all hoped that Mike, who showed the most interest in religion as a young boy, would follow in his uncle's footsteps, so his uncle devoted many afternoons to discussing theology with him. Reluctant to disappoint his family, Mike avoided telling them that he was not drawn to the ministry and that he was questioning his own beliefs in God and the Church.

Mike's parents never spoke about sex, and the Christian school Mike attended did not offer sex education classes. Thus, when Mike had his first nocturnal emission in early adolescence, he was ashamed, thinking that he had wet his bed. His older brother explained "the birds and the bees" to Mike, which helped him to understand what was happening to him. Shortly after, Mike began experimenting with masturbation and confiding in one of his close friends from church, who had access to erotic magazines, some of them homosexual. Mike borrowed the magazines and hid out in the basement of his house when no one was around to look at them. He was very apprehensive at those times that his mother would walk in on him and catch him masturbating, so he usually ejaculated quickly. He had a good deal of guilt over masturbating because his uncle had warned him that it was a sin. He was especially guilty that the homosexual erotica aroused him. When he was fifteen, the basement flooded during a particularly bad storm, and the magazines that Mike had forgotten about floated to the surface. His father discovered them and reprimanded Mike severely, and although he can laugh at the incident now, at the time Mike was mortified.

Girls were always comfortable around Mike because he wasn't loud and rough like the other boys. He had his first girlfriend very young, and they kissed in the woods near their neighborhood. After thirteen, Mike was never without a girlfriend, and he had his first sexual encounter at fourteen. That first experience was a "disaster" because after Mike ejaculated very quickly, the girl, two grades ahead of Mike, hinted that she would spread it around that he couldn't "keep it up." Mike was indelibly marked by this experience.

Subsequent girlfriends were more understanding, but Mike always experienced a great deal of tension when starting a new sexual relationship. He worried about his sexual performance and his ability to satisfy the woman. Sometimes, after he got to know a woman and he felt more comfortable being around her, he was able to control his ejaculation, and the sex would be pleasurable for him. He also tried a number of techniques to delay his orgasm during sex, including counting backwards and thinking of mundane topics, but none of them seemed to help. Nonetheless, he usually grew weary of his girlfriends after about a year, and he would end the relationship without provocation, quickly moving on to another woman. The endings were always friendly—he doesn't ever remember getting angry in his relationships.

That's why he was so devastated by Heather's betrayal. He was usually the one in control, the one to call it quits. He could not push away from his mind the image of Heather embracing their friend, and often in the middle of the night he awoke and imagined that Heather was making love to their friend at that very moment. He imagined that his friend was a virile lover, who could sustain her pleasure for great lengths of time. These thoughts disturbed him greatly. He was hurt and humiliated, and he was sure that at thirty-five, he would never find a woman he could marry and with whom he could raise a family.

He decided that he needed help with his sexual problem. He thought that maybe if he took care of that, Heather and he could have a better relationship.

▬ *WHAT DO YOU THINK?* ▬

1. Mike believed that his religious upbringing contributed to his sexual problems. Explain how this may be so.

2. What other factors in Mike's history may have contributed to difficulty delaying orgasm after penetration?
3. Mike describes splitting off from his body during sex. What do you suppose was happening to him psychologically at that point?
4. Mike saw himself as a sensitive man, in tune with women's feelings. Agree or disagree with Mike's assessment of himself.

Assessment

Mike's psychologist conducted a careful review of Mike's case. First, she referred Mike for a complete medical examination to rule out the presence of a physiologic explanation for his sexual dysfunction, since in rare cases problems with premature ejaculation are associated with multiple sclerosis and other degenerative neurologic diseases and also can be indicative of diseases of the posterior urethra (Kaplan, 1974). All Mike's medical tests were negative, and the physician assured Mike that he was in excellent health.

The psychologist next took a thorough history of the sexual problem, including the onset and extent, sexual history, family and cultural attitudes toward sex, medical and psychiatric history, relationship history, and use of alcohol and drugs. Mike explained that it was much more difficult for him to delay orgasm during intercourse than during masturbation. He admitted, however, that he had had problems with premature ejaculation from his first sexual encounter and that these problems usually were more persistent at the beginning of a relationship, when he felt less comfortable with the woman. He estimated the average amount of time before ejaculation after vaginal penetration to be about two minutes, but initial sexual encounters often resulted in orgasm seconds after penetration.

The psychologist noted that Mike fidgeted and smiled often while talking about his sexual experiences but claimed to be perfectly comfortable talking about his past. He described his first sexual experience quickly, and the psychologist had to probe Mike for more details about his feelings of embarrassment and sense of failure. He laughed easily about the floating pornography and alluded to the sexual excitement of looking at homosexual erotica. He denied any adolescent homosexual experiences. He admitted that his parents were inhibited sexually, that they never spoke about sex to him even as an adult, and that he always felt guilty about masturbating to pornography. Although he only remembers his uncle's admonitions about masturbation, his sister assures him that both his parents and his teachers at the Christian school warned against masturbation, pornography, and sex before marriage.

Mike denied current use of drugs or alcohol, but he admitted to experimentation with drugs and heavy use of alcohol during high school. He used alcohol in social situations, and he often found himself intoxicated, with occasional blackouts. He acted inappropriately toward women after drinking, often groping and aggressively pursuing women when they were not interested. His sexual performance did not improve with alcohol use.

Mike had no prior history of psychiatric treatment. He believed that his family was fairly stable, with the exception of his younger sister, who had recurring problems with depression and substance abuse. He denied any sexual abuse, although he has a vivid memory of seeing his father naked in the shower when Mike was about nine years old. To this day Mike remains struck by the size of his father's penis, much larger than his own.

His family relationships were loving for the most part. Mike reported feeling closer to his mother, who seemed to favor him, and being afraid of his father, who was stern and reserved. He perceived his role in the family as the "obedient son," who avoided conflicts and did what he was told. He often felt inadequate around his father, however, who was a pillar in the church community, highly regarded for his virtuous and selfless behavior. Mike disengaged himself from the church after high school.

Mike admitted being more comfortable around girls than boys as a child and later as an adult. He had a steady stream of girlfriends and recognized that he felt more secure with a girl on his arm. He believed that his relationships were fulfilling for him, but he wondered why he could not sustain a love relationship for more than a year at a time.

Mike remained in contact with Heather, who was willing to be interviewed by the psychologist. Heather described Mike as follows: "Mike is a mystery to me. At first I thought he was a sweet man, who was very concerned about my happiness and sensitive to my needs. But as our relationship developed, I realized how self-centered he was, especially during sex. He only wanted to experience pleasure; he wasn't interested in pleasuring me. And he pushed me away, refused to talk about our problems, and glossed over things to avoid any problems. I got very frustrated."

Case Conceptualization

Mike experienced difficulty with ejaculatory control, which is largely due to psychological rather than physiologic factors in the majority of cases (Bancroft, 1989). What were these components in Mike's situation? To begin with, a number of predisposing factors were present, including his restrictive upbringing and his learning and conditioning history with sex, all hypothesized to play an essential role in the development of premature ejaculation (Masters & Johnson, 1970) but which have not been adequately supported by research to date. The religious prohibitions against sexual pleasure outside marriage were made clear to Mike through a number of channels, including parents, the church, and school. His early experiences masturbating to sexual erotica were thus filled with trepidation and fear of discovery by his mother. Such anxiety can stimulate the sympathetic nervous system, which controls ejaculation, causing early ejaculation (McCary & McCary, 1982). In a sense, Mike trained himself to ejaculate quickly, fearful of being caught performing a forbidden act.

Yet many boys have similar experiences with early masturbation. Why was Mike unable to resolve his sexual anxiety? His first sexual encounter with a girl proved humiliating to Mike. Her hints at spreading his "secret" around the school petrified Mike (although the rumor would be false, since Mike had no difficulty "getting it up"; he simply could not delay his orgasm) and paved the way for subsequent anxiety around his sexual performance.

This anxiety served to maintain Mike's sexual difficulties throughout his young adult years and reinforced some of his beliefs formed early on about his inadequacy as a sexual partner. At the initial stages of most of his sexual relationships, Mike's thoughts were filled with intense fear of not satisfying his sexual partner, and he was eager to move quickly to intercourse to allay that anxiety. His anxiety was often physical, including muscle tension and gastrointestinal discomfort.

Mike also experienced depersonalization prior to and during the sexual act, feeling detached from his body, watching the sexual act as if someone else were performing. This estrangement from the physical realm prevented Mike from integrating the sensory and emotional aspects of the sexual act, making it difficult for him to develop the sensory awareness necessary for ejaculatory control. Typically, men with ejaculatory control problems lack knowledge of the excitement phase of sexual response and do not recognize the sensations that lead up to ejaculation (Kaplan, 1983). This lack of awareness does not allow for the voluntary control required to delay ejaculation. Although Mike mistakenly thought that distracting from sexual excitement would prolong the lovemaking, it only served to hasten the ejaculation.

Mike was exceedingly self-conscious of his sexual performance and projected a defensive stance to protect against embarrassment and vulnerability. Yet Mike appeared far from vulnerable to his sexual partners, who viewed his "let's get this over with" approach to intercourse as self-centered and insensitive to their needs. His behavior was misinterpreted as a desire for sexual release rather than for affection.

Further, Mike's shame about his lack of control prevented him from discussing his situation openly with his partner, making it difficult for him to attain closeness in the relationship. Poor communication was an additional maintaining factor. Mike waited for Heather to raise the issue of their sexual difficulties. Heather did not complain that the intercourse ended too soon but that she was unhappy that Mike lacked tenderness in their lovemaking. Yet Mike narrowly focused on the sex act itself, so when Heather turned to another man for sexual pleasure, Mike was certain it was because, unlike him, the other man was virile and could sustain their lovemaking.

Other psychological issues may have exacerbated Mike's problems with ejaculatory control. Mike's father was a paragon of virtue, and Mike often felt outshadowed by him. It is not surprising that Mike perceived his father's penis as much larger than his own when he glimpsed his father naked, a symbol of how "small" and inadequate Mike felt in comparison with his father. Although Mike's history and behavior indicate that he is heterosexual, he is among the 20 percent of males who report arousal to homosexual stimuli in adolescence (Bell, Weinberg & Hammersmith, 1981). The clinician assessing Mike wondered if those early arousal experiences confused Mike, or if he attributed any of his sexual difficulties to the notion that he may not be heterosexual.

Diagnosis

Mike's sexual history and presenting complaint were compatible with a diagnosis of premature ejaculation, lifelong type, situational type, due to psychological factors. According to *DSM-IV*, in order to meet the criteria for this diagnosis, the man must have recurrent ejaculation with minimal sexual stimulation before or shortly following penetration. The premature ejaculation must be before the man desires it and cause severe stress or interpersonal problems.

Mike often reached orgasm before he desired it, and although his girlfriends did not openly complain about his inability to delay ejaculation, his own defensive response interfered with their relationship. Mike's confidence in his ability to perform sexually was significantly lowered by this problem, which also served to impair his romantic ties. Mike was given the additional qualifier of *lifelong type* because his dysfunction had been present from his first experience with coitus. His diagnosis was further qualified by *situational type* because Mike was able to delay orgasm during masturbation and at times in his sexual experiences with women.

Despite the guidelines provided by *DSM-IV*, understanding of premature ejaculation has been limited by the lack of a commonly accepted definition of the disorder in the past (Grenier & Byers, 1997). Early researchers (Kinsey, Pomeroy & Martin, 1948) defined premature ejaculation as the inability to prolong orgasm for at least one minute subsequent to penetration. Later, Masters and Johnson (1970) defined the disorder as a partner's inability to delay ejaculation sufficiently to satisfy the partner for at least half their sexual encounters. In other cases, men have unreasonable expectations for maintaining an erection without ejaculation.

Despite the controversy regarding its precise definition, men disturbed by a lack of control over their orgasmic functioning often seek help from sex therapists or other nonprofessional sources on their own. Of course, premature ejaculation can occur occasionally for all men, but when the course is persistent, a diagnosis may be made. Premature ejaculation is a common sexual dysfunction, with high prevalence rates.

Most researchers agree that premature ejaculation is a dysfunction of the orgasmic phase of sexual response, as defined by Kaplan (1979). (The other two phases include desire and excitement.) Clearly, Mike had no difficulties with desire, since he was sexually attracted to women and desired sexual relations with them often. Nor was he impaired by erectile functioning; on the contrary, he was able to achieve an erection quickly. Mike's difficulty was in prolonging his pleasure during intercourse and maintaining ejaculatory control.

The clinician considered an additional diagnosis of anxiety, given the muscle tension, worry, and restlessness Mike experienced about his sexual performance. However, Mike's anxiety focused almost exclusively on his concerns about premature ejaculation and its effect on his relationships. He was confident and calm in other aspects of his life, and his worry did not significantly impair his work or nonsexual relationships, so this diagnosis was rejected.

Treatment and Outlook

The most common form of treatment for premature ejaculation is behavioral, made popular in the 1970s by Masters and Johnson. Such treatment addresses the sexual problem directly by having the couple perform various physical activities as homework. More recently, cognitive-behavioral and psychopharmacologic treatments have gained credence in the treatment of premature ejaculation (Haensel, Rowland & Kallan, 1996).

The psychologist treating Mike recognized that Mike had both sexual and relationship problems. Therefore, she planned a comprehensive treatment plan that targeted not only his inability to delay ejaculation but also his difficulty with communication and intimacy in his relationships and feelings of low self-worth.

Mike and Heather agreed to work together on repairing their relationship. The sex therapist assigned a number of homework assignments; the first, called *sensate focus* (Masters & Johnson, 1970), is excellent for relationships impaired by communication problems or repeated episodes of sexual "failure." Sensate focus requires couples to circumscribe the limits of their sexual contact and for partners to take turns inviting caressing of parts of the body that have been agreed on. Nongenital sensate focus excludes the genitals and the woman's breasts. The partner may guide the other person's hand to allow for touching in the desired area.

The therapist assigned these exercises to increase Mike's sensitivity to Heather's sexual needs, which Heather had identified as her principal complaint in the relationship. At the same time the sensate focus exercises increase communication about sexual needs because they require partners to articulate what they do and do not want. Finally, it was expected that the sensate focus exercises also would increase Mike's sensory awareness of his own arousal and orgasmic processes, key to developing ejaculatory control (Masters & Johnson, 1970).

The therapist also assigned the stop/start technique to increase Mike's control, which involves genital stimulation by the partner to the point of arousal, at which point the man indicates for his partner to stop the caressing. Heather and Mike had excellent success with this technique, and Mike was able to slowly increase his level of control. It also helped Mike gain awareness of his arousal process without depersonalizing or thinking anxious thoughts. The psychologist also provided some education regarding nonpenile methods of satisfying Heather and helped Mike to understand that women can be satisfied in other ways without vaginal penetration.

The psychologist helped Mike and Heather to improve their communication not only about sexual desires but also about their thoughts and feelings about the quality of the relationship. Mike learned to identify and verbalize unpleasant thoughts, which he had avoided in the past. He was able to stop blaming himself for Heather's transgression and to recognize that their relationship lacked interpersonal intimacy. He was able to express his angry feelings to Heather about her betrayal of their trust.

Mike explored early family issues in individual counseling, examining his feelings of inadequacy vis-à-vis his father. He revisited the early trauma of his first sexual experience with a female; recounting the story helped him to gain some distance and let go of the shame he had held on to. Cognitive techniques helped Mike to overcome his sense of failure as a sexual lover, which, together with more satisfying lovemaking with Heather, allayed a great deal of Mike's anxiety. The prognosis for Mike was excellent. By the end of twelve weeks, Mike reported a significant reduction in his anxiety level, greater control over ejaculation, and a deeper level of intimacy with Heather.

THINKING CRITICALLY

QUESTIONS FOR DISCUSSION OR WRITING

1. Explore how cultural factors may have affected Mike's sexual attitudes and behavior. As an example, in what way might media portrayal of sex affect a person's appraisal of his or her sexual performance?

2. Mike reported being intimidated initially by Heather's past sexual history. How would you account for his attraction to a woman whom he perceives as having greater sexual experience?

CHAPTER **11**

Pedophilia:
Predator of Youth

*The only purpose for which power can be rightfully
exercised over any member of a civilized community,
against his will, is to prevent harm to others. His own
good, either physical or moral, is not a sufficient
warrant.* JOHN STUART MILL

LEE'S STORY

Lee sat in his room one splendid spring day. It was early afternoon, and he
waited for the sound of the school bus that would signal the arrival of his
nephew and the two other little boys that usually came over to play after
school. Outside, the bright sunshine beckoned, promising a walk in the park
with the family dog. Inside, Lee's soul was tortured by the raging storm of emotions that threatened to tear him apart. To himself he thought, "I should just get
out of here until my sister gets home from work." Yet he seemed frozen to his
bed, ears craning for the sound of the bus. Finally, unable to make a decision,
Lee opted to let fate make the choice for him. He pulled out some magazines
that showed pictures of nude boys and started to masturbate. "If I come before
they get here," he thought to himself, "then I'll take the dog for a walk."

Just as he was selecting a magazine, he heard the familiar squeal of the
school bus's air brakes. Breathing a sigh of relief at having his conflict thus
resolved for him, Lee smiled and bounded down the stairs to pour milk and
put out a snack for the boys.

Scott and his friends burst through the door. "Uncle Lee," Scott yelled,
"We're home." Spying his uncle emerging from the kitchen with a plate of
cookies, Scott almost knocked him over as he ran to give him a hug. His
schoolmates threw down their backpacks and joined their friend at the table
for cookies and milk. The boys devoured their snack with a relish known
only to five-year-olds released from the confines of kindergarten on a perfect
spring day. Lee watched with amusement as the cookies disappeared.

Once the snack was finished, Lee invited the boys outside to play a game
of kickball. He knew that they would be too wound up to play inside, that

111

they needed to exorcise some of their excess energy. With the enthusiasm of a camp counselor and the direction of a gym teacher, Lee organized the boys into teams, using imaginary men to run the bases. The boys had a great time, cheered on by Scott's uncle who was the most fun adult any of them knew. Scott had been especially glad when his Uncle Lee moved in with him and his mother following his parents' separation a year ago. His dad had never been around much, and when he was, he was always in a bad mood. Uncle Lee always made time for him and never seemed to tire of playing video games, wrestling, or teaching him how to play baseball.

When the boys had exhausted themselves from running and laughing, Lee invited them inside to play hide-and-seek. The boys had all played this game at Scott's house before. They knew that at Lee's signal they were to hide in various parts of the house. Lee would take forever to find them, and when he did, he tickled them, but in a funny way.

Once he found each boy, Lee would join him in his hiding place. He'd start by tickling the boy under his arms until he squirmed with delight. Over and over Lee would tell the boy that part of the game was to keep as quiet as he could. Then he would tickle the boy's stomach. Finally, Lee would appear very serious, as he started rubbing the boy's pants over his genitals. When this occurred, the boys would become quiet, confused by the conflicting emotions this touching aroused. Although they all liked Lee and found that this type of "tickling" felt pleasurable, they all had a sense that somehow what they were doing was wrong. Lee always told them not to tell anyone, although he never seemed angry or threatening. And he always gave them a piece of candy or a quarter afterward. "This is for keeping our little secret," he would say. The boys never talked to anyone about what happened, not even to each other. They all assumed that they were the only one Lee did this with, his "special friend."

Sometimes Lee would end the game with rubbing the boy's genitals over his pants. On other days he would have the boy remove his pants and fondle him with his hand. Once in a while he had the boy touch his penis as well, and occasionally he had the boy put his mouth on his penis, pulling back and forth until he came. On these days Lee gave out a special award: a whole dollar. Although none of the boys really liked it when he had them suck his penis, they so wanted the money and Lee seemed so happy with them that it was OK.

After an hour of hide-and-seek, Lee invited all the boys into the television room to watch cartoons. The boys laughed, drank juice, and played around until they were picked up by their mothers. The parents of Scott's two friends were always grateful on the days that Lee would look after their sons; they didn't have to pay a babysitter, and their sons always enjoyed playing at Scott's house.

At 5:30 Scott's mother, Nancy, returned home from work. Lee and Scott were in the kitchen making hamburgers, Lee teaching his nephew how to shape the ground beef into perfectly round patties. The radio was playing oldies, the house was picked up and neat, and her son was happy. Nancy smiled as she thought how lucky she was to have such a great brother. So what if he stayed at home a lot and didn't have many friends? He had always been a shy kid growing up, depending on his big sister. Not much had really changed.

Lee was the youngest of three children. His parents were happily married, and there was no history of psychiatric disturbance on either side of the family. Both parents were professionals; his father was a social worker, and his mother was a nurse. They worked long hours and often left their children in the care of a babysitter after school. Lee was seven years younger than his sister Nancy, so by the time he came home from school to be cared for by the babysitter, he was often the only child there.

Babysitters came and went over the years. Lee's parents usually hired them from a local junior college, finding students reliable and often willing to make extra money in between classes. While the babysitters were usually women, occasionally a young man would answer their ad. His parents were pleased that some young men were comfortable taking care of children and welcomed the chance to expose their son to such admirable role models. It was one of these male babysitters that molested Lee.

Lee's victimization consisted primarily of being fondled and then having to watch as his perpetrator masturbated in front of him. After each episode, the older male would threaten Lee, telling him that he would kill Lee's dog if he told his parents. The perpetrator was cruel to Lee in other ways as well, one time preventing him from using the bathroom until he soaked his pants and then teasing him about being "a little baby." His victimization continued for about a year until the babysitter graduated and moved away. Lee never told anyone what had happened to him, feeling both ashamed and frightened. He was eight years old.

Lee's conception had been somewhat a surprise for his parents. His mother was forty-one when Lee was born. Her pregnancy, labor, and delivery were unremarkable, and Lee was born a healthy, active baby. Quiet and content from the beginning, Lee's parents often praised their good fortune for having such an easy going infant. Developmental milestones were reached as expected, with the exception of language development. Lee was delayed in speaking his first words and sentences, to the point that a speech therapist was consulted when he was three years old. While he was responsive to the therapy, his speech continued to be slightly slow, and Lee had difficulty expressing himself verbally. He enjoyed playing by himself or with his older siblings, had a friend or two at any given time while growing up, and was an average student who rarely caused any trouble. He saw a therapist for a few months when he was sixteen because his parents were concerned about his lack of ambition or interests. His therapist at the time concluded that Lee was most likely a "late bloomer" and told his parents not to worry about him. He enjoyed good health and had no significant history of illness or injury.

Following his own molestation, Lee developed a greater interest in sexual matters. He mimicked his perpetrator and started masturbating at the age of nine. He found his father's *Playboy* magazines, along with the one pornographic video that his parents kept in their closet. In the fifth grade he walked up to another boy on the playground and kissed him on the mouth. The boy was so stunned that he slugged Lee, knocking him to the ground. After that, Lee was ostracized from his class, some of whom referred to him as "homo" and "faggot."

At the age of thirteen, Lee experimented sexually with another boy his own age. At first they masturbated in front of each other and then took turns performing fellatio on each other. The other boy soon lost interest, and Lee was disappointed by the loss of his friend. Around the same time, Lee's older sister moved out, leaving him in essence an only child with parents who were often unavailable. With few friends his own age, Lee began playing more with some of the younger children in his neighborhood.

At first these young friendships were not sexual. However, when Lee was fourteen, one seven-year-old boy became especially attached to him. They became best friends, often playing "army" in the little boy's treehouse. Lee ate dinner at the boy's house at least two or three nights a week and occasionally was invited along on family outings. Once in a while the boys spent the night at each other's house, and it was during one of these times that Lee first molested the younger boy. The boy had climbed in bed with Lee in the middle of the night, saying that he was scared from a nightmare. Lee was surprised to find himself aroused as he held his friend. He began rubbing himself against the boy until he climaxed. This began a more or less regular pattern of sexual activity between the two boys. In Lee's mind, his young friend was always a willing participant in their "escapades," as he referred to them. Their sexual relationship continued for over a year and a half until the younger boy moved away.

Lee had little other sexual experience with other people. He had a girlfriend briefly in high school, but they broke up after a few weeks, having never done more than kiss. By the age of seventeen, Lee was masturbating at least twice a day, and he began collecting pornography to assist his habit. He most enjoyed looking at magazines and videos involving children, especially young boys. Despite his difficulty in obtaining these illegal materials, Lee began to amass a sizable collection. He moved out of his parents' home after dropping out of junior college at the age of nineteen, primarily because it was becoming increasingly difficult to hide his pornographic materials from them. He had molested several other young boys in the intervening years, victims he usually befriended while working at convenience stores. Bribing them with quarters for video games became a favored mode of seduction. Lee was twenty-five at the time he moved in with his sister, a loner who was devoted to Nancy and Scott. He would do anything for them.

Several weeks later, one of the boys who had played at Scott's house that spring afternoon was wrestling with his father. The father started tickling him, and the boy started to touch his father's genital area. "We don't do that," his father warned. "Scott's uncle lets us," piped up the boy without thinking. Alarmed, the boy's father stopped playing and convinced his son to tell him everything that went on at Scott's house. Furious, he wanted to go straight over to "that pervert's house" and shoot him. Instead, he called his wife and the police.

That evening Nancy was surprised to open her front door to find two policemen and a detective standing there. They asked for Lee, who was out with Scott getting ice cream. Lee and Scott soon walked in, laughing about something, and suddenly Lee's face went ashen when he spied the police. He was arrested on several counts of lewd and lascivious behavior with children under the age of fourteen, the legal term for child molestation. Lee began sobbing but did not resist arrest. Scott started screaming uncontrollably as the policemen took his uncle away. The detective saw that he would have to interview the boy later, since he was too upset to talk then.

▬ *WHAT DO YOU THINK?* ▬

1. Before the victims in this case arrived from school, Lee seemed conflicted when he thought about molesting the boys. What did he have to do in order to make it "OK" to follow through with his offense?

2. Lee seemed to genuinely love his nephew and his sister and did not ever wish to harm them. What would motivate him to molest Scott, knowing how his mother would react if she found out?

3. Lee knew the pain of being molested. Why would he do this to his nephew and his friends? How could he justify this to himself?

Assessment

Lee was eventually found guilty of multiple counts of child molestation. Prior to sentencing, he was referred to a forensic psychologist who specializes in the assessment of sex offenders for an evaluation. The results of this evaluation would assist the court in determining appropriate treatment for Lee, as well as his risk to reoffend and potential danger to the community.

Prior to meeting with Lee, the psychologist reviewed the statements of the three victims taken by detectives. Lee had confessed to his offenses to prevent his nephew and the other boys from having to endure the trauma of testifying in court. The evaluator also reviewed Lee's school records and spoke with the therapist who had seen him as a teenager. The probation officer's report contained information about the family history. Lee had no previous history of being arrested. He had worked some but usually as a store clerk where personnel files were minimal. In short, there was little objective information available about this perpetrator, and the psychologist was going to have to obtain information about Lee on his own. Much of the history outlined above resulted from the psychologist's interviews with Lee as well as his sister and other family members.

Lee was administered several psychological tests by the evaluator. On the Kaufman Brief Intelligence Test (Kaufman & Kaufman, 1990), he scored in the low-average range. There was a significant difference between his scores on the two parts of this instrument, since he did much better on the task that measures nonverbal reasoning than on the vocabulary measure. Noting his history of delayed language development, the psychologist gave Lee several other neuropsychological measures focusing on tests that assess language functions. In general, all aspects of his cognitive functioning appeared intact, although he scored in the mildly impaired range on tests of verbal fluency, verbal retrieval, and sentence repetition.

On the Millon Clinical Multiaxial Inventory (Millon, 1983), an objective measure of personality functioning, Lee showed strong dependent and avoidant personality traits along with passive-aggressive tendencies. He also showed marked elevations on scales that measure depression and anxiety. On the Multiphasic Sex Inventory (Nichols and Molinder, 1984), a self-report measure designed to assess a wide range of characteristics related to sex offenders, Lee most closely fit the criteria for what the authors call "the typical child molester (male victim) type." That is, Lee answered the questions in such a way as to suggest that he had an exclusive sexual interest in children rather than adults. He was open in acknowledging his offenses and did not attempt to minimize or deny his deviant behavior, as so many sex offenders often do. It was notable that he tended to justify his offenses, endorsing items that suggested that his victims were willing participants or had even initiated the offenses. He readily acknowledged his preoccupation with sexual matters and seemed to engage in a great deal of cognitive distortion around his behaviors. The psychologist concluded that Lee was at significant risk to reoffend and therefore represented a danger to the community. However, his sincere remorse and willingness to accept help were noted, along with his supportive family, including his sister Nancy. The evaluator recommended that rather than send Lee to a state hospital unit for sex offenders, he be placed out of state in a secure residential treatment facility for sex offenders.

Case Conceptualization

Pedophilia is one of the several different types of paraphilias, which are defined as recurrent, intense, sexually arousing fantasies, urges, or behaviors involving either nonhuman objects, suffering or humiliation of a partner or oneself, or directed toward children or other nonconsenting persons (APA, 1994). Some paraphilias have been criminalized, such as rape, exhibitionism, voyeurism, and child molestation. Others, such as fetishism and transvestic behaviors, do not involve an unwilling victim and so are not viewed as criminal. There is much professional debate about whether the paraphilias that do not involve an unwilling victim should be considered as socially deviant.

As a pedophile, Lee's sexual urges and fantasies were directed toward children, usually age thirteen or younger. Some individuals with pedophilia like Lee have an exclusive interest in children; others also may be attracted to adults. Pedophiles may prefer males, females, or both. Pedophiles generally report an attraction to children within a particular age range. Those attracted to females tend to prefer eight- to ten-year-olds, while those attracted to males prefer children who are slightly older. Every possible sexual activity may be engaged in by perpetrators with their victims, from undressing and looking to sexual intercourse. Varying degrees of force and coercion may be involved, and the perpetrator often uses a variety of excuses or rationalizations for the behavior.

Pedophiles may limit their activities to family members (incest), to victims outside their families, or to both. Some threaten their victims in order to keep them quiet, while others like Lee simply use bribes. Many perpetrators will go to great lengths to gain access to victims, such as choosing jobs or careers that put them in close proximity to children. They may become close friends with the mother of a potential victim, marry a woman with an attractive child, or even become a foster parent. Unless sadistic urges are also involved, the perpetrator is likely to be attentive to the child's needs in order to gain the child's trust and prevent disclosure.

Lee's disorder, like that of most pedophiles, began in adolescence, although some patients report the onset of symptoms at midlife. Pedophilia is a chronic disorder, especially in those attracted predominantly to males. The frequency of pedophilic activity may vary over a lifetime, often increasing during periods of stress. It is far more common in men than in women. The recidivism rate for pedophiles who prefer male children is roughly twice that for those who prefer females.

Nichols and Molinder (1984) point out that there is a behavioral progression that is universal to all sexual offenders. First is the stage of stalking or cruising. Here the pedophile has the thought to molest, followed by the thought that he is himself a victim, not a criminal. He then justifies his behavior in various ways, utilizing excuses, rationalizations, and distorted thinking in order to lower his inhibitions. Lee had to do little at this stage: simply be available when the boys arrived home from school, then leaving it up to a game of "fate" to decide if he would persist in his offense. The second stage is called pace and lead, where the pedophile "grooms" his victim for the eventual molestation. He assumes a role of relative power over the victim, develops a plan for carrying out his assault, and engages in "superoptimism," or the belief that he can get away with the offense along with the excitement of anticipating the deviant behavior. Lee set the stage by assuming a parental role with the boys, giving them a snack and organizing games. Hide-and-seek served his purpose of isolating the boys from one another and provided an excuse to be alone with each boy. The final stage is that of the sexual assault itself. The progression through the previous stages serves to corrode any internal or external deterrent or control, resulting in the inevitability of the offense. Once he had achieved his goal of isolating the boys and being alone with them, Lee was unable to stop himself from carrying out his offense.

A biological basis for this disorder has not yet been found. Some neurological investigations have found that perpetrators have smaller left frontal-temporal lobes, resulting in some disruption in language functioning. This finding was suggested both in Lee's history and in his neuropsychological test performance, since he was developmentally delayed linguistically and showed impairments on measures of expressive language functioning. Hypersecretion of the luteinizing hormone, stimulated by the gonadotropic hormone of the anterior pituitary gland, also has been found in many pedophiles. This finding serves as the basis for what is sometimes referred to as "chemical castration," or the use of luteinizing hormone-releasing hormone (LHRH) agonist to indirectly decrease production of testosterone (Ayd, 1995) and thus inhibit sexual urges.

Lee is typical of many pedophiles, who are often victims of either sexual or physical abuse themselves. His poor social skills, low self-esteem, and difficulty dealing with anger are also common findings. Pedophiles' ideas about sexuality and intimacy tend to be immature, stereotyped, and distorted. They often have had little positive interaction with opposite-sex peers. Interpersonally, they are likely to be passive-dependent and manipulative, with little awareness of their own feelings and a lack of empathy for others, including their victims. Common defenses include projection, denial, and rationalization, and occasionally, dissociative traits may be noted (Perry & Orchard, 1992).

Lee experienced a great deal of internal conflict regarding his attraction to young male children. While this is true of some individuals with pedophilia, it is not true for all. Most likely his sexual preference developed out of both his need to cope with his own victimization and his having acquired this preference based on his own experience. He had positive experiences with young boys, and he was either rejected or ostracized by his peers, in effect shutting off the latter avenue of sexual development. Both psychodynamic and social learning theories of personality development are often useful in conceptualizing individual cases and planning treatment interventions.

At a social level, family studies of pedophiles have found excessive rates of family disruption, conflict, substance abuse, physical abuse, and neglect

(Bard et al., 1987). Occasionally blame is placed on the portrayal of deviant sexuality in the entertainment industry (that is, music videos), pornography, or either overly restrictive or permissive societal values regarding sexual behavior in general, but these factors have not been studied adequately.

Diagnosis

To meet *DSM-IV* diagnostic criteria for pedophilia, the patient must be at least sixteen years of age or older and at least five years older than the victim. Clinical judgment must be used to decide if cases involving perpetrators in late adolescence meet the criteria for the disorder or not: The sexual maturity of the victim and perpetrator, the dynamics between them, and their age difference must all be taken into account. The intense and recurrent sexual urges, fantasies, and behaviors involving a prepubescent child must have occurred for at least six months and cause clinically significant distress or impairment in social, occupational, or other important areas of functioning.

It is common practice to augment the *DSM-IV* diagnosis of pedophilia by further classifying individuals as either fixated or regressed. This classification system was begun with the work of Nicholas Groth (1982). Groth distinguished the *fixated pedophile,* or what he termed a "true pedophile," by a primary sexual orientation to children, a relative lack of precipitating stressors, offenses that are planned and premeditated, an identification with the victim, a lack of sexual contact with peers, predominantly male victims, no substance-abuse history, passive-dependent traits, and a history of being abused or molested. *Regressed,* or *situational, pedophiles* are characterized by a primary sexual orientation to one's peers, evidence of a precipitating stressor, an impulsive initial offense, a victim who is essentially a substitute for a conflicted relationship, predominantly female victims, and continued sexual involvement with peers. Offenses may be related to drug or alcohol abuse as well. Given this dichotomy, Lee would best fit the fixated pedophile type.

Treatment and Outlook

The court agreed with the psychologist's recommendations regarding Lee's placement and treatment, and he was sent to a residential treatment facility specializing in the rehabilitation of sexual offenders. Lee's prognosis was positive with regard to treatment, in that he was highly motivated to change and lacked the complications of antisocial personality traits or substance-abuse problems. Many sexual offenders deny or minimize their problems, are forced into treatment involuntarily, and are not motivated to change.

The treatment program Lee attended was highly structured and included individual and group therapy. In Lee's case, occupational training also was employed, since he had little ability to support himself financially. The program was largely cognitive-behavioral and multidimensional in philosophy. Aversive conditional procedures were used to help Lee alter his sexual preference. In this therapy, Lee was shown slides and films of young boys and concurrently administered an electric shock, while slides and films of adult women were accompanied by pleasurable stimuli, and he was encouraged to stimulate himself sexually while viewing these slides. Other groups focused on improving his social skills, including his ability to communicate, problem-solve, and resolve conflict. Assertiveness skills were a large focus of this group. Finally, another type of group focused on the examination and changing of distorted thinking relative to his offenses, in particular the rationalizations that undermined any effort he might make to inhibit his sexual acting out.

Following his completion of the program, which took over three years, Lee was considered for release by the treatment staff. Lee and the staff agreed that while he had made significant progress in improving his social skills and correcting his distorted thinking, he continued to find young males sexually attractive. At his request, he was tried on an antiandrogen medication, Depo-Provera (medroxyprogesterone acetate, or MPA), which, like the LHRH agonists mentioned above, reduces sexual drive by suppressing the body's production of testosterone. While treatment results with these medications are mixed and treatment compliance is a major problem, Lee fit the profile of offenders for whom such drugs are most indicated. That is, he is not antisocial, he is nonviolent, and his sexual preferences are very specific and consistent (Marshall et al., 1991).

Of course, during this time, Scott also was in therapy. The nontraumatic nature of his victimization, his mother's supportive reaction, good premorbid adjustment, and his not having to endure ongoing questioning in court procedures all aided his recovery. He had displayed minimal regression, and actually, it seemed that the worst part of the whole experience for Scott was the loss of his relationship with his favorite uncle. When Lee was released from residential treatment, it was arranged for him to meet with Scott several times in Scott's therapist's office. Both participants were well prepared for their meeting, in which Lee took responsibility for his actions, apologized for them, and explicitly told Scott that he was not to blame for what happened. Scott was able to say how much he had missed his uncle and how angry he was that Lee had done something that caused them to be separated so long and which caused him to lose his friendships with the other two boys. Over time they were able to reconcile their relationship, although it was many years before Nancy let them be alone together. Lee now lives alone and works in a hardware store. He has several friends and continues to take Depo-Provera. He has accepted that he may never have a long-term relationship but enjoys the close relationships he has with his family.

For many pedophiles the outcome of treatment is not so good. Recidivism rates are high, although one study found that a prison-based cognitive-behavioral program resulted in a reconviction rate of 25 percent after four years compared with a rate of 64 percent for untreated pedophiles (Marshall et al., 1991). Much continued understanding is necessary in this often neglected but very dangerous population.

▬ *THINKING CRITICALLY* ▬
QUESTIONS FOR DISCUSSION OR WRITING

1. Given the high recidivism rates for this patient population, many in our society believe that pedophiles should never be returned to the community. What are the arguments for and against this position?
2. What do you think of a man in his late twenties who forms a long-term consensual sexual relationship with a girl aged fourteen or fifteen? Is he a pedophile?

CHAPTER **12**

Borderline Personality Disorder: *One Side Wins—The Other Side Loses*

Enduring an emotional roar that no one else can—or wants to—hear.   JANICE CAUWELS, Imbroglio

ANNA'S STORY

Anna leaned against Enrique, traced the tattoo on his arm with her finger, and closed her eyes, infused with a calmness and safety in his embrace. Their lovemaking had been particularly passionate that afternoon, and Anna was surprised by the force of her sexual response to him. Even now, as she rested her cheek against his shoulder, she felt a twinge of pleasure at the memory and giggled. "It's good to be loved by such a kind man," she thought. She glanced over at the clock on the kitchen wall, suddenly remembering that she had promised her mother to be home by 5:00. Anna's mother was old-fashioned, "from the old world," Anna often said to her friends when they wondered why a 22-year-old woman had a curfew.

Enrique remained sprawled on the couch, smoking a cigarette, while Anna rushed around his apartment, gathering up her shoes, jacket, and purse. "See you later, babe," he said as Anna darted out the door. "Give me a call about this weekend." While Anna was inserting the key into her car, the tranquillity that had washed over her minutes earlier suddenly vanished. The thunder began to roll inside her again, quickly gaining momentum, exploding in rage when she realized what had happened. The voice in her head started pestering her, encircling Anna like a twister: "He doesn't love me. He's just using me. Over and over. I'm like his mistress. He couldn't even get off the couch to say goodbye to me the way he should. If he loved me, he would never treat me this way. I'm gross to be with him like that. I gave him my virginity. I gave up my dream for him."

She stormed back into the apartment and screamed at him. Enrique was startled by the abrupt change in Anna, but he had seen this happen to her before. He tried to reassure her and tell her he loved her, but he knew that it

123

was useless once she got into one of her tirades. He figured she was still angry at him for seeing Joleen ten months ago. He had forgiven *her* for stalking his apartment for hours until they emerged and then breaking in through the window and smashing pictures and trashing the place. He didn't understand why she couldn't just put the whole thing behind her.

Anna cried all the way home, driving at top speed. At home, when she noticed that her younger sister, Marja, was wearing one of her shirts, Anna once again flew into a rage. She hurled paperback books at her, pulled her hair, and punched her. "I do everything for you. You do nothing for me. I hate you," she screamed. Marja pulled herself away from her sister and slammed her bedroom door behind her.

Slam! To Anna that closure was like a steel door locking her out of the world and trapping her in a room of emotional pain. She wanted to scream to her sister to stay and not leave, but the words would not come out of her mouth. No one understood anyway. "You're too sensitive," her parents, sisters, friends, and boyfriends had always told her, and Anna knew those lines were a code that really meant: "We can't take you anymore." Anna believed that she had two sides of her: a "good me" and a "bad me." The good side, however, was trapped, like now, and the bad side faced the world.

If she could just get away from her own pain, put it away, or dig it out. Anna pulled out the pocket knife she had from camp in the sixth grade and made small slices on her arm. She watched the blood form red spots on her white skin. As it had in the past, the sight grounded her in some strange way, and she began to calm down.

Anna often wondered why she was so sensitive. Is it because she was born in Poland and moved to this country when she was five? She has only vague memories of Poland, but she can recall the terror she felt boarding the plane for the United States with her mother, father, and two sisters. Her mother cried when the plane took off, and her father sat next to her, impassive while he read the newspaper. At other times she wonders if being so weak and sick when she was small made the difference. Her father had to take time off of work to drive her to her medical appointments because her mother didn't drive. She loved those days when her father would stay by her bed, read her stories from Poland, and sing her songs from his childhood. He always worried about her health. Perhaps he worried about losing her the way he had lost his four brothers to sickness in Poland.

After Anna got stronger, her father reverted to his former behavior. They had little money, and he worked hard. He put in sixty-hour weeks on the line at a manufacturing plant, and when he was home, he rarely talked to his wife or daughters, spending most of his free time off in his room building model airplanes. Anna missed their special times together, and she tried hard to draw his attention to her, without success.

Anna's mother never seemed to mind that her husband gave her little attention, focusing on raising her daughters and keeping the house instead. She was charged with disciplining the children because her husband did not want to be burdened with that. Most of the time she was patient with her daughters, perhaps too lenient at times, but occasionally she would become overwhelmed. It was not easy to raise three girls in a small apartment without any money in a foreign country. Sometimes she spanked them with a hairbrush or a belt when they didn't obey.

She did her best to treat all the girls equally, but she had particular problems with Anna, who was irritable even as a baby. On countless occasions her mother had to referee fights Anna started with her sisters for inconsequential reasons. She prayed that Anna would grow out of her difficult stage as she got older, but it only seemed to worsen. Anna's friendships were rocky throughout junior and senior high school. Her mother knew the pattern well: Anna would become enamored of a new friend, and the two would spend all their free time chatting on the phone or going shopping at the mall together. Suddenly, without warning, Anna would become furious at her best friend, cut her out of her life, and rant and rave about her to her mother. Anna would be hard to handle at these times. At other times Anna adored her family and friends and was willing to do anything for them.

Anna was embarrassed by her mother and wished that her mother had been more like her "American" friends' mothers, who could drive and were busy with activities outside the home. Her mother dressed "funny" and spoke English with a thick accent. Anna also resented her mother for being passive and helpless. Anna wished that her father wouldn't criticize her mother so often, but she always thought her father was so much smarter than his wife. She sometimes wondered secretly why he had married her. His family had had status in their little Polish town, and her mother was a poor girl from the "other side of the tracks." Her mother's family didn't approve of her father, and shortly after their marriage, her father began feuding with her mother's side of the family. Her father tells Anna that he just "cut them out" of his life, and he has never spoken to those family members since.

Anna wished she could get along better with her sisters, but their calm and rational approach to life infuriated her at times. When they told her to "calm down" or to "stop being so psycho," Anna hated them. Why didn't they feel as intensely as she did? Anna repeatedly asked herself. Stella, who is two years older than Anna, planned to attend graduate school in another city in the fall. Anna admired her sister for being so smart and beautiful that she never had trouble finding or keeping a boyfriend. Marja, her younger sister and her mother's favorite, annoyed Anna because she always wanted to tag along with her. Anna fought with both her sisters, although the most bitter conflicts were with Stella. She was particularly angry with Stella because she had advised her to abandon her dream of being an actress. Looking up to her sister, Anna believed that she knew what was best for her, so she did not pursue an acting career. Now Anna is resentful because she thinks that her sister's advice was wrong but that it's too late for her to have a future as an actress. Anna wants Stella out of her life, which is why she cut her face out of the photographs taken at the family reunion last year.

Anna's eyes grow misty as she thinks about Mr. Thompson, her high school acting teacher, the only person who could understand her. He praised her abilities, making her believe that she was special and talented. She can still recall the excitement of being on stage, the lights shining on her and the audience paying full attention to her.

Anna blushes when she recalls Mr. Thompson's kind face, because he was her first "crush." The boys in high school were immature and only after one thing, in Anna's estimation. She thought she loved her first boyfriend in high school, but when he tried to get her dress off one night, Anna ended the relationship abruptly because she realized he only wanted her for sex. She became despondent following that breakup and took a bottle of aspirin. She had so much stomach pain that she begged Stella to take her to the emergency room. After pumping her stomach, the physician insisted that Anna be admitted to the psychiatric unit for further evaluation. Anna spent the night in the locked unit, throwing a tantrum and furious at her sister for allowing the doctor to incarcerate her. The next day Anna's mother and father arranged for her to come home.

Shortly after that incident, Anna met Enrique, who was a substitute math teacher at her high school and eight years older than she. Even though he had a steady girlfriend, he consoled Anna following her breakup. Anna felt she had finally met someone who could understand her and comfort her. At first, she only wanted to be his friend, but it got to the point where she couldn't stop thinking about him, and she continued to monitor his whereabouts for one year.

After Anna graduated from high school, Enrique and Anna began dating. Anna thought Enrique was older and wiser and could teach her a lot about life. She didn't want to lose her virginity to him, but he told her it would make her a more powerful actress if she tapped into her sexual energy, so she relented. Although their lovemaking was passionate and fulfilling, Anna experienced a great deal of guilt over it. She became clingy and jealous of Enrique and suspected that he had another girlfriend, so she began parking her car outside his apartment, keeping surveillance for hours. One evening he exited his apartment with another woman, and Anna broke in through a window after they had driven away, smashed photographs of him, and took her pictures and things away.

Enrique forgave Anna and severed ties with the other woman, but the turbulence in their relationship did not remit. Anna tried to go on with the relationship, but she had difficulty controlling her insecurity and jealousy, and eventually her feelings became so intense that she would erupt in anger. Enrique became exasperated with Anna's outbursts, and he often ignored her at those times. This only angered Anna further. She didn't understand how she could love and hate a person so powerfully like that, and she didn't know what to do with these conflicting feelings. "It's as if one side wins and the other side loses," she explained it to herself.

She loved Enrique, but she knew he was making plans to leave the city to take a better job. Anna panicked at the thought of his leaving, and she was angry that he could betray her in this way. After the incident at his apartment, she decided to remove any reminders of herself from his home, so he wouldn't have a hope of being her boyfriend. As far as she was concerned, as long as he was going to leave her, she had to obliterate him from her life. She told her sister that Enrique was dead to her.

She wished that she could go to church like her mother and pray for help. Anna's family was devoutly Catholic, and Anna moved in and out of involvement with the Church. At one point she became immersed in a fringe group of Charismatic Catholics, participating in marathon weekend retreats and extensive service to the organization. She cut off ties with the group rather abruptly when one of the group leaders chose another woman to assist him with one of the outreach activities. After that, Anna rejected the Catholic religion and declared herself an atheist.

Her mother was very worried about her daughter's outbursts. She had pleaded with her to do something, but Anna was worried about the financial burden of professional help. She only worked part time as a nanny for a Polish family from her mother's church. She hadn't worked full time since she was fired from her clerical job because of a "personality clash" with her boss. When her mother agreed to pay for some counseling, Anna finally made an appointment to see a counselor.

▰▰▰ *WHAT DO YOU THINK?* ▰▰▰

1. Personality disorders are pervasive patterns of maladaptive functioning that often impair interpersonal relations. If you were Anna's friend, how would you explain to her why she had difficulty getting along with people? What "maladaptive" behaviors would you point out to her?

2. What role, if any, did the family's migration experience play in Anna's development? What about her early illness? How might these events have contributed to difficulties in interpersonal functioning?

3. Enrique had cheated on Anna and taken advantage of her naivete to have sex with her. Could Anna's vehement response to him be a normal reaction to a dysfunctional relationship? Why or why not?

Assessment

After an initial structured interview with Anna, the psychologist arranged for a number of assessment procedures. She also arranged for a family consultation in order to meet with Anna's sisters and parents.

The psychologist juggled two preliminary hypotheses. She noted from the initial intake interview that Anna had a history of strained relationships and difficulty controlling her angry responses, the precipitant to her seeking treatment. Clearly, her difficulties in interpersonal functioning were far from transitory. Although Anna was concerned about her temper, she placed a good deal of the blame for her social difficulties on the deficits of others. This information led the clinician to wonder about the presence of a personality disorder. She also noted a recent exacerbation in Anna's anger and despair and questioned whether Anna's current struggles with emotional control were related to a mood disorder. Recognizing that anger and interpersonal difficulties also can be part of a mood disturbance, the clinician was careful to assess for both Axis I and Axis II disorders. She also was careful to take the cultural background of the client into consideration during the assessment process.

Anna completed two personality inventories that are used widely by psychologists for diagnostic purposes: the Minnesota Multiphasic Personality Inventory (MMPI-2) and the Millon Clinical Multiaxial Inventory 2 (MCMI-2). The MMPI-2 revealed that Anna was not guarded in her response and that she was willing to disclose her emotional difficulties. The MMPI-2 reports T-scores on nine clinical scales, with a T-score of 65 or above considered to be clinically significant. Anna scored highest on the scales relating to family discord and impulsive and rebellious behavior (Scale 4; T = 75), to unusual thinking and social alienation (Scale 8; T = 70), and to anxiety and obsessions (Scale 7; T = 75). People who have a similar profile to that of Anna often have come from chaotic family situations and thus have learned that the world around them is not safe and that the people around them are untrustworthy and rejecting. Such individuals lash out angrily first, to guard against real or imagined rejection. They may be viewed as odd because their thinking is peculiar. They sometimes engage in unlawful activities. Understandably, the combination of these features makes personal relationships difficult for a person of this profile.

On the MCMI-2, which assesses personality clusters and severe personality disorders, Anna obtained a significantly high score on borderline personality disorder, with elevated scores in the narcissistic and histrionic personality pattern categories. Anna's scores for severe and chronic depression were low on both the MCMI-2 and the MMPI-2. Her score of 17 on the Beck Depression Inventory (BDI) was not significant, particularly since she did not elevate on the depression scale of the objective personality tests.

The structured interview indicated that Anna had made suicidal gestures on at least one occasion and that these gestures usually followed a relationship upset. Anna indicated that these were impulsive and desperate reactions that were not intended to end her life. She also admitted to using self-injurious behavior such as cutting herself to manage her overwhelming feelings. She admitted to occasional feelings of panic, with increased pressure on her chest and a tightening in her throat. She denied any ritualized behavior or need to check. She denied having visual or auditory hallucinations, although she did describe experiencing negative voices in her head that degrade her and attack people close to her. Anna maintained that she recognized these voices as part of her and not coming from outside herself. She did say that at times she felt removed from her body, as if she were watching herself in a movie. There were no indicators of substance abuse, from either the objective test results or the interview data.

Case Conceptualization

The clinician noted that interpersonal relationships had presented special challenges for Anna at least as early as adolescence. Initially hopeful and excited about a relationship, Anna inevitably would experience conflict and/or betrayal, resulting in a rupture in the relationship. Feeling abandoned, Anna would experience overwhelming rage or depression. These deficits in sustaining close ties, coupled with impulsive behavior and unstable moods, suggested the presence of a personality disorder to the clinician, with the features of a borderline personality disorder (BPD) most prominent.

Borderline personality disorder has long intrigued researchers and clinicians, and a number of explanations for its development have been offered. Current conceptualizations embrace a multifaceted approach to understanding this disorder, which considers genetic predisposition, constitutional vulnerability, early childhood development and object relations, social and cultural factors, and cognitive schemas.

Anna's mother told the clinician that Anna was different from her sisters and that as a baby she was irritable and very difficult to soothe. It is likely that Anna had a constitutional vulnerability to abnormally high levels of irritability, which has been hypothesized in people with BPD (Stone, 1995). Other research (Coccaro, 1989) points to low serotonin levels, which are associated with difficulties in modulating aggression, in conjunction with high norepinephrine levels, which are associated with increased risk taking and sensation seeking, to account for the impulsive behavior typically found in people with BPD. Anna's difficulties in controlling her intense emotions and the impulsive behavior that she engages in when these feelings overwhelm her may in part be explained by these constitutional and biologic factors.

It is unlikely, however, that Anna's predisposition to aggressive and impulsive behavior alone can account for the development of this disorder in Anna. There is a hypothesized link between childhood sexual and physical abuse and the subsequent development of BPD (Herman, Perry & van der Kolk, 1989; Ogata, et al., 1990). Was Anna abused as a child? She denied any sexual abuse, and her mother's physical punishment was intermittent. Her father was emotionally unavailable and uncomfortable with intimacy, but from the interview data, the clinician could not conclude that he physically or sexually abused his daughter. Anna's family could be characterized as what noted researcher Linehan (1993) has called an "invalidating environ-ment," an unempathic and occasionally physically abusive family. The un-spoken parental message that Anna internalized was that displays of emotion were unacceptable, an unfortunate situation for Anna, who was tempera-mentally prone to intense emotions. When Anna's father explained to Anna that he had "erased" his wife's family from his life following a transgression, Anna further learned that conflict was equally intolerable and to be avoided. The sum of this was that Anna began to mistrust her own feelings, which were labeled as unacceptable, and did not learn how to soothe herself when they arose in her.

On the other hand, when Anna did display intense emotions, she occa-sionally would receive the attention and help she needed, especially from her mother. Her mother rescued her, but she also was the "disciplinarian" who doled out physical punishment in an erratic manner. While healthy individu-als are able to integrate divergent aspects of people, Anna could not reconcile her mother's contradictory nurturing and punitive behavior, and she resorted to splitting the good and the bad to cope with it. In this way, Anna's mother became all good, until she did or said something that "hurt" Anna; then she became mean. Anna viewed other people in her life in a similar way: her sis-ters, her high school boyfriend, and Enrique.

When people failed to meet her expectations, Anna's "all or none" think-ing did not allow her to integrate these negative experiences with past posi-tive ones, so people became all good or all bad to Anna. This is what often happened with her sisters. One week Anna idealized Stella and admired her wisdom and intelligence. The next week Stella fell off the pedestal, lost her credibility, and became the object of Anna's ire. Anna also had difficulty inte-grating the negative and positive parts of herself; this is what she meant when she said that she had a "good me" and a "bad me," two parts that occupied completely separate rooms.

Other events in Anna's family may help to explain why her normal devel-opment was impaired. The family's early migration experience from Poland to the United States placed undue strain on the family system, isolating the mother and placing financial pressures on the father. This rupture from their homeland had hardly begun to heal when Anna became sick. The father pro-vided Anna with unprecedented attention during her illness, forming an inti-mate bond that was later denied once she was restored to health. A less rejection-sensitive individual would experience disappointment that her fa-ther could not be with her more, but she would eventually accept and under-stand this change as part of her getting better. Anna could not recover easily from this experience and interpreted her father's behavior as rejection and abandonment, forming early schemas of intimacy with others as dangerous. Such disturbances in early attachment patterns are common among people with BPD (Kernberg, 1988; Kohut, 1977).

Later, as an adolescent and a young adult, the slightest hint of rejection or betrayal activated Anna's cognitive schema of mistrust, which triggered overwhelming feelings of rage and despair. When Anna suspected Enrique of cheating on her, she was consumed by a blind fury and turned to extreme measures of stalking and breaking into his house. At other times, Anna directed her intense emotions at herself. She had a history of cutting herself with a knife following breakups with boyfriends and interpersonal disappointments. Often these attempts in BPD patients are intended to regulate the emotional pain and not to end life (Linehan, 1993). People around Anna would state that she was "overreacting" and "too emotional" or "just trying to get attention," but Anna would say that the intense feelings welled up in her so quickly and so vehemently that she had no control. She often felt shame after such outbursts and suicidal gestures. Although Anna's history indicated that she used these strategies to ease her hurt, she is nonetheless at risk for suicidal behavior given her swift mood changes and her difficulties with impulse control.

Further, Anna had a tenuous grip on her own identity. It is quite normal at age twenty-two to have some confusion about identity, but Anna's sense of herself was fragile. She wavered between divergent images of herself: as good, as bad; as religious, as atheist; as seductive, as modest; and so on. She had poor personal boundaries and was easily influenced by those around her. Anna's identity was diffuse, which was puzzling for those who lived and worked with her, and lent a certain unpredictability to their interpersonal relations.

Diagnosis

Anna's history and the results of the personality testing were consistent with a diagnosis of borderline personality disorder (BPD). BPD is one of the personality disorders in Cluster B, the so-called dramatic and emotional group, which also includes narcissistic, histrionic, and antisocial personality disorders. Note that Anna's test results pointed to narcissistic and histrionic traits. It is not uncommon for a person to share a number of traits from all three personality disorders in this cluster; approximately two-thirds of individuals diagnosed with one personality disorder meet the criteria for an additional one (Pilkonis et al., 1995). Michael Stone (1990) has called them "fellow travelers" (p. 222).

Generally speaking, BPD refers to a long-standing pattern of unstable interpersonal relationships, shifting moods and self-image, and impulsive behavior that begins by early adulthood. *DSM-IV* requires five (or more) of the following to be present for a diagnosis of BPD:

1. Intense efforts to avoid real or imagined abandonment
2. Unstable interpersonal relationships marked by idealization and devaluation
3. Unstable self-image

4. Impulsive self-destructive behavior (for example, shopping, sex, reckless driving, substance abuse, binge eating, and so on)
5. Repeated suicidal gestures or self-mutilating behavior
6. Unstable moods, characterized by sudden shifts
7. Feelings of emptiness
8. Intense anger with poor control over angry outbursts
9. Transient paranoid thinking or dissociative symptoms

Anna's signs and symptoms fulfilled at least six of the nine criteria set out by *DSM-IV*. The most prominent features were her wavering perceptions of both her own identity and others' and her inability to regulate her emotions, especially her anger. This made Anna extremely vulnerable to disappointment, since the slightest hurt erased all memory of previous positive interactions, leaving Anna full of anger and desperate to relieve the unrelenting pressure and pain. Linehan (1993), a noted researcher of BPD, has likened this vulnerability to having third-degree burns over 90 percent of the body. A person with BPD has no "emotional skin" (p. 69). A mere brush against that burn can send a person with BPD into emotional agony. Another hallmark of the BPD patient is a series of "parasuicidal" behaviors, which are suicide gestures and self-injurious behavior not intended to end the person's life. Anna had been hospitalized for ingesting aspirin and had engaged in self-injurious behavior following interpersonal hurts.

This vulnerability is further exacerbated by the increased impulsivity characteristic of many people with BPD. When Anna was in pain, she had grave difficulty controlling her responses, so she engaged in inappropriate, hurtful, and at times unlawful activity. Her breaking into Enrique's apartment is an example. Although Anna's behavior does not reflect a respect for others' feelings and property, it differs from antisocial behavior, for she felt shame and guilt after her angry outbursts. (See Chapter 13 for a discussion of antisocial personality disorder.)

Did Anna have a coexisting mood disorder? Although this is a common occurrence among people with BPD, she did not display the signs and symptoms of a depressive disorder at the time she sought treatment. (See Chapter 5 for a discussion of major depressive disorder.) The clinician was careful to monitor her mood, however, since she had fallen into periods of despondency in the past.

Treatment and Outlook

Treatment for BPD has been problematic for therapists. A number of studies (McGlashan, 1986; Stone, 1990) suggest that there are no advantages to one type of treatment over another for the patient with BPD. Many other studies have shown that patients with BPD end their therapy prematurely (as judged by the psychotherapist) and often continue the search for a therapist with whom they feel a "fit" (Stone, 1995). This results in "therapist hopping."

Patients with BPD have long been dubbed "the most difficult patients"; this has been a most unfortunate stigma, since these patients experience enormous pain and require a great deal of support. Linehan (1993) has developed a form of therapy specifically for patients with BPD that she has called "dialectical behavior therapy" (DBT), which takes into consideration the opposing forces at work in people with BPD. Linehan advocates both acceptance of the person and a movement toward helping the patient change the maladaptive behaviors. DBT offers individual sessions for supportive therapy to convey the acceptance and mandates that clients also attend classes that teach cognitive and behavioral strategies for this change. Research studies examining the effectiveness of DBT support its effectiveness (Linehan, 1993).

The prognosis for Anna is fair. Her clinician, in keeping with Linehan's suggestion that support and skills training be distinct, saw her for one hour a week in supportive therapy and enrolled her in a cognitive skills class for mood management. The individual therapy attempted to build a trusting alliance, but this was slow to emerge and was checkered by stormy outbursts and disappointments. The clinician worked with Anna to gently confront her use of "all or none" thinking, which Anna used to manage her contradictory feelings toward others. Initially, she was quite compliant and complimentary toward her therapist, but when she ended the session on time and resisted Anna's attempts at running over the hour, Anna bristled. She sent the therapist a letter during the week accusing her of only wanting Anna's money and not caring about her. She expressed frustration that the therapist did not reveal more of herself to Anna but simply stared at her blankly while she poured out her most secret thoughts. She was unable to integrate the notion that the therapist could be quite concerned about Anna and also set limits around the therapeutic relationship. Her initial interpretation of the therapist's silence was attentiveness, but later she construed it as withholding and reminiscent of her father's distant relationship with her.

The next session Anna came dressed in a long-sleeved sweatshirt, even though it was a sweltering summer day. She opened the session: "You see, I'm wearing long sleeves. I'll tell you later why." She had made superficial cuts to her forearms with a razor in response to her last interaction with the therapist. She was angry and hurt that the therapist would not make special exceptions for her, and she used the self-mutilation to manage those fierce emotions. She maintained that when she could see her pain that way, it made it more manageable. The therapist pointed out Anna's black-and-white opinion of her, and although Anna initially protested, over time she was able to identify some of her extreme thinking.

The cognitive-behavioral class taught Anna some useful skills for managing her anger and sadness, as well as for challenging her black-and-white thinking. Anna learned to keep an "anger journal" and to put words to her rageful feelings.

Anna remained in individual, supportive therapy for six months. As her alliance with the therapist became strengthened, Anna was less guarded. However, after a particularly emotional and positive session, she canceled her appointments and never returned. It is possible that the emerging intimacy with the therapist frightened her, so "one side wins" with intimacy, but "the other side loses" to fears of betrayal and abandonment.

■■■■ *THINKING CRITICALLY* ■■■■

QUESTIONS FOR DISCUSSION OR WRITING

1. Borderline personality disorder is claimed by some to be associated with a history of sexual or physical abuse in the majority of cases (Herman, Perry & van der Kolk, 1989). Some psychologists have argued that the sickness of BPD may reside less within the person and more in the abusive environment in which the person existed. Since Anna did not report any history of abuse, as the treating clinician, would you search for repressed memories of sexual or physical abuse in Anna's case? What are the pitfalls in doing so? What are the arguments for and against probing for these?

2. Unfortunately, a diagnosis of BPD often stigmatizes an individual, who is branded as angry and manipulative. This negative stereotype fails to capture the pain that a person with BPD experiences. If a close family member or friend were diagnosed with BPD, would you want him or her to know the diagnosis? Why or why not?

3. What kind of future does Anna have?

CHAPTER **13**

Antisocial Personality Disorder: *Bad to the Bone*

Evil is wrought by want of Thought
As well as want of Heart   THOMAS HARDY, *The Lady's Dream*

KURT'S STORY

The child's scream sliced through Kurt's nap, waking him abruptly. He looked out the window and saw Desiree, his girlfriend, pleading with her three-year-old son to get out of the car and come in the house.

"Fine, just sit in the car for all I care," yelled Desiree, storming into the house.

Seeing Kurt standing in the hall, Desiree started to complain about her son, who continued to whine in the front seat. Before she could say anything, Desiree found herself on the floor, her jaw aching and the taste of blood in her mouth. It took her a second to realize that Kurt had just hit her across the face.

Now he stood over her, berating her as a parent. "Stupid bitch! You can't even take care of your stupid kid," Kurt bellowed. Desiree tried to get up, but Kurt put his foot on her chest, holding her down. Angry now, Desiree dug her nails into Kurt's foot until he yelped in pain and staggered backward. Desiree seized the moment to bolt for the door.

Almost to the car, Desiree knew she had to get away. "Kurt's a maniac when he's like this," she thought. She hesitated at the car door, fumbling for her keys. Tackled from behind, she slammed into the car. Desiree felt her left arm snap from the impact. She fell to the ground and closed her eyes as her boyfriend punched and kicked her in a fit of rage.

Several minutes later, Desiree came to, her head, ribs, and arm throbbing in pain. "Why am I at the hospital?" she wondered, before realizing that Kurt, after beating her up, had now driven her to the emergency room. "Oh man, here we go again," thought Desiree, before wincing from a new ache in her hip.

As a doctor and a kind nurse Desiree had met before tended to her wounds, they asked what had happened. Desiree concocted a story about falling from her bicycle. She noticed the subtle glance exchanged between her two caretakers and knew they didn't believe her. The doctor suggested that her description of what happened did not match the type of injuries she had, and the nurse urged her to tell them what really happened.

Desiree stuck to her story, despite the fact that everyone knew she was lying. It wasn't the first time she had had to endure this type of inquisition, and to herself she cursed at Kurt for humiliating her like this. After several hours, Desiree walked out to the parking lot to look for Kurt. She found him asleep in the car.

Kurt woke up as Desiree climbed in the passenger's seat. She could tell that he was high on something, probably that hashish and opium he loved to smoke.

"How are you, babe?" asked Kurt, concerned. He was always like this after he hit her, and Desiree knew as he stared at the bright new cast on her arm that several good days would come out of this as he tried to make it up to her.

"I'm OK," she replied. "Where's Max?" she asked, referring to her son.

"He's at Nathan and Jill's," Kurt replied, starting the car. "They said they'd watch him while you and I go to Mexico for a couple of days. I figure you deserve at least that." It was then that Desiree noticed the camping equipment in the back seat.

"Like hell you're taking me to Mexico to be nice," she thought. "You were going anyway to score some dope." Desiree smiled weakly, closed her eyes, and said, "Great, let's go."

Several days and three drug deals later, Desiree and Kurt returned to the United States. Both of them were high on crystal meth, and Kurt yelled at Desiree about what a lousy mother she was. The conflict escalated until Desiree retorted that Kurt's mother was lousy, too. The minute the words escaped her mouth, she knew she had gone too far.

Suddenly, Kurt became eerily calm. He walked back to the kitchen and returned with a knife. Desiree's eyes widened in fear, and she lunged for the door. Kurt followed and managed to stab her twice before Desiree could free herself and get outside. She was able to drive herself back to the emergency room, where she told the kind nurse that her boyfriend had tried to kill her.

Kurt was arrested later that day and charged with domestic violence, assault, possession of illegal drugs, and attempted murder. He eventually was found guilty on all counts. During the sentencing phase of his trial, the court requested that a psychological evaluation be conducted in order to assist the court in determining appropriate placement and any treatment needs. A psychologist was appointed, and Kurt was evaluated over a period of several days.

As part of the evaluation, the psychologist asked Kurt a number of questions about his life. Because of the circumstances under which the assessment was performed, and because of Kurt's tendency to lie, the psychologist also obtained information from police reports, Desiree's court testimony, probation reports, school records, and interviews with Kurt's mother and other relatives.

Kurt was born in a large Midwestern city. He has an older brother who has a history of offenses related to drug abuse. His parents divorced when Kurt was a toddler, but not before he had both witnessed and fallen victim to his father's physical abuse. His mother took him and his brother to Colorado to get away from the father. After several years, the father found them and kidnapped the two boys from school. Federal investigators located him several weeks later, living with his sons in a hotel. Kurt and his brother were malnourished, dirty, and bruised from being beaten.

Kurt and his brother returned to live with their mother. She and her friends drank heavily and abused drugs, and it was not long before Kurt began to use drugs as well. While still in grammar school, he began failing classes, engaged in frequent fights with his peers, and often was truant. He was expelled from two schools and placed in classes for the severely emotionally disturbed.

Kurt's mother tried to get help for her son through the school system. She was referred to a counselor but was inconsistent in keeping appointments. At one point Kurt was diagnosed with attention-deficit hyperactivity disorder, but his mother refused to let her son take medication. Despite all Kurt's behavioral problems, his mother stood by him, defending him as best she could.

Kurt first was arrested at the age of twelve for shoplifting. His mother convinced the storeowner to drop the charges as long as she paid for the missing items and agreed to keep her son out of the store. The shoplifting continued, however, and by the age of fourteen Kurt and his friends were breaking into houses in their neighborhood. He was apprehended and placed in juvenile hall. After serving thirty days, Kurt was released and put on probation. During this time, he ran away from home and lived in Denver, supporting himself by stealing and selling drugs. He had long since abandoned school. Following an assault on a gas station attendant who caught him stealing, Kurt was sentenced to two years in a residential treatment facility for juvenile offenders. His mother drove two hours every weekend to see him.

Kurt was released from the juvenile facility on his eighteenth birthday. He continued to live a transient lifestyle, supporting himself primarily by selling drugs. He spent much of his time in Arizona and New Mexico, transporting drugs between Mexico and Colorado. He had several minor arrests as an adult, including driving offenses, weapons possession, and violation of probation, which resulted in several months of prison time.

Although Kurt made good money selling drugs, he could never hang on to it. Good looking and charming, he always seemed able to find some woman whom he could convince to let him move in. Although he was often abusive to these women, his generosity, his sense of fun and adventure, and, ultimately, his ability to seduce them with his promises to change and his tales of being victimized himself often won them back. His relationships were short-lived, however, and it was not uncommon for Kurt to be involved with more than one woman at a time. At the time of his arrest for attempted murder, he was twenty-six years old.

▬ *WHAT DO YOU THINK?* ▬

1. Many criminals have histories of being physically or emotionally abused by their parents. Is there a relationship between being abused as a child and developing an antisocial lifestyle later in life?
2. There is a phrase that is popular in our culture, that of a "cold-blooded killer." Kurt became very calm before he attacked his girlfriend. What do you think happened?
3. There is much public policy debate over whether to simply warehouse criminals or to spend the money to treat them. What is the research evidence for either position?

Assessment

In addition to learning about Kurt's history, the psychologist also administered a number of psychological tests. When interpreting tests given to people involved with the legal system, caution must be used because of criminals' tendencies either to try to appear "crazier" than they really are or to minimize and deny their problems. Some hope that by appearing to have a major mental illness they can avoid serving time in prison and be incarcerated in a psychiatric facility instead. Others cannot tolerate the idea that there is anything wrong with them and so either try to answer questions as they think a "normal" person would or offer as little information as possible. Kurt fit into this latter category.

During his assessment, Kurt was hostile and negative toward the examiner. He wore his long brown hair in a ponytail and sported a sparse goatee. Tattoos covered both his arms. He was agitated and restless throughout his interviews. He demonstrated little tolerance for frustration and would not attempt to solve problems that did not come easily to him. When asked to do something he didn't want to, he simply refused. His most frequent response to test questions was, "I don't care."

On the Wechsler Adult Intelligence Scale–Revised, Kurt scored in the low-average range. He did much better when asked to solve nonverbal problems of the type not usually associated with school, while doing poorly on tasks that assess his fund of knowledge, vocabulary, and common sense. He also did poorly on tasks that measure attention, concentration, and speed of mental processing. Because he had not used drugs for several months while in jail, these deficits were assumed to be reflective either of Kurt's problems in these areas or of his lack of motivation. His test performance suggested that he was potentially of average intelligence and that it was very likely that he had one or more learning disabilities.

Kurt refused to participate in the examination of his skills in reading, writing, or math, exclaiming, "I don't want to do these tests. I know how I am, and I'll deal with it. I read my Bible." He scored in the mild to moderately impaired range on several tests associated with frontal lobe functioning, suggesting that the diagnosis of attention-deficit hyperactivity disorder made during his childhood was accurate.

On personality measures such as the Minnesota Multiphasic Personality Inventory 2 (MMPI-2) and the Rorschach Inkblot Test, Kurt responded in such a way that showed that beneath his indifferent facade was a man who felt inadequate and inferior to others. Despite his hostility and bravado, Kurt was childlike in his needs for attention and affection. When these needs were not met, he became enraged. Once angered, he was unable to control himself, and he acted out aggressively and violently. Once his anger was spent, he felt bad and attempted to reconcile with the person he had harmed. The object of his rage was most likely to be a girlfriend who would inevitably fail to live up to the idealized standard of overindulgence and tolerance set by his mother.

Kurt also was found to have little tolerance for stress. He avoided dealing with problems whenever possible and used drugs as a way of turning off unwanted feelings and relieving tension. Living within the drug subculture also allowed him to act out his rejection of societal values and standards. He justified his own attempts to manipulate and control others by pointing to similar behaviors on the part of everyone he knew. He had little capacity for empathy and was likely to be self-centered, dishonest, and opportunistic in his relationships. He was depressed and had been since the time of his incarceration.

Case Conceptualization

Antisocial personality disorder (APD) is the most reliable diagnosis among the personality disorders. Approximately 6 percent of males and 1 percent of females evidence a lifetime risk for the disorder (Meloy, 1995). Over three-fourths of all convicted felons meet the criteria for APD. However, not only do criminals manifest the disorder, but so do many people who might be considered valued members of society, some business executives, politicians, and salespeople among them. Although delinquent behavior prior to age fifteen is a precondition for APD, the diagnosis cannot be made formally until age eighteen. Interestingly, the disorder normally goes into spontaneous remission by the fourth decade of life and has an average duration of nineteen years from first symptom to last.

There is no consensus on the underlying cause of APD. Biologically, chronic cortical underarousal has been identified as one possible substrate for the APD patient's limited emotional repertoire. In particular, reduced skin conductance along with increased heart rate when exposed to intense or aversive stimuli defines the physiologic signature of the person with APD, especially if that person has psychopathic tendencies (Hare, 1978). While the emotional life of those with APD is likely to be dominated by anger, shame, boredom, contempt, and the need for exhilaration and pleasure through domination, such persons experience little or no gratitude, empathy, joy, affection, guilt, remorse, or reciprocal pleasure. This pattern of emotional reactivity may be genetically transmitted, related to having a relative who is APD, as found consistently in studies of twins and adopted children. While adopted children with an APD parent resemble the biologic parent more than the adoptive one, environmental factors play an important role in influencing the risk of developing the disorder (Meloy, 1995). In addition, violence by those with APD has been shown to be either of the affective type, accompanied by high levels of sympathetic nervous system arousal, or of the predatory type, accompanied by minimal or no sympathetic arousal. Kurt's aggressive behavior was typically more of the affective type, aroused by intense levels of anger or fear.

Psychologically, Kurt and others with APD experience little anxiety, have a limited capacity for emotional attachment, display a significant need for self-aggrandizement, and demonstrate a lack of conscience. Kurt relied on the relatively primitive defenses of projection, denial, rationalization, splitting, omnipotence, and devaluation. Narcissism and hysterical traits are also associated with APD. Such patients do not have an ability to relate to other people as whole, real, or meaningful but instead experience others as objects to manipulate into meeting their needs.

From a social perspective, family studies have occupied a great deal of research attention. While many studies conclude that lack of affection, parental rejection, or inconsistent discipline may result in an adult with APD, other studies find little relationship between these factors and later delinquent or antisocial behavior. This may be due in part to the nature of some of these studies, which rely on the APD subject's perception of his or her own past. One consistent finding is that a disciplinary pattern in which there are strict, unrealistic expectations accompanied by a lack of supervision and/or behavioral consequences tends to produce delinquent behaviors in youth (Singer, 1974). This was certainly true for Kurt, whose abusive father and doting, inconsistent mother combined to provide both a model of and a lack of consequences for antisocial behavior. A family history of substance abuse, poverty, domestic violence, and child abuse also has been associated with the development of APD, but in ways as yet unspecified. It is obvious that not all children who grow up under such circumstances develop the disorder, suggesting that other factors are more central. Finally, the values of one's subculture, such as that of a gang, can contribute to the development of APD. There is some controversy, however, as to whether behavior that is antisocial to society at large but may be adaptive or self-protective within a given subculture is really evidence of APD.

Diagnosis

APD is defined in *DSM-IV* (APA, 1994) by a pervasive pattern of disregard for and violation of the rights of others that begins in childhood or early adolescence and continues into adulthood. As with all personality disorders, the individual must be at least eighteen years of age for this diagnosis to be given. A diagnosis of conduct disorder is often applied to those who display consistent antisocial traits prior to age eighteen.

Kurt qualified for a diagnosis of APD by displaying at least three of the seven possible symptoms since the age of fifteen. He failed to conform to social norms by repeatedly engaging in illegal activities, selling drugs in particular. He engaged in a pattern of consistent deceitfulness, lying in order to meet his needs. He was impulsive, acting without regard for the consequences of his behavior. He also was prone to irritability and aggressiveness, being quick to anger and resolving most conflicts by fighting. Kurt showed reckless disregard for the safety of himself or others, most dramatically when he attacked Desiree. He showed consistent irresponsibility by not supporting himself and manipulating others into taking care of him. Finally, he displayed a lack of remorse for his actions, often making up an excuse for his offenses, such as, "They were going to get me; I just got them first."

The label of *psychopath* is often used interchangeably with that of APD in common parlance, but in truth it should be applied only to a minority of patients with APD (Hare, 1991). Psychopathy represents a more severe form of APD and is typified by a superficial charm, a grandiose sense of self-worth, a need for stimulation, shallow affect, a lack of empathy, a parasitic lifestyle, promiscuity, and irresponsibility in addition to the other features of APD. While mood disorders and substance abuse may accompany APD, only substance abuse is associated with psychopaths.

Kurt clearly met the diagnostic criteria for APD. He also demonstrated a mild form of psychopathy. The severity of his condition was somewhat mitigated by the presence of depression and his strong attachment to his mother.

Treatment and Outlook

There is no demonstrably effective treatment for APD or psychopathy, although several factors have been identified that improve the prognosis, as in

Kurt's case. On the other hand, Meloy (1995) has identified five clinical features that contraindicate treatment of any kind: a history of sadistic and violent behavior, total absence of remorse, extremely high or extremely low intelligence, no history of emotional attachment, and fear on the part of the experienced clinician in the absence of any overtly threatening behavior by the patient. Kurt did not meet these criteria, and in the recommendations made to the court, the psychologist suggested that he be confined in a prison setting that offered the possibility of psychological treatment. Despite the presence of significant psychopathic symptoms, it was felt that he demonstrated several positive prognostic indicators.

First, Kurt had been moderately depressed since being incarcerated. Indeed, he ruminated about his mistakes and failures and admitted to entertaining thoughts of suicide. Once in prison, he was treated with one of the newer antidepressant medications, along with cognitive-behavioral treatment, and he showed significant improvement.

Second, although he lacked much experience of anxiety and the motivation to change that accompanies such discomfort, Kurt's capacity for emotional attachment suggested that he might be able to form a therapeutic alliance with a therapist. Indeed, following several months of resistance to treatment, he was able to accept his therapist's attempts to support and help him. Over time, he came to value the opinions of the therapist and used the therapist's observations to make changes in the way he behaved.

Cognitive-behavioral therapy that focused on relapse prevention was used in a daily group therapy format with other APD patients. Thoughts, feelings, perceptions, and fantasies that stimulate antisocial behaviors were painstakingly and systematically examined so that the chain of events leading to a discrete antisocial act could be understood. Members of Kurt's group were then taught new ways of thinking and acting to break the maladaptive progression of events.

One ongoing difficulty for Kurt was his narcissistic need to devalue others as a means of shoring up his own grandiosity and repairing old emotional wounds. This need led to continual provocation of other inmates, especially those perceived as smaller or weaker. The inmate would eventually attack Kurt, who would then feel justified in beating up his victim. This behavioral pattern proved resistant to treatment efforts despite repeated attempts to help Kurt understand and change it. Eventually, Kurt seemed to develop a greater sense of adequacy and self-confidence as he became proficient in a job-training program studying to be an auto mechanic.

Kurt was released from prison after eleven years. Now in his late thirties, he remains on probation and continues to attend group and individual therapy on an outpatient basis. He also goes to Narcotics Anonymous groups and works in an auto repair shop. He lives with his mother and stepfather in a small town in western Colorado. In treatment he is working on preparing himself to have a relationship with a woman, but he knows that this situation is the one most likely to trigger assaultive behavior on his part. For now he is content to enjoy his freedom and the prospects of a future brighter than he ever imagined.

▬▬ *THINKING CRITICALLY* ▬▬

QUESTIONS FOR DISCUSSION OR WRITING

1. Therapists often complain that they cannot form a therapeutic relationship with those who have antisocial or narcissistic personalities. Why do you think this is, and what effect might this inability to form meaningful relationships have on the psychotherapy process?

2. Some people who grow up in a racially segregated, economically oppressed, urban subculture say that antisocial behavior is adaptive to survival. How might such traits be adaptive, and would living in such conditions ever justify, say, a drive-by shooting in retaliation for the death of a fellow gang member?

CHAPTER 14

Attention Deficit/Hyperactivity Disorder: *All Wound Up and Out of Control*

The most turbulent, the most restless child has, amidst all his faults, something true, ingenious, and natural, which is of infinite value, and merits every respect. FELIX A. DUPANLOWP

RICHARD'S STORY

The second period bell rang. The teacher asked her fourth-grade class to take out their homework assignment from last night and pass it to the front of the class for collection. Richard panicked as he searched through his notebook, pages falling out all over his desk. He knew he did his homework. Where was it?

As he continued to rummage through his notebook, he noticed the classroom had become still. He looked up and saw twenty-four pairs of eyes converge on him. "Can't find your assignment again, Richard?" his teacher asked.

"No, Ms. Berman," replied Richard, sheepishly. This was becoming all too common. The teacher moved on, discussing the short story they were to have read over the weekend.

After a few minutes, Richard found it difficult to pay attention to his teacher's lecture. He gazed out the window, lost in reverie. A small commotion next to him caught his eye. He glanced over to find two of his friends smiling about a note they had just passed to each other. "Hey, what's up?" blurted Richard.

"Richard," called the teacher. "Do you have something you want to share with the class?"

Richard denied having any contribution to make and soon found himself placed in a familiar desk away from the rest of his classmates. After a few minutes, he was again daydreaming.

"Richard," the teacher chimed. "Are you going to join us?" Richard looked confused and noticed that everyone else had a pencil and paper lying on their desk tops. He lunged into his backpack, hoping to find some clean paper. When he could not, the teacher brought him several pieces on which to write.

Richard began the in-class writing assignment. It concerned a topic in which he was interested, what it would be like if computers ruled the world, but he had trouble figuring out an introductory sentence. Aware that it was a timed writing assignment, he scratched out some sentences related to the subject. As usual, his paper was poorly organized, and his handwriting was difficult to read. The bell rang, signaling the end of the assignment and of second period. As Richard dropped his paper on his teacher's desk, she reminded him that she was meeting with him and his mother that afternoon after school. His face bright red, Richard scuttled out the door, dreading yet another teacher conference where his academic underachievement and disruptive classroom behavior were the topics of the day.

To Richard's surprise, this conference was different. Not only was his mother there, but so were several of his teachers and the school counselor. No one scolded him, and it was clear that he was not in trouble. The school counselor summarized his academic history: "It is the same for Richard each year. He scores well on the standardized tests, very well in fact. He is a good reader, and he is especially good in physical education and art. He has consistent difficulties in math, and his handwriting is atrocious. The anecdotal teacher remarks on his report cards all comment on his lack of organization, his distractibility, his tendency to daydream, talking out of turn in class, and trouble getting along with his peers. At least he stays in his seat now. Reports from first and second grade talk about how he was always touching other kids' things and getting up all the time. The increased structure, consistent negative consequences, and isolation of Richard from his peers have improved his behavior somewhat, but his academic performance continues to be less than what we would expect. We need to get to the bottom of this."

Everyone agreed. The teachers then took turns talking about Richard's behavior and performance in their classrooms. Each of them talked about how much they liked him, finding him creative and talented artistically but inconsistent in his academic performance and often causing minor disruptions in the classroom. The counselor then asked his mother about Richard's behavior at home.

His mother agreed that it often seemed as though Richard was not listening to her when he was asked to do something. His room was a "pig sty," and no matter what she tried, she could not get Richard to keep it clean. Getting him to do his homework was a nightly battle. He loved to play Nintendo, however, and using this as a reward for getting him to do just about anything sometimes worked. He was the star of his basketball and soccer teams at the YMCA, but in baseball his coaches were always yelling at him to stay focused on the game. He did better playing infield; in the outfield he often could be found doing cartwheels or picking dandelions. However, she added, "He's basically a good kid, and I always thought he'd just grow out of this."

Attention then moved to Richard, who was asked what he thought. "I don't know," he began. "I just get bored with some things real easy. I know my Mom has to yell at me a lot, and I get in trouble in school for stupid stuff. My Dad always says I need a new brain. Maybe I do."

The school counselor quickly responded that Richard had an excellent brain, one that allowed him many talents in sports and in his artistic efforts. She said that while he did well in many situations, there were simply some settings, such as the classroom and perhaps center field, that were difficult for him to deal with. Richard smiled, and his mother asked what the counselor suggested. "I believe that Richard could benefit from a psychological evaluation," said the counselor. "I would like to refer you to someone I know who specializes in assessing children who have trouble in school. After the evaluation is complete, we can all meet again and talk about where to go from here."

Richard and his mother felt reassured that perhaps something could be done to help him with his problem. Everyone at the meeting had been so supportive and interested in helping. Richard's mother agreed to contact the psychologist that afternoon.

▨ *WHAT DO YOU THINK?* ▨

1. The problems Richard has do not sound all that unusual. What specific behaviors might the school counselor have noticed that made her think that Richard could benefit from a psychological assessment?

2. In addition to not being terribly unusual, Richard's behavior could be caused by all kinds of factors. How might the evaluating psychologist sort through all the possibilities to determine the underlying cause of Richard's difficulties?

3. Richard's problems are not of recent onset. Why do you think his mother may have resisted previous efforts to identify his problem?

Assessment

The psychologist met with Richard's mother a few days later to obtain a complete history of his family background, course of development, and medical record. Richard's parents had met while his father was in the Navy and serving in Guam. His mother, who was from Guam, had immigrated to the United States after marrying his father. After ten years and two children together, Richard's mother had divorced his father because of his drinking.

Richard continued to see his father every other weekend but did not enjoy these visits when his father was intoxicated. His older sister had trouble reading and had received remedial instruction to help her learn to read at grade level.

Richard's mother was twenty-seven when Richard was born. She admitted to smoking while pregnant but did not drink or use other drugs. Her pregnancy was uncomplicated, and Richard was delivered naturally at thirty-seven weeks' gestation. He was a small baby at five pounds eleven ounces, and he was kept in the hospital for a few days to make sure that he could feed adequately before being released to go home.

As an infant, Richard was an active baby. His mother reported that he had colic and often was difficult to soothe. He had difficulty establishing a regular sleeping pattern and kept his parents worn out for the first eighteen months of his life.

When Richard was a toddler, his mother noticed that he had a short attention span. He continued to be very active and wore out his shoes, clothing, and toys quickly. His mother often described him to her family as like a "spinning top," moving from one thing to another in a constant blur of motion. As a result, he often fell down and ran into things. He was always getting scrapes and bruises, but he seemed heedless to danger. Although generally a good-natured child, when he threw a temper tantrum, it was a major event. More than once Richard's mother had to abandon a shopping cart full of groceries in a store in order to carry her son out to the parking lot kicking and screaming.

Richard's mother went to work as a bank teller when he was four, and he was placed in preschool. There he was always in trouble. He failed to follow directions, talked out of turn, and could never be found in his seat. His teachers liked him but often joked that they had to "tie him to his chair" in order to maintain control.

Richard's medical history was largely unremarkable. He had contracted the usual childhood diseases and was allergic to dog hair. Despite his tendency to be accident-prone, he had no significant head injuries. He also had had no serious illnesses, and a recent medical examination had shown him to have normal vision and hearing.

The psychologist then proceeded to have the mother complete two behavior rating scales that asked questions about a wide variety of behaviors on Richard's part. She was asked to have the same scales completed by Richard's father, and permission was asked to send a similar scale to the school for his teachers to fill out. The psychologist also asked for permission to talk directly with Richard's school to learn what his teachers had to say about him and to collect samples of his schoolwork. Another appointment was scheduled so that Richard himself could be assessed.

A week later Richard's mother brought him to the psychologist's office. Although initially apprehensive, Richard soon warmed to the doctor's relaxed manner. After some discussion of Richard's interests in basketball and art, the psychologist asked Richard about his life in general and about school in particular. There were several questions about how he was disciplined, his usual mood, and how he got along with his friends. The psychologist also asked some questions Richard thought were really weird, like did he ever hear voices. But mostly Richard thought that for a visit to the doctor, this wasn't too bad.

The psychologist gave Richard a number of tests. These included an intelligence test, some achievement tests to see how much he had learned in school, and some neuropsychological tests that were sensitive to frontal lobe functioning. During his evaluation, Richard appeared to try his hardest on all tasks. He showed an adequate tolerance for frustration when faced with tasks that were difficult for him. Although some part of his body was always in motion, such as shaking his leg or tapping his fingers, in the testing setting Richard did not seem distractible.

Richard scored in the high-average range of intellectual ability on the Wechsler Intelligence Scale for Children, 3rd Edition (Wechsler, 1991), confirming his teachers' assumptions that he was very bright. He did much better on tasks that measured visuospatial abilities, abstract reasoning, and common sense than he did on tasks that were sensitive to attention, concentration, and speed of mental processing. He did terribly on a test where he was asked to recite backwards a random list of numbers presented orally. His fund of information and vocabulary were within the average range, suggesting that despite his problems in school, Richard was still managing to learn.

On the Wechsler Individual Achievement Test (1992), Richard scored in the high average range in reading and spelling. Receptive and expressive language abilities and reading comprehension were within the average range, and written expression and math skills were below average. Richard did better when presented with math problems that were already set up on paper, but he had more difficulty when presented with word problems that he had to first understand, then weed out extraneous information, and finally set up to solve himself. His written paragraph describing his ideal house contained many creative ideas but was poorly organized with weak sentence structure.

It was on the neuropsychological tests that Richard performed the most poorly. The Hand Movements subtest from the Kaufman Assessment Battery for Children (Kaufman & Kaufman, 1983) has children mimic a series of hand gestures (fist, palm down, karate chop) by the examiner. Richard did very poorly on this task, reflecting a deficit in the temporal ordering of motor sequences that apparently did not arise spontaneously when he played sports. On the Stroop Word and Color Test, children are first asked to read a long list of four words (*tan, green, red,* and *blue*) printed in different colors. Next, they are asked to read the color of the ink in which each word is written; for example, the word *red* might be written in green ink, with the correct response then being "green." Richard had great difficulty with this interference task, taking far more time and making many more errors than do most children his age. His performance suggested that he might have great difficulty preventing distraction when there were competing factors vying for his attention. Finally, he was given the Continuous Performance Test, a computer program that presents a series of random letters on the screen, with the instruction to hit the space bar after each letter except the letter X. Richard had great difficulty with this measure of vigilance, often hitting the space bar after seeing the X and then failing to correctly respond for a few letters while he became frustrated with himself.

Case Conceptualization

Based on Richard's history, presenting symptoms, and test results, the psychologist concluded that Richard suffered from attention-deficit hyperactivity disorder (ADHD). What was unusual in Richard's case was that his hyperactivity was quite mild, which is often not a typical finding for boys. While there is no single definitive assessment strategy or instrument for making the diagnosis of ADHD, a pattern of at least average intelligence; achievement deficits in reading comprehension, math, and handwriting; and difficulty with sequencing, organization, and disinhibition of behavior on neuropsychological tests sensitive to frontal lobe and executive functioning serves as a useful guide in making an accurate diagnosis (Pennington, 1991). Since the presenting symptoms of ADHD also can be symptoms of numerous other types of learning disabilities and emotional disorders, careful assessment is warranted to prevent misdiagnosis.

ADHD has been a perplexing disorder to conceptualize over the years. In the past it was known as "hyperkinetic impulse disorder" and "minimal brain dysfunction." The confusion surrounding the disorder has been magnified by whether the researcher investigating ADHD has thought of it as a collection of behavioral symptoms or as a type of cerebral dysfunction. In addition, no two people with ADHD look alike. While Richard's case is mild and he is not very hyperactive, another child with ADHD may act as though he or she is "bouncing off the walls." It is also a very situation-dependent disorder, in that it responds positively to the optimal environmental conditions of structure, novelty, freedom of movement, individual attention, and immediate gratification. This is why Richard does so well playing Nintendo games. Finally, virtually everyone exhibits some of the behaviors associated with ADHD some of the time. The diagnosis is reserved only for those who exhibit many of these behaviors with an intensity and chronicity that is extreme in relation to developmental norms (Greene & Barkley, 1995).

There is no consensus about the cause of ADHD. Twin and adoption studies suggest a genetic component. In addition, ADHD has been associated with Turner syndrome, fragile X syndrome, XYY syndrome, early treated phenylketonuria and neurofibromatosis. Drug or alcohol exposure in utero, including maternal smoking as in Richard's case, also has been associated with increased frequency of ADHD. Neurotoxin exposure (especially to lead), infections, and pediatric head injury have all been shown to result in an increased incidence of the disorder. Finally, family histories of ADHD, mood disorders, learning disabilities, substance abuse, and antisocial personality disorder have all been noted in the literature.

At the present time, ADHD is believed to arise from abnormalities in the structure and function of the prefrontal cortex and its networks with other brain regions, especially the striatum. This part of the brain is concerned primarily with what is known as executive functioning, or the self-regulation and modulation of behavior. As a result, the behavior of those with ADHD is controlled more by their immediate environment and its consequences than is the behavior of others. The behavior of others, by comparison, tends to be more controlled by internally represented information, such as hindsight, forethought, time, planning, rules, and self-motivating stimuli (Barkley, 1997). The inability of ADHD patients to effectively inhibit their behavior makes it less likely that they can utilize these internal resources to help them achieve their goals. A better name for ADHD might be behavioral disinhibition disorder, since the attentional deficits highlighted by the disorder's current name are more of a secondary by-product than a primary disability.

Cognitively, then, Richard and others with ADHD have difficulty with several tasks necessary to efficiently produce goal-directed behavior. Working memory, or the ability to hold and manipulate information mentally, is often impaired. This difficulty was reflected in Richard's performance in math generally and in his problems reciting numbers presented to him orally in reverse order. The higher activity level seen in ADHD children is reflected in their talking more, both to themselves and to others, as well as in their making more nonvocal sounds, such as Richard's leg shaking and finger tapping. ADHD children have trouble delaying gratification and resisting temptation, requiring a great deal of structure in order to succeed. Perhaps this is why Richard did better at basketball and soccer than baseball, which requires much more internal motivation to stay focused on the often monotonous or slow-paced game. Finally, motor control problems are evident in those with ADHD, as reflected in Richard's difficulty in mimicking a series of hand movements by the examiner.

These deficits in executive functioning and self-regulatory behavior display themselves in other common psychological problems, including a low tolerance for frustration, outbursts of temper, and stubbornness. People with ADHD often display an excessive and frequent insistence that their needs be met. They are easily demoralized and hold a belief that they are prone to fail at whatever they try. Depression and low self-esteem are observed commonly, and rejection by one's peers is also noted at least half the time. Children with ADHD are often seen as oppositional, lazy, and irresponsible by parents and teachers. They are at increased risk for developing antisocial personality disorder and mood disorders such as anxiety and depression. In addition, ADHD symptoms often precede the onset of Tourette's disorder, another syndrome associated with impaired frontal lobe functioning.

Diagnosis

ADHD is defined in *DSM-IV* as "a persistent pattern of inattention and/or hyperactivity-impulsivity that is more frequent and severe than is typically observed in individuals at a comparable level of development" (APA, 1994). Richard met the defining criteria for the disorder in that he displayed evidence of symptom onset prior to age seven, and his impairment was observable both at school and at home. False-positive reporting rates of as high as 30 percent have been noted when researchers rely on parent statements alone (Pennington, 1991). Additionally, Richard presented evidence of impairment in his social and academic functioning, and other possible causes for these symptoms (such as mental retardation, abusive or neglectful environments, mood disorders, a medical condition, pervasive developmental disorder, psychosis, or substance abuse) were ruled out in his case.

Interestingly, *DSM-IV* continues to rely on behavioral evidence of inattention, hyperactivity, and impulsivity rather than neuropsychological test performance, which may be more reliable. The matter is complicated by evaluators' past tendencies to use untrained observers, such as parents and teachers, to both identify and operationalize concepts such as "distractibility" or "attention span" while trusting their ability to not misinterpret any undesirable behavior on the part of the child in this context (Connors et al., 1995). Such symptoms as forgetfulness, distractibility, restlessness, difficulty organizing tasks and behaviors, and avoidance of tasks that require sustained mental effort, such as homework, form much of the basis for this diagnosis.

DSM-IV also recognizes subtypes of the disorder. Richard manifested the predominantly inattentive type of ADHD. Distractibility is the primary manifestation of this subtype, with academic underachievement a frequent by-product. Underarousal has been hypothesized as the basis for this type of ADHD, with resulting passive off-task inattention, failure to adequately monitor the environment for cues and feedback, failure to self-monitor, and poor sustained performance. In the predominantly hyperactive-impulsive type, more pervasive impairment is noted outside the academic sphere. The inability to inhibit inappropriate behavior, or impulsive responding, is the primary manifestation of this ADHD subtype. Schachar and colleagues (1993) observe that those with this subtype are unable to stop or modify their behavior once it is started, even if the behavior is clearly going to result in a negative outcome. A combined type of ADHD is also possible, and some researchers have hypothesized the existence of an aggressive subtype, which has yet to be distinguished adequately from other subtypes (Schwean, Saklofske, Yackulic & Quinn, 1995). For adults in whom ADHD symptoms persist, the residual subtype is appropriate.

Treatment and Outlook

Richard and his mother attended another meeting with his teachers and the school counselor, but this time the psychologist who conducted the evaluation also was present. The results of the assessment were presented, along with the diagnosis of ADHD. The diagnosis was explained to Richard and his mother, and they were given several articles and books to read along with encouragement to become "expert" in their knowledge of this disorder.

In the questions that followed, Richard's mother expressed concern that she might be responsible somehow for his condition. She was reassured that there was no way to know for certain what caused ADHD and that at any rate what was more important was to find ways to help Richard to ensure that he could take advantage of his many gifts and talents. Richard also wondered if there was something seriously wrong with his brain, and it was explained to him that while his brain did not function as efficiently as most people's in some respects, there was nothing seriously wrong with him. Indeed, there was much reason to believe that in his case the relatively mild nature of his symptoms, the possibilities for treatment, and the passage of time might all work in concert to minimize the impact of his disorder.

Richard was referred to a psychiatrist for medication evaluation and was soon started on Ritalin (methylphenidate), the most common medicine used in the control of ADHD symptoms. Effective in 70 to 90 percent of all cases, this medication is structurally related to amphetamine and is an indirect dopamine agonist (Pennington, 1991). Its advantages include a quick response, although its effects wear off after several hours, necessitating readministration at least once during the day to allow a child to make it through the school day. Ritalin has been reported to have growth-suppressant effects in young children, which can be minimized by using "drug holidays" during weekends and holidays when behavioral inhibition is less important than during school hours (Ayd, 1995). Other popular medications in the treatment of ADHD include other psychostimulants such as Cylert (pemoline) and Dexedrine (dextroamphetamine). Antidepressant medication, neuroleptics, and anticonvulsants also have been used in the treatment of this disorder.

While treatment with medication is important and even necessary in most cases of ADHD, it is hardly ever sufficient as a complete treatment (Pelham, 1993). Richard proved to be responsive to Ritalin, which made the educational and psychological interventions much more successful. In relation to school, it was decided to try to maintain him in a regular classroom, given his level of intelligence, the absence of other learning disabilities, and his positive response to medication. Almost half of all those with ADHD can be kept in a regular classroom setting, and this is generally agreed to be a worthwhile goal if at all possible. Richard was indeed better able to pay attention in class and control his behavior. Both his grades and achievement test scores showed improvement over the next two years, until he was at or above grade level in every subject.

Richard also began individual psychotherapy. Here, the focus of treatment was on improving his social skills and addressing his cognitive self-perceptions that affected his self-esteem. He was taught strategies to increase his ability to organize his environment, to think in logical, sequential steps, and to talk through a decision-making process to improve behavioral self-control. These interventions proved beneficial, with the result that Richard got in less trouble both at home and at school, and he also was able to make and keep friendships with his peers.

Finally, Richard's mother also was involved in his treatment in two ways. First, she was referred to a support group for parents with ADHD children. Here she was able to listen to other parents who had children similar to her son. This helped her feel less isolated and also provided helpful advice on dealing with the kinds of problems parents of ADHD children often run into. Second, she was taught by Richard's therapist how to decrease problems at home by increasing structure. Behavioral charts that provided both time requirements for certain activities and more immediate rewards for appropriate behaviors were set up. She was shown how to be consistent in her communication and discipline with her son, with the result that she had fewer occasions where she felt that Richard did not listen to her. Activities that Richard enjoyed, such as playing Nintendo, were made contingent on the completion of activities he did not like so much, such as doing homework. Both Richard and his mother were pleased with these interventions, because it meant that they did not argue so much.

While some children apparently outgrow the symptoms of ADHD, most do not. The outcomes vary greatly, depending on a wide variety of factors, including the severity of the disorder, responsiveness and compliance with medical treatment, and environmental factors. Between 10 and 25 percent of ADHD adults develop serious psychiatric or antisocial pathology that often results in hospitalization or incarceration. As a group, ADHD adults suffer from lower levels of education and occupational achievement and tend to choose jobs where high levels of activity are required. They are typically no less self-supporting or employed than the general population, but they may have inferior work records and are more prone to being fired and having difficulty getting along with co-workers and supervisors (Barkley, 1990; Weiss & Hechtman, 1993).

Richard went on to graduate from high school and is now enrolled in a four-year college. He continues to enjoy sports and is majoring in physical education with the plan of becoming a high school teacher and coach. He hopes that with the insight provided by his own struggles, he will be able to be effective as an instructor and role model for other young people. He continues to draw and is the cartoonist for the university newspaper. Students and faculty alike appreciate his witty barbs at campus and academic politics. While he no longer takes medication, he continues to use some of the strategies he learned in school and therapy to organize his life, although, as he reported in a recent letter, his room is still a "pig sty."

▬▬▬ *THINKING CRITICALLY* ▬▬▬

QUESTIONS FOR DISCUSSION OR WRITING

1. Richard's story demonstrates the importance of a correct diagnosis and a supportive educational and home environment in the treatment of ADHD. What might be the impact on a child's development if his or her ADHD is not diagnosed or treated correctly?

2. Some parents and teachers are quick to label any child they find active, oppositional, or difficult to control as having ADHD. Why might it be tempting to do this, and what impact might this incorrectly and prejudicially applied label have on a child?

CHAPTER 15

Bulimia Nervosa:
The Self-Destructive Diet

Everything in excess is opposed to nature.   HIPPOCRATES

DANA'S STORY

It was Dana's twenty-second birthday. To celebrate, she and her boyfriend, Matt, were joining her family at a plush Cambridge restaurant for dinner. As they pulled in the parking lot, Dana noticed her parents talking with another couple outside the entrance. She thought to herself how often she had witnessed this little scene: Her mother, impeccably coifed and dressed, throwing her head back in feigned laughter, while her father told one of his stupid jokes for the zillionth time. Her father, an attorney, and her mother, an executive in a large computer firm, were both very popular in the community, and it was a rare evening out that they failed to run into several people whom they knew.

As she walked into the restaurant with Matt and her parents, Dana saw that her older sister, Joanie, and her boyfriend were already seated. Her older brother was not going to be there; big surprise, he never was. He always seemed to escape the dreaded family gatherings with one excuse or another. Ever since he dropped out of law school and joined the Peace Corps, the tension between him and their parents was almost unbearable. No matter that he was now a big success in designing software products; all the Wilson children knew that if you weren't doing what Mom and Dad wanted you to do, you might as well be a serial killer for all the grief they gave you.

As Dana walked to her table, conversations stopped, and staring men were prodded under the table by their disapproving dates. Her long, light-brown hair, high cheek bones, and dark complexion never failed to draw attention. Her petite figure and large, piercing blue eyes often invited comparisons with a porcelain doll, with the attendant wish to take care of her. As her grandmother was fond of saying, Dana was so pretty "her beauty entered the room before her." Rather than enjoy this attention, however, it always made Dana extremely anxious and self-conscious. She immediately thought, "My God! These people must think I'm so fat. They're staring at me!" She walked stiffly to her seat, trying her hardest to disappear.

Joanie, as usual, was not going to let Dana get away with so much attention. "Hey, Bubble-butt," she called so that half the Eastern seaboard could hear. "Come here and congratulate me. I just got accepted to grad school at BU." Dana could tell that Joanie was high on something; she usually was. It always amazed Dana that her sister managed to succeed academically while being perpetually intoxicated. Dana herself had barely survived high school and had dropped out of junior college two years ago after a half-hearted attempt, mostly to appease her parents. It seemed that she and Joanie were always competing. Joanie usually won the awards, while Dana won the guys.

"Joanie," scolded their mother. "This is Dana's party. You save your absolutely fantastic news until later." Then, to her husband, she added, "Oh, dear, remind me to call the Rothsteins. They'll be so thrilled to hear Joanie was accepted."

Dana rolled her eyes at Matt, who winked at her and grabbed her hand. How could he be so patient with her and her family, she wondered. They're all nut cases: My mother just cares about appearances. World War III could break out, and she would run down to Neiman's to make sure she had plenty of dresses. My sister's an addict whose sole purpose in life is to screw me over. My brother's disappeared, and my father doesn't have a clue. He still treats me like I'm five or something. He gave me a stuffed animal for my birthday! And me! If he ever found out about me, it would be all over. If it wasn't for Matt, I don't know what I'd do.

Throughout dinner Joanie and her mother vied for center stage. Each was a master at garnering attention, usually at someone else's expense. Joanie would occasionally make a remark to Dana, usually prefaced by an affectionate term such as "Thunder Thighs" or "Porky." Her mother, with a mysterious rhythm all her own, could interrupt herself in midsentence to comment on how little Dana was eating, how she should do something else with her hair, how unflattering her dress was, or how much more interested in her Matt would be if she had her breasts enlarged and then proceed with whatever piece of gossip she was engaged in. Dana endured this familiar torture with her characteristic withdrawal. She sat quietly and pushed her food around, drinking lots of water and wishing she had smoked more pot before leaving her apartment. Finally she excused herself and went to the bathroom.

Thank God! Dana breathed a sigh of relief at getting away from her mother and sister's banter. She entered the last stall and locked the door. Gently touching the back of her throat, Dana proceeded to vomit, ridding herself of the few morsels of food she had managed to force down. It was the third time she had thrown up that day, and it didn't take much to start the process. She began to scheme how she would binge later. She had already purchased or shoplifted everything she needed, anticipating how awful tonight was going to be. Who was she kidding, she would have binged tonight no matter what was going on!

Dana came back to the table to find that after-dinner drinks had been or-dered, and Matt and her father had retired to the bar to smoke cigars. Joanie and her mother were huddled together, discussing some obscure fashion topic, and Joanie's boyfriend looked as though he would die of boredom. He moved over to sit next to Dana and told her how great she looked. Dana's immediate thought was, "How can he say that? My hips hardly fit in this oversized chair, and my stomach is bulging from dinner." She felt horrible and proceeded to down her drink and then Matt's.

After leaving the restaurant, Dana cried the whole way home. Matt did his best to comfort her. They finally made love, which Dana detested. She hated sex, hated having Matt see her naked, hated intimacy of any kind. She did it only so that Matt would go to sleep, leaving her free to raid her hidden stash of cereal, raisin bread, snack pies, and eclairs. She shivered outside on the fire escape, gorging herself on fistfuls of food. When she finally felt so full that she would explode, she went inside and threw up, this time without even having to induce vomiting. She hugged the toilet as she repeatedly coughed and gagged. What a relief! She sat on the bathroom floor for an hour before returning to bed, staring at the wall, her mind a blank.

WHAT DO YOU THINK?

1. What role do you think Dana's family played in the development of her eating disorder?
2. Matt's love for Dana is clear, and she acknowledges how important it is to her that he loves her. Why do you think that even though she is happy in her relationship, she continues to binge and purge?

Assessment

A few weeks after her birthday dinner, Dana made an appointment to see a therapist. Matt had discovered her throwing up one night, had figured out what was going on, and had threatened to break up with her if she did not seek help. Humiliated and ashamed, she had reluctantly agreed. She had kept her terrible secret for so long, and now the only person in the world that mattered to her had found out. Part of her was glad, relieved not to carry her burden alone, but mostly she was frightened. Afraid of giving up her binging and purging, afraid of getting fat, afraid of giving up control, Dana perched in the therapist's waiting room, huddled in the corner of the couch, wishing she could disappear.

Dana said very little during her first visit with the psychologist. She liked the therapist's warm and reassuring manner but was afraid to trust her and feared her criticism. She was able to squeak out the reason for making an

appointment but then concocted an excuse to leave the session early, promising to return in a couple of days. She went straight to a convenience store,
shoplifted two large bags of chips, wolfed them down, and threw up.

Dana skipped her next appointment but then called to reschedule after
being confronted by Matt. Over the next two sessions the therapist had her
talk about her life and family. The youngest of three, Dana had been in-
dulged and infantilized throughout her childhood. Her successful parents
could never be pleased: Neither her appearance, so important to her mother,
nor her achievements, of value to her father, were ever good enough. She and
her sister had fought and argued since the day Dana was brought home from
the hospital. She idealized her big brother and cherished the time he spent
with her, but he had left for college by the time she was in sixth grade. In addition to her mother's incessant sniping, her grandmother was forever harp-
ing on her weight and what she ate. For years she cut out articles on dieting
with pictures of thin models and sent them to Dana. Dana had long been
used to this and routinely threw them away without even opening the en-
velopes any more.

Dana had been depressed for a number of years. At the age of fourteen,
she began abusing drugs and alcohol, introduced to both by her adventurous
sister. Quaaludes and marijuana rapidly became her favorites, along with
vodka, since they served to help numb her painful feelings.

Described as "chunky" by her father when she was a little girl, Dana had
grown up being teased by her sister and classmates for being slightly overweight. Although at puberty she had become better proportioned, by then
she loathed her body and was convinced that she was the fattest person on
the planet. Her mother was obsessed with what she ate and constantly insti-
tuted new diets. At the age of sixteen, Dana was told by a friend about a
great way to lose weight while still being able to eat whatever she wanted.
Although the thought of making herself throw up disgusted her at first, Dana
quickly came to rely on her new method of weight control.

Dana had seen a psychiatrist for her depression for several years but had
never told anyone about her eating disorder. Twice during her senior year of
high school she had tried to kill herself by overdosing on her antidepressant
medication and had been hospitalized each time. She managed to complete
high school but failed out of her junior college classes because her binging
and purging had begun to consume so much of her time. For the past two
years she had worked as a secretary for her father's law firm, a position that
was tolerant of her frequent absences and late arrivals. She continued to
abuse drugs but was able to support herself on the rather generous salary
provided by her father. She had become adept at stealing most of the foods
she binged on, only once being apprehended for shoplifting. She dated little,
preferring occasional brief, wild sexual excursions during periods of intoxication, often during a bar-hopping spree with her sister. It was only through
Matt's persistence and, as Dana put it, her few remaining grains of common

sense that she had finally consented to go out with him. Their one-year relationship had proven to be the best part of her life.

The therapist began to ask more questions related to Dana's eating disorder. She was now binging and purging an average of five times a day. While vomiting was her preferred method of purging, she occasionally tried starving herself and had periods where she exercised for several hours a day. She preferred carbohydrates and sweets as foods to binge on. She had a morbid preoccupation with her weight and held a grossly distorted perception of her body. Much of her day was consumed with thoughts of food, eating, and how she looked. Although she was intelligent and popular, most of Dana's relationships were superficial because she tended to isolate herself from her friends and co-workers. She had not had a period in several years and in fact could not recall the last time she had one. At five feet six inches tall and weighing 112 pounds, Dana believed that she was overweight. When asked by her therapist to pick a movie star whose body type she thought resembled hers, Dana immediately answered "Rosie O'Donnell."

The psychologist asked Dana to stay after her fourth session, when she seemed more comfortable talking about herself, to complete several objective tests. On the Revised Hamilton Rating Scale for Depression (Warren, 1995), Dana indicated through her answers that she was severely depressed, with features of melancholia. Although she denied any current intention or plan to kill herself, she admitted to wishing that she would simply not wake up one morning. She complained of excessive guilt, a lack of interest in sexual activity, difficulty falling asleep, feelings of restlessness and agitation, worry, and somatic preoccupation. On the Millon Multiaxial Clinical Inventory III (Millon, 1983), Dana demonstrated predominant personality traits of avoidance and competitiveness. Hypersensitive to rejection, she is distrusting and suspicious of others, believing that she must be tough and self-reliant in order to survive.

Dana also was administered the Eating Disorder Inventory-2 (Garner, 1991). This self-report measure surveys symptoms typically displayed by those with anorexia or bulimia, providing information useful in understanding the individual patient, planning treatment, and assessing progress. Not surprisingly, Dana's profile was consistent with that of other young women with bulimia nervosa. In addition to her preoccupation with being thin and her dissatisfaction with her body, Dana also scored highly on scales related to feelings of general ineffectiveness, perfectionistic thinking, distrust of others, difficulty in knowing what she is feeling, and fears of growing up and coping with the demands of adulthood. On another part of the EDI-2, Dana identified her ideal weight as 105 pounds. In discussing these results with the therapist, she stated her belief that if she could just reach her ideal weight, she would no longer worry about the way her body looked. She admitted that her self-esteem tended to rise and fall with her weight, which she checked at least once or twice each day. When the therapist gently expressed skepticism that reaching her ideal weight would solve her problem, Dana sheepishly admitted that she was probably right.

Case Conceptualization

Dana is one of the thousands of young women in the United States who suffer from bulimia nervosa. While it is difficult to determine the prevalence of eating disorders generally, it is estimated that approximately 1 to 3 percent of all adolescent and young adult women meet the *DSM-IV* criteria for this disorder. Among certain groups, such as female graduate and medical students, the incidence is higher. Some professions expose their members to heightened pressure to diet or maintain a thin appearance. It has become commonplace in recent years for well-known actresses, models, athletes, and dancers to confess to journalists their eating disorders, and indeed, the increased incidence of bulimia in these occupations has been well documented by researchers (Garner, 1991).

Men also can manifest the symptoms of bulimia, although they do so in much fewer numbers than women. Their clinical picture is very similar, and an increased incidence is also found among certain athletes and professional groups, such as wrestlers and jockeys.

Like Dana, most bulimics develop their initial symptoms in late adolescence or early adulthood, although the occasional onset in children has been observed. Dana began her binge-purge cycle as part of an effort to diet or lose weight. Without treatment, her symptoms were likely to persist for at least several years and could be either chronic or intermittent. Intermittent bulimic episodes are usually precipitated by external stress. Concurrent depressive symptoms or major mood disorder is common, and about one-third of bulimics also have a substance abuse problem. Personality disorders, especially of the borderline type, also occur frequently.

Dana's bulimia is presently understood to be a multidetermined disorder, with the defining symptom pattern representing a final common pathway resulting from a number of distinctly different developmental routes. Biological, psychological, familial, and sociocultural factors all contribute to the development of this eating disorder, although the relative contribution in each individual case is likely to vary widely.

Kendler and colleagues (1991) conducted twin studies to determine the possible role genetics might play in bulimia. These researchers reported a concordance rate of almost 23 percent for identical twins, while fraternal pairs had a concordance rate of just under 9 percent. These results suggest a modest genetic influence. In addition, since rates of affective disorders are higher in the relatives of persons suffering from bulimia, some investigators have speculated that eating disorders may be an expression of an affective disorder, which is well known to be genetically transmitted (Rutter et al.,

1990). As in Dana's case, an increased incidence of substance abuse and dependence also has been reported in the families of bulimics.

Psychological factors contributing to the development of bulimia have been much better documented. Poor self-esteem is often a contributing factor, nurtured by a perfectionistic attitude that one can never live up to. In her case, Dana constantly felt like a failure, a belief that was fostered by her family. Immaturity, passivity, and self-defeating behavior patterns are common and contribute to feelings of not having control over one's life (Dykens & Gerrard, 1986). Other traits, such as obsessional thinking, hostility, somatization, confusion regarding sex role identity, and impulse control problems also have been reported in many bulimic patients (Garner, 1991). Dana harbored feelings of anger and resentment toward her family but was unable to express them directly. The press has recently made popular the notion that sexual abuse is often a cause of bulimic symptoms, with the resulting unfortunate assumption from some therapists that all eating disorder patients must have been sexually molested. Two recent literature reviews have found no such connection between the two disorders (Conners & Morse, 1993; Pope & Hudson, 1992).

For Dana, her symptoms represented a struggle for autonomy, independence, and individuality, which would suggest one reason why the disorder so often begins in adolescence, when the resolution of these conflicts is a primary developmental task. Parents and families who do not manage the task of relinquishing control appropriately may inadvertently contribute to the development of symptoms. In Dana's family, her parents' need to control her life in a manner more suitable for a much younger child led to a passive-aggressive expression of hostility and rebellion on her part. Feeling powerless to determine her own future or meet her parents' expectations, she engaged in self-defeating behaviors that indirectly caused her parents much pain while also justifying their infantilizing attitudes and behaviors toward her.

In understanding the psychological purpose of the two aspects of bulimia, binging and purging, several factors contribute to compulsive overeating. Dana's intense fear of becoming fat led to dietary restraint, which paradoxically increased the likelihood of her binging when she was hungry or stressed. In addition, food was soothing for Dana, initially helping her to relieve anxiety. Overeating also had a distracting or numbing emotional effect, causing Dana to focus more on the physical discomfort of being full rather than on the emotional pain of some life event. It has been shown that bulimics are emotionally "out of touch" with themselves, that they have difficulty identifying internal sensations or feelings, including hunger, satiety, distinguishing pleasure from pain, and other emotional states (Garner, 1991). Finally, while vomiting provided immediate relief from the physical discomfort of overeating and reduced the fear of becoming fat, it typically was followed by feelings of self-reproach and guilt, further promoting Dana's low self-esteem. Feelings of failure occurred especially when Dana was trying to resist the temptation to binge and purge. Dana once said that she enjoyed the dreamy, emotionally bland state that often accompanied an episode of vomiting, so the inducement of vomiting took on an almost addictive quality.

On a sociocultural level, it is well known that our society promotes thinness and attractiveness in young women through advertising, often pairing the image of being thin with being professional, intelligent, or successful. In addition, most men prefer women who are thin and attractive, which places additional pressure on women who define themselves in part by men's interest in them. Sociological studies have found a relative paucity of eating disorders in non-Western cultures, leading some researchers to conclude that it is our Western preoccupation with thinness that contributes to the prevalence of bulimia and anorexia in the United States and Europe. Dana identified this aspect of her upbringing as a crucial factor causing her symptoms, since the popular girls in her high school were mostly thin and attractive, and she wanted to be included in that group despite her fear of male attention.

Diagnosis

Bulimia nervosa (usually referred to simply as *bulimia*) is one of the two primary types of eating disorders identified in *DSM-IV*, the other being anorexia nervosa. While they are often distinguished conceptually as two different disorders, in practice, it is not uncommon to see symptoms from each disorder in the same patient, either coexisting or occurring sequentially over the course of the disorder. The dynamics of each disorder are similar, and some studies have found that bulimic patients often have lost as much weight as anorexics, the difference being that bulimics started out at higher initial weights (Garner, 1991). Obesity is not defined as an eating disorder, since there is little evidence that the obese eat more than those not obese, nor is it defined as a psychiatric disorder. There are some patients who are identified only as compulsive overeaters who deny any efforts to purge. While this latter group would not qualify for a diagnosis of bulimia, some observers have found that in most instances the so-called compulsive overeating is in fact an adaptive response to a prolonged period of excessive dieting or weight loss.

Dana's disorder was characterized by a pattern of binge eating accompanied by reliance on an inappropriate compensatory method to prevent weight gain, in her case, vomiting. This pattern of binging and purging must occur at least twice a week for a period of three months before the diagnosis can be made. A binge is generally defined as eating more food than most people would, given the context, within a two-hour time period. Overeating on Thanksgiving would not be considered a binge, since most people engage in this behavior. Dana's binges usually were conducted discreetly or in secret, and she felt ashamed of her eating problems. Her binges were both planned and occurred spontaneously, triggered by the context, such as a salad bar.

They often continued until she was painfully full and occurred in response to feelings of depression, external stressors, intense hunger, or fears of being fat.

During the binge itself, Dana experienced an uncharacteristic lack of control. She described her binges as occurring within a state of frenzy. Dissociative states may occur either during or immediately after the binge, as when Dana sat on the bathroom floor for an hour after her late-night binge. Once the disorder is established, sufferers often report that they are unable to resist the urge to overeat, or once they have started to binge, they are unable to stop unless fearful of being interrupted and discovered.

Purging can be accomplished by several means, although self-induced vomiting is the preferred method in well over three-quarters of all bulimics. Sometimes bulimics will vomit after consuming only a small amount of food, as Dana did during her birthday dinner. She did not fear becoming fat from overeating at that point; she merely wanted to induce the numbing state that accompanies vomiting to avoid dealing with her feelings toward her family that night. Many individuals become quite proficient at inducing the gag reflex and may reach the point where they can vomit at will. Other purging methods include the use of laxatives, diuretics, or diet pills. Excessive exercise or fasting is occasionally the method of choice, and enemas or ipecac syrup is used in a small number of cases. Sometimes a combination of methods is employed, and up to one-third of bulimics will abuse laxatives at some point in their disorder.

An additional requirement for the diagnosis of bulimia is the excessive emphasis on body shape and weight as a factor in the determination of one's self-esteem. Bulimia shares this feature with anorexia along with the fear of gaining weight, the desire to lose weight, and dissatisfaction with one's body.

Dana is typical of many bulimics who do not appear to be notably over- or underweight. Many, like Dana, were overweight at some point in their lives prior to the onset of symptoms. Between binges, it was not unusual for Dana to restrict her calorie consumption by eating "diet" foods and avoiding foods she identified as fattening or likely to trigger a binge.

Finally, bulimia can result in a number of medical problems, including cardiac arrhythmia and arrest, esophageal tears, electrolyte disturbances, and gastric rupture. Recurrent vomiting can result in a significant and permanent loss of dental enamel, giving rise to an increase in tooth decay and front teeth that appear chipped and ragged. Vomiting also can cause swollen parotid glands, which result in a puffy facial appearance. Menstrual irregularity or amenorrhea is not uncommon, as in Dana's case. The cause of this disturbance is unclear. Perhaps not surprisingly, Dana had been told of these medical risks by her physician, but it did not stop her from binging and purging.

Treatment and Outlook

One of the few things therapists agree on in the treatment of bulimia is that the therapy must be individualized to meet the needs of individual patients.

While the various methods of treatment are well defined, some amount of trial and error is often necessary to find the right approach for a given patient.

It was decided that Dana would be referred to a residential treatment center specializing in eating disorders. Level of intervention is often the first treatment choice made, since decisions must be made about whether to treat a patient as an inpatient, in a residential program, in an outpatient program that might meet several hours a day four or more times a week, or in a combination of outpatient therapies. Given the severity of her disorder, her substance abuse problems, and her level of depression and lack of adequate social support, a residential program seemed best suited to meet Dana's needs. Dana agreed that she would not be able to stop abusing drugs or end her cycle of binging and purging without a great deal of external structure and support.

Dana moved into a house with six other young women with eating disorders. The program at the house utilized a number of treatment approaches, predominantly derived from the cognitive-behavioral and recovery or social models. First, Dana was told that the only condition of being able to remain at the house was to remain abstinent from any drug abuse and not to engage in any unplanned eating or purging behaviors. She was told to eat three planned, balanced meals along with a snack daily. Rigid rules involving her food, such as counting calories, eating only "fat free" foods, and avoiding desserts, were challenged, and she was encouraged to eat prepared meals with the other residents, each of them taking turns fixing meals. She was told to stop weighing herself and engaging in other "body image" behaviors but rather instead to concentrate on exercise, sleeping, and eating in moderation with a goal of being healthy.

Dana and the other residents met for daily group therapy, sharing support and decreasing the isolation each of them felt. They praised one another for who they were, not what they looked like, and searched for new bases on which to build their self-esteem. They also attended lectures on assertiveness, conflict resolution, and communication skills. Art and dance therapy was used to assist Dana in developing more appreciation for and attunement to her body. Participation in twelve-step groups also was encouraged, and the principles applied both to her drug abuse and to her eating disorder. Individual therapy also was used to address Dana's lack of coping strategies and to help her separate emotionally from her family.

Both because of her severe mood disorder and on the basis of positive outcome studies utilizing medication in the treatment of bulimia, Dana was prescribed Prozac (fluoxetine), one of the newer antidepressant medications that also has been proven effective in the remission of symptoms of bulimia (APA, 1993). Other medications that have proven successful in double-blind studies include Tofranil (imipramine), Norpramin (desipramine), and Desyrel (trazodone). Within a few weeks, Dana's depressive symptoms showed great improvement, and she found that she experienced less intense urges to binge.

Little is known about the natural course or long-term outcome of bulimia. Those treated as outpatients seem to maintain symptomatic improvement over follow-up periods of up to six years (APA, 1993). Dana remained at the residential treatment center for nine months but continued to attend evening groups there for several more months. She and Matt married and relocated in order to minimize contact with her family. Her only relapse to date, ten years later, occurred during a stressful time when she had discontinued use of her medication. She quickly sought help and was able to prevent her bulimia from getting out of control. Dana realized from this episode that maintaining vigilance over her symptoms was going to be a lifetime job.

▬ *THINKING CRITICALLY* ▬
QUESTIONS FOR DISCUSSION OR WRITING

1. Some people believe that bulimia is primarily a Western disease, caused by our society's preoccupation with thinness in women. What role do you think this factor might have played in the development of Dana's symptoms?

2. As we become more familiar with the issues involved in eating disorders, it is often easy to perceive ways in which we use food for other reasons besides gaining energy and health. What are some of the ways people use or abuse food?

CHAPTER 16

Dementia of the Alzheimer's Type: *Descent into Darkness*

This is the way the world ends,
Not with a bang, but with a whimper.
T. S. ELIOT, "The Hollow Men"

BETTY'S STORY

Betty was fuming. How dare her supervisor force her to take an administrative leave of absence! Hadn't she been the most popular and efficient secretary at work for years? Weren't her past performance evaluations exemplary, and hadn't the company rewarded her with salary increases and once made her employee of the year in her division? Shoot, Sandy, the supervisor, and she were good friends. How could she do this?

Betty stared at the letter Sandy had written outlining her offenses. She struggled to concentrate, as her mind kept drifting to memories of growing up in Texas. She thought fondly of her father, a skilled artisan, building a swing set for her and her siblings. "No," she said to herself, "I've got to focus on this letter."

Sandy's letter stated that for the past several months Betty had fallen asleep at her desk and required increased supervision as she tried to leave work early or stay on her breaks longer than allowed. Betty could not remember ever falling asleep at work but thought that if she did, it was because of those darn pills the doctor had given her because of her "spells." She could only remember one "spell," and then only because her boyfriend kept bringing it up. She had gone to the train station, become overwhelmed in the confusion, and lost contact with her boyfriend and daughter. When they found her, she was sitting on the floor crying. That's when they had taken her to the doctor, and she had given Betty the pills. "For your depression," the doctor had said.

The letter went on to relate that Betty would sometimes forget how to use her telephone and operate her computer. "No one forgets to use a telephone. The darn thing doesn't work half the time," she snapped. Betty was surprised to hear herself speak out loud. "I'm not usually like this," she thought. "It's just that they make me so mad at work. They don't teach me the new computer program, and then they expect me to know how to use it."

Betty's eyes moved to the bottom of the page in front of her and read the sentence: "She has twice been incontinent and nonchalantly continued to work as though nothing had happened." Although she read and reread this sentence, she couldn't make sense of it, because she couldn't remember what *incontinent* and *nonchalantly* meant. "I know those words," Betty thought to herself. "They are on the tip of my tongue. That's been happening a lot lately," Betty consoled herself. "I must be getting old."

Just then Betty's boyfriend, Herbert, walked in the room and asked how much she had written a check for at the grocery store that afternoon. Betty's mind went blank, but she said, "Oh, about thirty dollars," in a carefree, it-doesn't-really-matter tone of voice. Herbert gave her a doubting look, and Betty was relieved when he seemed to accept her answer.

"Don't forget you have a doctor's appointment tomorrow," Herbert said.

"Oh, I haven't," Betty cheerfully replied. To herself, Betty panicked. "What doctor's appointment?" she wondered. Then she looked once more at her supervisor's letter. "They're sending me to see a shrink!" Betty closed her eyes and started to cry softly.

Betty had lived a long and full life. At sixty-one she was in good physical health. Just last year she had been diagnosed with hypertension, but she was taking no medication for this condition. She had never required surgery and rarely missed a day of work because of illness. True, it was hard to get up now when she was sitting down, and she walked with short, wide steps. Slightly built, she had bright, wide eyes and a ready smile. When spoken to, she would display a warmth and sense of humor that made her popular with her co-workers. When she was not the focus of attention, however, she would lower her eyes and sit quietly.

Betty had grown up in Texas. Her father died of a stroke. Her mother, who had stayed home to raise Betty's five brothers and sisters, was now "senile" and living in a "home." Always a good student, Betty had completed high school. She soon married and raised four children. Her husband had died twelve years ago, and she now lived with Herbert, her boyfriend of the past seven years.

Betty worked as a secretary for most of her adult life. Although she could no longer recall the exact dates of her employment, she had held each position for several years and had always prided herself on her skill and efficiency.

Usually, Betty could remember detailed information about her remote past. She could recall much of her childhood and adolescence, the years of her marriage, and her move from Texas to California. However, her memory for more recent events was abysmal. She could not remember what day she had last worked, what she had watched on television the night before, or even what she had eaten for breakfast that morning. Although Betty would never admit it, without the assistance of Herbert and her co-workers, she could not have gotten along as well as she had. The people who cared about her seemed to compensate for her when she forgot things or became confused.

Betty had never received psychiatric treatment before. She had enjoyed a life relatively free of anxiety, and she had become depressed only briefly following the death of her husband. Over the past few months, however, she had started to display several symptoms of depression. These included a lack of energy, poor appetite, difficulty concentrating, hypersomnia (she would sleep fourteen hours a day if Herbert allowed it), and a lack of interest in her usual activities. However, inconsistent with depression was Herbert's observation that Betty tired and became more confused in the afternoon (depressed people are generally worse in the morning) and that she tended to minimize her problems (depressed people tend to complain a lot and exaggerate their difficulties). The family physician had prescribed Paxil, a relatively new antidepressant medication that is well tolerated by the elderly. Herbert was not sure if the medication had been helpful or not but knew that if he did not remind Betty to take it, she would never remember to.

When Betty arrived at the psychologist's office the next day, accompanied by Herbert, she was very frightened. She tried not to show her fear. She had worn a dress she thought made her look pretty, and she was determined to be pleasant and sociable. She was relieved when the psychologist seemed friendly and did her best to cover up when she was asked something she could not remember. She became irritated with Herbert when he corrected her about something she had forgotten. Outwardly, however, she smiled and acted like it was of no importance.

Once during the interview, however, Betty came unglued. The psychologist asked her about a statement in Sandy's report alleging that several recent company visitors complained that she was difficult to understand when answering questions. Betty casually replied that the company visitors could not understand her because they were "foreigners." When corrected on this point by Herbert, she became angry and snapped, "They just didn't like what I had to say to them," and began to cry. She was soon able to be consoled by Herbert, and the interview resumed as though nothing had happened.

▬ *WHAT DO YOU THINK?* ▬

1. Some of Betty's problems (poor memory, difficulty recalling words, personality changes) are common as people move into their sixties and beyond. How do we tell if these problems are part of the normal aging process or symptomatic of a psychiatric or neurologic disease?

2. In the elderly, depression and dementia present with a very similar symptom picture. To complicate matters more, as the demented person becomes

aware of his or her gradually eroding abilities, depression is a typical and understandable response to these losses. How do we distinguish the difference between which is primary, especially since one condition is reversible?

3. There are several different types of dementia, each with a different cause. How do we distinguish between the different types?

Assessment

Betty's examination by the psychologist proceeded with a thorough review of her personal, family, occupational, academic, and medical histories. In addition, a thorough review of her neuropsychological symptoms was conducted. Betty complained of occasional difficulty with blurred vision but denied any other sensory-perceptual problems. She wore glasses for reading and had astigmatism in her left eye. She denied any motor problems or problems with her thinking, communication, or relationships. She initially denied having any problems with her memory, but when challenged by Herbert, she admitted that she often forgot "unimportant things." Herbert reported that until she had received an administrative leave from work, he had attributed Betty's failing memory to "old age."

The psychologist conducted a mental status examination (MSE), a formal way of observing or asking about certain aspects of a patient's behavior. The examination usually consists of six parts and addresses:

1. The patient's general appearance and behavior
2. Characteristics of the patient's speech
3. The patient's mood and manner of emotional expression
4. Content of the patient's thought (hallucinations, delusions, obsessions, phobias, suicidal ideation, and so on)
5. The patient's cognitions (how alert the patient is, ability to attend and concentrate, capacity for abstract thought and motor functioning, and so on)
6. The patient's capacity to make judgments and level of insight into his or her condition

Betty's MSE was notable for her unusual gait, her fluent speech, her euphoric mood, and labile affect (a way of expressing emotions in which the person shows a wide range of intense feelings during a short period of time, often laughing and crying during the same interview). Usually, she answered the examiner's questions in a direct manner but on occasion would go off on a tangent, laughing and saying that she was "just joking" when this was pointed out to her. She denied any unusual ways of thinking, such as hallucinations or delusions, as well as any suicidal thoughts. She was fully aware of where she was and of the date, day of the week, and time of day. She had difficulty concentrating when asked to perform simple math problems in her head. Betty showed difficulty in abstract thinking. When asked what the saying "The grass is always greener on the other side" might mean, she replied, "You stay where you are; things could be worse." Her judgment was poor. When asked what she would do if she were stranded in the Denver airport with only a dollar in her pocket, she stated that she would buy a cup of coffee and try to figure out what to do next. She also lacked insight into her condition.

The psychologist gave Betty a battery of neuropsychological tests. These tests are designed to measure specific aspects of a person's sensory-perceptual, attentional, memory, language, visual-spatial, conceptual, and motor functioning. A person's scores are compared with the scores of others of the same gender, age, and level of education to ensure that any deviation from the norm is due to actual cerebral impairment and not normal sexual differences, normal aging, or level of formal schooling. In addition to the actual scores that a person receives, careful observation of the person's performance on the specific tasks can provide more detailed information that can be useful in understanding strengths and weaknesses in performance.

Because this evaluation sought to determine if Betty's cognitive functioning had deteriorated, the psychologist first had to assess what Betty's cognitive abilities were prior to the onset of symptoms noted by her supervisor. There are several ways to do this, including the use of tests that measure functions that are resistant to cerebral deterioration (such as vocabulary and fund of information tests) (Zimmerman & Woo-Sam, 1973), demographic data formulas (Barona, Reynolds & Chastain, 1984), and the best-performance method (Lezak, 1995). This latter technique uses the highest scores or set of scores from all tests, nonscorable behavior not necessarily observed during formal testing, and evidence of premorbid achievement as the best estimate of premorbid ability. In addition, recent findings have shown that a person's ability to correctly pronounce irregularly spelled English words is resistant to the deterioration usually found in dementia and other forms of brain damage. This observation has been incorporated into a standardized test, the National Adult Reading Test (Nelson & Willison, 1991). Based on her history and performance on tests of vocabulary, reading, and fund of information, Betty's premorbid level of intelligence was estimated to be within the average range.

Betty was given several subtests from the most commonly used measure of intelligence, the Wechsler Adult Intelligence Scale–Revised (Wechsler, 1981). Except for the measures of vocabulary and fund of information mentioned earlier, Betty's performance was mostly in the mildly impaired range, at least a standard deviation below average. Her lowest scores were on tests that measure visual-spatial functioning and abstract concepts.

Further evaluation of Betty's visual-spatial functioning was conducted using the Rey Complex Figure Test (Meyers & Meyers, 1995). This test involves having the patient copy a complicated line drawing. The patient's rendition is then scored for accuracy and completeness. Betty's drawing, although complete, contained several inaccuracies. Her score of two standard deviations below the norm reflected her difficulties in this area. She complained about the quality of her work throughout her performance and afterwards cried, "How could I make anything so dreadful. My grandson could do better."

The Rey Complex Figure Test also serves as a test of visual memory. Patients are asked to reproduce the drawing at intervals of three and thirty minutes after the copy trial. During this time, intervening tests, usually verbal in nature, are given. These reproductions are also scored and compared with a normative sample. In Betty's drawing of the complex figure after three minutes, she omitted most elements of the original drawing and, unlike her copy trial, committed several inaccuracies. Her drawing after a thirty-minute delay was similar. Both demonstrated rapid forgetting and poor recall. Her performance improved only slightly when she was asked if she recognized elements of the original drawing.

Betty also was given a test of verbal memory, the Rey Auditory-Verbal Memory Test (Spreen & Strauss, 1991). On this test she was asked to listen to a list of fifteen words over several trials and to learn as many as she could. Over five trials she was able to learn only six words (most women her age can learn ten or more). After a thirty-minute delay, she could recall only five words. However, when reciting her word lists, Betty gave ten to twelve words, at least half of which were fabricated. To herself, then, she appeared satisfied that she had been able to recall most of the words from the list. When asked to identify the original fifteen words she had been asked to learn from a list of about fifty, Betty was only able to identify four words correctly (the average is fourteen). Her performance suggested that she was unable to encode new memories into short-term storage. Little wonder that she was having difficulty performing her duties at work.

On the Trail Making Test (Reitan & Wolfson, 1993), one of the most sensitive measures of all types of cerebral dysfunction, Betty showed severe impairment. The first part of this test consists of twenty-five circles printed on a sheet of paper, each containing a number from one to twenty-five. She was asked to connect the circles in numerical order with a pencil line as quickly as possible. She performed this portion of the test in eighty-eight seconds (the average for women of her age and level of education is around thirty-five seconds). On the second, more difficult part of the test there are again twenty-five circles. This time half are numbered one through thirteen, and the other half are lettered from A through L. The task in this second part is to connect the circles, in order, alternating between numbers and letters. She performed this portion of the test in 372 seconds (average for women of her age and level of education is around 91 seconds). Her performance on this test showed poor mental flexibility, a deficit in visual scanning, and a tendency to become confused and overwhelmed by too much stimulation.

On other tests Betty displayed an average span of auditory attention, as measured by her ability to recall a string of random numbers. However, her speed of mental processing was mildly impaired. She displayed dysnomia, or the inability to name common objects, calling a triangle a rectangle and a fork a spoon. She had difficulty understanding the meaning of what she read or heard and then responding appropriately. For example, when asked why we have to get a license in order to be married, Betty said, "I don't know. There has to be money involved. Everything is based on money." Finally, Betty was asked to complete a self-report measure of depression in the elderly (Yesavage, 1986). She was unable to understand the simple instructions, which were to circle the "Yes" or "No" following each statement. She drew a line through all the "No's" down the page.

Case Conceptualization

There are several types of dementia, all of which are characterized by the death of nerve cells in the brain. It is the selective nature in which the nerve cell death occurs in these diseases that gives them their characteristic symptoms (Agid, Ruberg, DuBois & Pillon, 1987). Pick's disease, frontal lobe dementia, Huntington's disease, and progressive supranuclear palsy are examples of other types of dementia. Patients with Parkinson's disease sometimes can develop symptoms of dementia. Dementia also can be caused by cerebrovascular accidents when brain cell death occurs as the result of the loss of blood supply to a certain part of the brain. Korsakoff's dementia, usually associated with chronic alcoholism, is caused by a deficiency in thiamine (vitamin B). It is through the pattern of symptoms and speed of onset that distinctions between the various types of dementias are made in the early stages of these diseases. As the dementia progresses, the various types become indistinguishable, and all result in complete disability and eventual death (Lezak, 1995).

Betty's disorder, dementia of the Alzheimer's type (DAT), is the most common form of dementia, since more than half of all dementias are of this type (Mortimer, 1983). The probability of developing DAT increases with age, and it affects approximately 7 percent of all persons over the age of sixty-five (Terry & Katzman, 1983). It afflicts an equal number of men and women and appears unrelated to racial or cultural background (Lezak, 1995). Heredity has been implicated in some cases of DAT, especially if onset is prior to age seventy, since about half of all children of an affected parent develop the disorder (Shalat, Seltzer, Pidcock & Baker, 1987). DAT also has been linked to Down syndrome and has been associated in some studies (but not all) with older maternal birth age (Lezak, 1995). A history of head trauma and chronic exposure to neurotoxic substances also has been associated with DAT. Other suspected causes include a slowly growing virus or immunologic abnormalities (Ogden, 1996). The time from diagnosis to death ranges from three to twenty years, with an average survival of seven years (Lezak, 1995).

As is typical of DAT, Betty's first symptom was forgetfulness, which may be impossible to distinguish from the normal memory loss associated with aging. Other common early symptoms include depression and irritability, word-finding problems, difficulty at work, and problems associated with any change in routine (Lezak, 1995). The patient also may be displaying inappropriate behavior and verbal comments, a tendency toward grandiosity and euphoria, and mild confusion and lapses in attention (Ogden, 1996). The absence of motor problems and other focal neurologic signs helps distinguish DAT from other types of dementia at this point in the illness. As in Betty's case, during the early stages, DAT may be undiagnosed through the usual medical or neurologic examination procedures and may require neuropsychological testing in order to be accurately assessed (Reitan & Wolfson, 1992).

In the middle stages of DAT, speech and language problems become more noticeable. Patients may have trouble staying on the topic being discussed, and the content of their speech may become limited and concrete. Abstract thinking becomes difficult, until the patient has trouble comprehending new situations and subtle nuances of language and nonverbal expression. Disturbances in gait, disorientation, and an increasing inability to perform customary functions are common. In the early and middle stages, patients are aware of these difficulties and may try to deny their problems by minimizing them or avoiding new situations. It is also not uncommon for patients to become depressed at this stage as they realize what is happening to them. As the disease progresses, the frontal lobes of the brain become involved, resulting in patients gradually losing awareness of their condition until they become unconcerned about their behaviors and problems. At this point depression may be alleviated, and poor judgment, a lack of impulse control, and inappropriate behaviors may become more prominent. Personality changes, including the onset of psychotic symptoms (especially paranoid delusions and visual hallucinations), are also common. Institutionalization is often required for patients at this stage of their illness (Lezak, 1995; Ogden, 1996; Reitan & Wolfson, 1992).

In the later stages of DAT, patients may lose the capacity to speak spontaneously and finally may become mute. They eventually lose the ability to care for themselves in even rudimentary ways, often becoming bedridden and incontinent and spending most of their time staring blankly ahead. They may not recognize even their closest family members. Sucking and licking movements of the tongue are not uncommon, and some patients develop seizures and involuntary jerks. Death is often the result of any of a variety of illnesses to which those with dementia are especially susceptible, such as pneumonia or urinary tract infection (Reitan & Wolfson, 1992).

Diagnosis

Betty's history, presenting symptoms, and test performance are all consistent with an impression of dementia, most likely of the Alzheimer's type. The essential feature of dementia is the development of multiple cognitive deficits that include memory impairment and at least one of the other higher cognitive functions (APA, 1994). Examples of these other cognitive functions include aphasia (a loss of the ability to speak or understand oral or written language), apraxia (an inability to carry out certain motor activities despite being physically able to), agnosia (failure to recognize or identify objects despite intact sensory functioning), or a disturbance in executive functioning (the ability to plan, organize, sequence, and think abstractly). Dementia is typically progressive and irreversible.

In order to qualify for a diagnosis of dementia, these deficits must be severe enough to significantly impair the patient's work, social activities, or relationships. Other causes for the symptoms must be ruled out. For example, there could be an underlying medical condition, such as normal-pressure hydrocephalus (when the normal flow of cerebrospinal fluid is blocked, usually by scarring from old head injuries or hemorrhage), or the symptoms could be due to the effects of medication the patient is taking. Delirium and depression always must be ruled out, since these conditions can mimic dementia. The effects of normal aging are sometimes mistaken as evidence of dementia. Misdiagnosis and overdiagnosis of dementia are common problems, and reversible conditions must be identified through medical examination and laboratory tests.

Treatment and Outlook

There is no specific treatment for DAT. Betty was immediately referred for a thorough medical and neurological examination to rule out any type of reversible cause of her symptoms. Finding none, she and her family were invited back to the psychologist to review the findings of her neuropsychological tests and to discuss her diagnosis and future plans. They were told that Betty was probably in the early to middle stages of DAT and that her condition had gone undetected as long as it had both because of her efforts to deny her problems and because of the willingness of those around her to compensate for her deficits. They also were told that Betty would be unable to return to work and that she would eventually require more supervision and care than that currently provided by her boyfriend.

Betty's family was both distressed and relieved at this news. While they felt sad for their mother and loved one, having a diagnosis helped them make sense out of what was happening and allowed them to begin making plans. The family had been through this already with Betty's mother, who already lived in a home for those with dementia. They were aware of the support groups and community resources for caregivers and immediately planned to attend meetings to obtain additional information and needed emotional support.

Betty was referred to a neurologist, who could follow the progress of her dementia and prescribe medication to assist with symptoms of depression, psychosis, paranoia, or agitation as they developed. She also was referred to a community research project that was involved in testing new medications for the treatment of DAT. These medications work on the cholinergic system and have shown limited but promising success (Ogden, 1996). Betty felt grateful to be able to participate in the study, somewhat hopeful that the new medications might help her, but mostly glad that she could still make a contribution despite her illness. She also participated in short-term therapy to monitor suicidal ideation and to assist with her depression by "putting all my ducks in a row," as she put it. Betty discussed her wishes regarding her future care with her family, thus relieving them of the burden of having to guess at what she wanted and the guilt of having to admit that they could no longer care for their loved one. She completed her will and discussed the details of her funeral. She seemed to get the most satisfaction out of writing a series of letters to her children and grandchildren that she intended to be read after her death. She enjoyed reviewing family photographs and telling stories about the past, which one of her sons decided to record for future generations.

Betty remained with her boyfriend for another year. When it became clear that she could no longer live independently, the family moved her to the same residential care unit that had housed her own mother. Exhausted from taking care of her, they occasionally returned to therapy for support and assistance in coping with the stress of watching their mother deteriorate, having to wash, dress, and feed her. While Betty was at the rest home, they developed a visitation schedule that they continued until she died six years later, long after she had stopped recognizing them. They returned to therapy one final time to share the letters that their mother had written soon after she was diagnosed.

No matter what its cause, dementia is a tragedy for both the victim and their family. It is also a difficult disorder for the professionals involved with these patients, since they must watch helplessly as a vibrant, alert person deteriorates into a vegetative state. It is this feeling of ineffectiveness that makes it so stressful to live or work with those afflicted with dementia. Interventions are best directed at increasing self-control for the patient and giving caregivers some way of improving the quality of the victim's daily life.

Betty was fortunate to have such a supportive and well-informed family. Her diagnosis also was made easier because her condition was so advanced. It is not uncommon for a patient to undergo a series of neuropsychological assessments before arriving at a definitive diagnosis during the early stages of the disease. Caregivers also can be given rating scales and questionnaires at regular intervals to monitor how well the patient is coping with the demands of everyday living. This practice provides another measure of deterioration and allows the therapist to organize appropriate in-home care and/or institutionalization at the appropriate time. Caregivers' stress levels also need to be monitored so that they can receive assistance before becoming "burned out." While the burden for caregivers often increases as the disease progresses, the impact on patients actually decreases as their awareness of their condition deteriorates.

Perhaps it is only when we watch as a loved one gradually loses his or her independence, sense of humor, intelligence, imagination, and personality that we begin to appreciate the wonder and complexity of the human brain. It is this sense of wonder that sustains us as we continue to search for ways to understand, treat, and prevent the devastating effects of DAT.

THINKING CRITICALLY
QUESTIONS FOR DISCUSSION OR WRITING

1. Often the best way to determine how to help someone else is to imagine that you are the one afflicted with the problem. How would you want your family to respond if you were the one in the early stages of Alzheimer's disease?

2. What do you think it would be like if you were the psychologist who had to tell Betty and her family about her diagnosis and what it means?

REFERENCES

Agid, Y., Ruberg, M., DuBois, B., & Pillon, B. (1987). Anatomoclinical and biochemical concepts of subcortical dementia. In S. Stahl, S. Iverson & E. Goodman (Eds.), *Cognitive neurochemistry*. Oxford: Oxford University Press.

Ainsworth, M. D. (1972). Attachment and dependency: A comparison. In J. L. Gewirtz (Ed.), *Attachment and dependence*. Washington, DC: Winston.

Ainsworth, M. D. (1989). Attachments beyond infancy. *American Psychologist, 44,* 709–716.

Albert, M., Naeser, M., Levine, H., & Garvey, J. (1984). Ventricular size in patients with presenile dementia of the Alzheimer's type. *Archives of Neurology, 41,* 1258–1263.

American Psychiatric Association. (1993). *Practice guidelines for eating disorders*. Washington, DC: APA Press.

American Psychiatric Association. (1994). *Diagnostic and statistical manual of mental disorders* (4th ed.). Washington, DC: American Psychiatric Press.

Angst, J. (1993). Comorbidity of anxiety, phobia, compulsion and depression. *International Clinical Psychopharmacology, 8* (Suppl.), 21–25.

Ayd, F. (1995). *Lexicon of psychiatry, neurology and the neurosciences*. Baltimore: Williams & Wilkins.

Ballenger, J. C., Burrows, G. D., Dupont, R. L., Lesser, I. M., Noyes, J., Pecknold, J. D., Rifkin, A., & Swinson, R. P. (1988). Alprazolam in panic disorder and agoraphobia: Results from a multicenter trial. *Archives of General Psychiatry, 45,* 413–422.

Bancroft, J. (1989). *Human sexuality and its problems* (2nd ed.). Edinburgh: Churchill-Livingstone.

Bard, L., Carter, D., Cerce, D., Knight, R., Rosenberg, R., & Schneider, B. (1987). A descriptive study of rapists and child molesters: Developmental, clinical and criminal characteristics. *Behavioral Sciences and the Law, 5,* 203–220.

Barkley, R. (1990). *Attention deficit hyperactivity disorder: A handbook for diagnosis and treatment*. New York: Guilford Press.

Barkley, R. (1997). Behavioral inhibition, sustained attention, and executive functions: Constructing a unifying theory of ADHD. *Psychological Bulletin, 121,* 65–94.

Barona, A., Reynolds, C., & Chastain, R. (1984). A demographically based index of premorbid intelligence for the WAIS-R. *Journal of Consulting and Clinical Psychology, 52,* 885–887.

Beck, A. T. (1967). *Depression: Clinical, experimental and theoretical aspects*. Philadelphia: University of Pennsylvania Press.

Beck, A. T., Rush, A. J., Shaw, B. F., & Emery, G. (1979). *Cognitive therapy of depression.* New York: Guilford Press.

Beck, A. T., & Steer, R. A. (1996). *Beck Depression Inventory–II.* San Antonio: Psychological Corporation.

Bell, A. P., Weinberg, M. S., & Hammersmith, S. K. (1981). *Sexual preference: Its development in men and women.* Bloomington: Indiana University Press.

Bellack, A., & Mueser, K. (1993). Psychosocial treatment for schizophrenia. *Schizophrenia Bulletin, 19,* 317–336.

Bowlby, J. (1969). *Attachment and loss,* Vol. 1, *Attachment.* New York: Basic Books.

Bowlby, J. (1973). *Attachment and loss,* Vol. 2, *Separation: Anxiety and anger.* New York: Basic Books.

Brandsma, J. M., Maultsby, M. C., & Welsh, R. J. (1980). *The outpatient treatment of alcoholism: A review and comparative study.* Baltimore: University Park Press.

Briere, J. (1995). *Trauma Symptom Inventory.* Odessa, FL: Psychological Assessment Resources.

Brown, G., Birley, J., & Wing, J. (1972). Influence of family life on the course of schizophrenic disorders: A replication. *British Journal of Psychiatry, 121,* 241–258.

Brown, S. (1988). *Treating adult children of alcoholics: A developmental perspective.* New York: Wiley.

Brown, S. (1995). A developmental model of alcoholism and recovery. In S. Brown (Ed.), *Treating alcoholism* (pp. 27–53). San Francisco: Jossey Bass.

Clark, D. M. (1988). A cognitive model of panic attacks. In S. Rachman & J. D. Maser (Eds.), *Panic: Psychological perspectives* (pp. 71–90). Hillsdale, NJ: Lawrence Erlbaum.

Cloninger, C. R. (1987). Neurogenic adaptive mechanisms in alcoholism. *Science, 236,* 410–416.

Clum, G. A., & Knowles, S. L. (1991). Why do some people with panic disorders become avoidant: A review. *Clinical Psychology Review, 11,* 295–313.

Coccaro, E. F. (1989). Central serotonin and impulsive aggression. *British Journal of Psychiatry, 155* (Suppl. 8), 52–62.

Conners, C., March, J., Erhardt, D., Butcher, T., & Epstein, J. (1995). Assessment of attention deficit disorders: Conceptual issues and future trends. *Journal of Psychoeducational Assessment,* 185–204.

Conners, M., & Morse, W. (1993). Sexual abuse and eating disorders: A review. *International Journal of Eating Disorders, 13,* 1–11.

Corkin, S. (1981). Brain acetylcholine, aging and Alzheimer's disease: Implications for treatment. *Trends in Neuroscience, 4,* 287–290.

Coryell, W., Scheftner, W., Keller, M., Endicott, J., Maser, J., & Klerman, G. (1993). The enduring psychosocial consequences of mania and depression. *American Journal of Psychiatry, 150,* 720–727.

Cotton, N. S. (1979). The familial incidence of alcoholism. *Journal of Studies on Alcohol, 40,* 89–116.

Dager, S. R., Cowley, D. S., & Dunner, D. I. (1987). Biological markers in panic states: Lactate-induced panic and mitral valve prolapse. *Biological Psychiatry, 22,* 339–359.

Devor, E. J., & Cloninger, C. R. (1989). Genetics of alcoholism. *Annual Review of Genetics, 23,* 19–36.

Dobson, K. S. (1985). An analysis of anxiety and depression scales. *Journal of Personality Assessment, 11,* 522–527.

Dykens, E., & Gerrard, M. (1986). Psychological profiles of purging bulimics, repeat dieters, and controls. *Journal of Consulting and Clinical Psychology, 54,* 283–288.

Fenichel, O. (1945). *The psychoanalytic theory of neurosis.* New York: Norton.

Fowles, D. (1992). Schizophrenia: Diathesis-stress revisited. *Annual Review of Psychology, 43,* 303–336.

Freud, A. (1958). Adolescence. *Psychoanalytic Study of the Child, 16,* 225–278.

Galaif, E. R., & Sussman, S. (1995). For whom does Alcoholics Anonymous work? *International Journal of the Addictions, 30,* 161–184.

Garner, D. (1991). *Eating disorder inventory-2 professional manual.* Odessa, FL: Psychological Assessment Resources.

George, M. S., & Ballenger, J. C. (1992). The neuroanatomy of panic disorder: The emerging role of the right parahippocampal region. *Journal of Anxiety Disorders, 6,* 181–188.

Goodman, W., Rasmussen, S., Price, L., Mazure, C., Heninger, G., & Charney, D. (1989). *Yale-Brown obsessive compulsive disorder scale.* New Haven: Clinical Neuroscience Research Unit.

Goodwin, F., & Ebert, M. (1973). Lithium in mania: Clinical trials and controlled studies. In S. Gershon & B. Shopsin (Eds.), *Lithium: Its Role in Psychiatric Research and Treatment.* New York: Plenum Press.

Gottesman, I. (1991). *Schizophrenia genesis: The origins of madness.* New York: Freeman.

Green, B., Lindy, J., Grace, M., & Leonard, A. (1992). Chronic posttraumatic stress disorder and diagnostic comorbidity in a disaster sample. *Journal of Nervous and Mental Disorders, 180,* 760–766.

Greene, R., & Barkley, R. (1995). Clinic-based assessment of attention deficit/hyperactivity disorder. *Journal of Psychoeducational Assessment, 61–73.*

Grenier, G., & Byers, E. S. (1997). The relationships among ejaculatory control, ejaculatory latency, and attempts to prolong heterosexual intercourse. *Archives of Sexual Behavior, 26,* 27–47.

Grotevant, H. D., & Cooper, C. R. (1985). Patterns of interaction in family relationships and the development of identity exploration in adolescents. *Child Development, 56,* 415–428.

Groth, A. (1982). The incest offender. In S. Sgroi (Ed.), *Handbook of clinical interventions in child sexual abuse.* Lexington, MA: Lexington Books.

Haas, K., & Haas, A. (1993). *Understanding human sexuality.* St. Louis: Mosby.

Haensel, S. M., Rowland, D. L., & Kallan, K. T. (1996). Clomipnamine and sexual function in men with premature ejaculation and controls. *Journal of Urology, 156,* 1310–1315.

Hare, R. (1978). Electrodermal and cardiovascular correlates of sociopathy. In R. Hare & D. Schelling (Eds.), *Psychopathic behavior: Approaches to research.* New York: Wiley.

Hare, R. (1991). *The Hare Psychopathy Checklist-Revised.* North Tonawanda, NY: Multi-Health Systems.

Hathaway, S., & McKinley, J. (1989). *Minnesota multiphasic personality inventory-2 manual.* Minneapolis: National Computer Systems.

Herman, J. L., Perry, C., & van der Kolk, B. A. (1989). Childhood trauma in borderline personality disorder. *American Journal of Psychiatry, 146,* 490–494.

Holen, A. (1993). The North Sea oil rig disaster. In J. P. Wilson & B. Raphael (Eds.), *International handbook of traumatic stress syndromes.* New York: Plenum Press.

Hollon, S. D., Shelton, R. C., & Loosen, P. T. (1991). Cognitive therapy and pharmacotherapy for depression. *Journal of Consulting and Clinical Psychology, 59,* 88–89.

Hughlings-Jackson, J. (1931). In J. Taylor (Ed.), *Selected writings.* London: Hodder and Stoughton.

Janet, P. (1925). *Psychological healing* (Vols. 1–2). New York: Macmillan. Originally *Les medication psychologiques* (Vols. 1–3). Paris: Felix, Alcan, 1919.

Jenike, M. (1992). New developments in the treatment of OCD. In A. Tarman & M. Riba (Eds.), *Review of psychiatry* (Vol. 2). Washington, DC: American Psychiatric Press.

Jenike, M., & Rauch, S. (1994). Managing the patient with treatment-resistant OCD: Current strategies. *Journal of Clinical Psychiatry, 55* (Suppl. 3), 11–17.

Josselson, R. (1988). The embedded self: I and thou revisited. In D. K. Lapsley & F. C. Power (Eds.), *Self, ego, and identity* (pp. 91–106). New York: Springer-Verlag.

Kagan, J., Reznik, J. S., & Snidman, N. (1988). Biological bases of childhood shyness. *Science, 240,* 167–171.

Kaplan, H. S. (1974). *The new sex therapy.* New York: Brunner/Mazel.

Kaplan, H. S. (1979). *Disorders of sexual desire.* New York: Simon & Schuster.

Kaplan, H. S. (1983). *The evaluation of sexual disorders*. New York: Brunner/Mazel.

Kaplan, H., & Sadock, B. J. (1985). *Modern synopsis of comprehensive textbook of psychiatry*. Baltimore: Williams & Wilkins.

Kaufman, A., & Kaufman, N. (1983). *K-ABC: Kaufman assessment battery for children*. Circle Pines, MN: American Guidance Service.

Kaufman, A., & Kaufman, N. (1990). *K-BIT: Kaufman brief intelligence test*. Circle Pines, MN: American Guidance Service.

Kendler, K., MacLean, C., Neale, M., Kessler, R., Heath, A., & Eaves, L. (1991). The genetic epidemiology of bulimia nervosa. *American Journal of Psychiatry, 148*, 1627–1637.

Kendler, K. S., Kessler, R. C., Neale, M. C., Heath, A. C., & Eaves, L. J. (1993). The prediction of major depression in women: Toward an integrated etiologic model. *American Journal of Psychiatry, 150*, 1139–1148.

Kernberg, O. F. (1988). Object relations theory in clinical practice. *Psychoanalytic Quarterly, 57*, 481–504.

Kinsey, A., Pomeroy, W., & Martin, C. (1948). *Sexual behavior in the human male*. Philadelphia: Saunders.

Klein, D. F., & Fink, M. (1962). Psychiatric reaction patterns to imipramine. *American Journal of Psychiatry, 119*, 432–438.

Klerman, G. L., Weissman, M., Rounsaville, B., & Chevron, E. (1984). *Interpersonal psychotherapy of depression*. New York: Basic Books.

Kohut, H. (1977). *The restoration of the self*. New York: International Universities Press.

Kovacs, M., Gatsonis, C., Pollock, M., & Parrone, P. L. (1994). A controlled prospective study of DSM-III objectives: Using DSM-III criteria for adjustment disorder. *Archives of General Psychiatry, 51*, 535–541.

Laing, R. (1967). *The politics of experience*. New York: Ballantine Books.

Lezak, M. (1995). *Neuropsychological assessment* (3rd ed.). New York: Oxford University Press.

Linehan, M. (1993). *Cognitive-behavioral treatment of borderline personality disorder*. New York: Guilford Press.

Marmar, C. R., Weiss, D. S., Schlenger, W. E., Fairbank, J. A., Jordan, K., Kulka, R. A., & Hough, R. L. (1994). Peritraumatic dissociation and posttraumatic stress in male Vietnam theater veterans. *American Journal of Psychiatry, 151*, 902–907.

Marshall, W., Jones, R., Ward, T., Johnston, P., & Barbaree, H. (1991). Treatment outcome with sex offenders. *Clinical Psychology Review, 11*, 465–486.

Martin, R. L., Cloninger, C., & Guze, S. (1985). Alcohol misuse and depression in women criminals. *Journal on Study of Alcohol, 46*, 65–71.

Masters, W. H., & Johnson, V. E. (1970). *Human sexual inadequacy*. Boston: Little, Brown.

Maxmen, J. S. (1986). *Essential psychopathology.* New York: Norton.

McCary, J., & McCary, S. (1982). *Human sexuality.* Belmont, CA: Wadsworth.

McFarlane, A. C. (1992). Multiple diagnoses in posttraumatic stress disorder in the victims of a natural disaster. *Journal of Nervous and Mental Disorders, 180,* 498–504.

McGlashan, T. H. (1986). The Chestnut Lodge follow-up study: III. Long-term outcome of borderline patients. *Archives of General Psychiatry, 43,* 329–334.

McGue, M., Pickins, R., & Svikis, D. (1992). Sex and age effects on the inheritance of alcohol problems: A twin study. *Journal of Abnormal Psychology, 101,* 3–17.

McNally, R. J., & Eke, M. (1996). Anxiety, sensitivity, suffocation fear, and breath-holding duration as predictors of response to carbon dioxide challenge. *Journal of Abnormal Psychology, 105,* 146–149.

Meloy, R. (1995). Treatment of antisocial personality disorder. In G. Gabbard (Ed.), *Treatments of psychiatric disorders* (2nd ed.). Washington, DC: American Psychiatric Press.

Merikangas, K. R., Fentorn, B. T., Cheng, S. H., Stolar, M. J., & Risch, M. (1997). Association between migraine and stroke in a large-scale epidemiological study of the United States. *Archives of Neurology, 54,* 362–368.

Meyers, J., & Meyers, K. (1995). *Rey complex figure test and recognition trial, professional manual.* Odessa, FL: Psychological Assessment Resources.

Miller, G. (1994). *The substance abuse subtle screening inventory-2.* Bloomington, IN: Sassi Institute.

Millon, T. (1983). *Millon clinical multiaxial inventory manual* (3rd ed.). Minneapolis: National Computer Systems.

Mortimer, J. (1983). Alzheimer's disease and senile dementia: Prevalence and incidence. In B. Reisberg (Ed.), *Alzheimer's disease.* New York: Free Press.

Mueser, K., Bellack, A., Wade, J., Sayers, S., Tierney, A., & Haas, G. (1993). Expressed emotion, social skills and response to negative affect in schizophrenia. *Journal of Abnormal Psychology, 102,* 339–351.

Nelson, H., & Willison, J. (1991). *National adult reading test (NART)* (2nd ed.). Windsor, Eng.: NFER-Nelson.

Newcorn, J. H., & Strain, J. (1992). Adjustment disorder in children and adolescents. *Journal of the American Academy of Child and Adolescent Psychiatry, 31,* 318–326.

Newman, S. C., & Bland, R. C. (1994). Life events and the one-year prevalence of major depressive episode, generalized anxiety disorder, and panic disorder in a community sample. *Comprehensive Psychiatry, 35,* 76–82.

Nichols, H., & Molinder, I. (1984). *Multiphasic sex inventory.* Tacoma, WA.

Nolen-Hoeksema, S. (1990). *Sex differences in depression.* Stanford: Stanford University Press.

Ogata, S. N., Silk, K. R., Goodrich, S., Lohr, N. E., Westen, D., & Hill, E. M. (1990). Childhood sexual and physical abuse in adult patients with borderline personality disorder. *American Journal of Psychiatry, 147,* 1008–1013.

Ogden, J. (1996). *Fractured minds: A case-study approach to clinical neuropsychology.* New York: Oxford University Press.

Pelham, W. (1993). Pharmacotherapy for children with attention deficit hyperactivity disorder. *School Psychology Review, 22,* 199–227.

Pennington, B. (1991). *Diagnosing learning disorders: A neuropsychological framework.* New York: Guilford Press.

Perry, G., & Orchard, J. (1992). *Assessment and treatment of adolescent sex offenders.* Sarasota, FL: Professional Resource Press.

Perse, T. (1988). Obsessive-compulsive disorder: A treatment review. *Journal of Clinical Psychiatry, 49,* 48–55.

Pilkonis, P. A., Heape, C. L., Proietti, J. M., Clark, S. W., McDavid, J. D., & Pitts, T. E. (1995). The reliability and validity of two structured diagnostic interviews for personality disorders. *Archives of General Psychiatry, 52,* 1025–1033.

Pope, H., & Hudson, J. (1992). Is childhood sexual abuse a risk factor for bulimia nervosa? *American Journal of Psychiatry, 149,* 455–463.

Reitan, R., & Wolfson, D. (1992). *Neuroanatomy and neuropathology: A clinical guide for neuropsychologists* (2nd ed.). Tucson, AZ: Neuropsychology Press.

Reitan, R., & Wolfson, D. (1993). *The Halstead-Reitan neuropsychological test battery: Theory and clinical interpretation* (2nd ed.). Tucson, AZ: Neuropsychology Press.

Riggs, D., & Foa, E. (1993). Obsessive compulsive disorder. In D. Barlow (Ed.), *Clinical handbook of psychological disorders: A step-by-step treatment manual.* New York: Guilford Press.

Rimm, D., & Masters, J. (1974). *Behavior therapy: Techniques and empirical findings.* New York: Academic Press.

Root, M. (1992). Reconstructing the impact of trauma on personality. In L. Brown & M. Ballou (Eds.), *Personality and psychopathology: Feminist reappraisals* (pp. 229–265). New York: Guilford Press.

Rothbaum, B., & Foa, E. (1996). Cognitive behavioral therapy for PTSD. In B. van der Kolk, A. McFarlane & L. Weisaeth (Eds.), *Traumatic stress: The effect of overwhelming experience on mind, body, and society* (pp. 491–509). New York: Guilford Press.

Rutter, M., MacDonald, H., LeCouteur, A., Harrington, R., Bolton, P., & Bailey, A. (1990). Genetic factors in child psychiatry disorders: II. Empirical findings. *Journal of Child Psychology and Psychiatry, 31,* 39–83.

Schachar, R., Tannock, R., & Logan, G. (1993). Inhibitory control, impulsiveness and attention deficit hyperactivity disorder. *Clinical Psychology Review, 13,* 721–739.

Schneier, F. R., Liebowitz, M. R., Davies, S. O, Fairbanks, J., Hollander, E., Campers, R., & Klein, D. F. (1990). Fluoxetine in panic disorder. *Journal of Clinical Psychopharmacology, 10,* 119–121.

Schwean, V., Saklofske, D., Yackulic, R., & Quinn, D. (1995). Aggressive and nonaggressive ADHD boys: Cognitive, intellectual and behavioral comparisons. *Journal of Psychoeducational Assessment,* 6–21.

Sergeant, J. (1994). Brain-imaging studies of cognitive functions. *Trends in Neurosciences, 17*(6), 221–227.

Shalat, S., Seltzer, B., Pidcock, C., & Baker, E. (1987). Risk factors for Alzheimer's disease: A case-control study. *Neurology, 37,* 1630–1633.

Shuckit, M. A. (1994). A clinical model of genetic influences in alcohol dependence. *Journal on the Study of Alcohol, 55,* 5–17.

Shuckit, M. A., & Smith, T. L. (1996). An eight-year follow-up of 450 sons of alcoholic and control subjects. *Archives of General Psychiatry, 53,* 202–210.

Singer, M. (1974). Deliquency and family disciplinary configurations: An elaboration of the superego lacunae concept. *Archives of General Psychiatry, 31,* 795–798.

Solomon, S. D., Gerrity, E. T., & Muff, A. M. (1992). Efficacy of treatments for posttraumatic stress disorder: An empirical review. *Journal of the American Medical Association, 268,* 633–638.

Spreen, O., & Strauss, E. (1991). *A compendium of neuropsychological tests: Administration, norms and commentary.* New York: Oxford University Press.

Stewart, W., Lipton, R. B., Celentano, D. D., & Reed, M. L. (1992). Prevalence of migraine headache in the United States. *Journal of the American Medical Association, 267,* 64–69.

Stone, M. (1995). *Abnormalities of personality: Within and beyond the realm of treatment.* New York: Norton.

Stone, M. H. (1990). Treatment of borderline patients: A pragmatic approach. *Psychology Clinics of North America, 13,* 265–283.

Terry, R., & Katzman, R. (1983). Senile dementia of the Alzheimer's type. *Annals of Neurology, 14,* 497–506.

Timko, C., Moos, R. H., Finney, J. W., & Moos, B. S. (1994). Outcome for treatment of alcohol abuse and involvement in Alcoholics Anonymous among previously untreated problem drinkers. *Journal of Mental Health Administration, 21,* 145–160.

Tohen, M., Shulman, K., & Satlin, A. (1994). First-episode mania in late life. *American Journal of Psychiatry, 151,* 130–132.

van der Kolk, B., McFarlane, A., & van der Hart, O. (1996). A general approach to treatment of posttraumatic stress disorder. In B. van der Kolk,

A. McFarlane & L. Weisaeth (Eds.), *Traumatic stress: The effect of over-whelming experience on mind, body, and society* (pp. 417–440). New York: Guilford Press.

Viney, L. L., Clark, A. M., Bunn, T. A., & Benjamin, Y. N. (1980). Crisis intervention counselling: An evaluation of long and short-term effects. *Journal of Counselling Psychology, 32,* 29–39.

Warren, W. (1995). *Revised Hamilton rating scale for depression manual.* Los Angeles: Western Psychological Services.

Wechsler, D. (1981). *Wechsler adult intelligence scale-revised (WAIS-R) manual.* New York: Psychological Corporation.

Wechsler, D. (1991). *Manual for the Wechsler intelligence scale for children* (3rd ed.) (WISC-III). San Antonio: Psychological Corporation.

Wechsler individual achievement test-manual. (1992). San Antonio: Psychological Corporation.

Weiss, G., & Hechtman, L. (1993). *Hyperactive children grown up.* New York: Guilford Press.

Weissman, M. M., Sholomkas, D., & John, K. (1981). The assessment of social adjustment: An update. *Archives of General Psychiatry, 38,* 1250–1258.

Welch, K. (1993). Drug therapy of migraine. *New England Journal of Medicine, 329,* 1476–1483.

Wetzler, S., & Sanderson, W. C. (1995). In G. M. Asnis & I. M. van Praag (Eds.), *Panic disorder and clinical, biological and treatment aspects.* New York: Wiley.

Yehuda, R., Southwick, S. M., Krystal, J. H., Bremner, D., Charney, D. S., & Mason, J. W. (1993). Enhanced suppression of cortisol following dexamethasone administration in posttraumatic stress disorder. *American Journal of Psychiatry, 150,* 83–86.

Yesavage, J. (1986). The use of self-rating depression scales in the elderly. In L. Poon (Ed.), *Handbook for clinical memory assessment of older adults.* Washington, DC: American Psychological Association.

Zimmerman, I., & Woo-Sam, J. (1973). *Clinical interpretation of the Wechsler adult intelligence scale.* New York: Grune & Stratton.

INDEX